UNDER SIEGE

ADVANCING STUDIES IN RELIGION
Series editor: Sarah Wilkins-Laflamme

Advancing Studies in Religion catalyzes and provokes original research in the study of religion with a critical edge. The series advances the study of religion in method and theory, textual interpretation, theological studies, and the understanding of lived religious experience. Rooted in the long and diverse traditions of the study of religion in Canada, the series demonstrates awareness of the complex genealogy of religion as a category and as a discipline. ASR welcomes submissions from authors researching religion in varied contexts and with diverse methodologies.

The series is sponsored by the Canadian Corporation for Studies in Religion whose constituent societies include the Canadian Society of Biblical Studies, Canadian Society for the Study of Religion, Canadian Society of Patristic Studies, Canadian Theological Society, Société canadienne de théologie, and Société québécoise pour l'étude de la religion.

UNDER SIEGE

Islamophobia and the 9/11 Generation

JASMIN ZINE

McGill-Queen's University Press

Montreal & Kingston • London • Chicago

© McGill-Queen's University Press 2022

ISBN 978-0-2280-1118-7 (cloth)
ISBN 978-0-2280-1119-4 (paper)
ISBN 978-0-2280-1217-7 (ePDF)
ISBN 978-0-2280-1218-4 (ePUB)

Legal deposit second quarter 2022
Bibliothèque nationale du Québec

Printed in Canada on acid-free paper that is 100% ancient forest free
(100% post-consumer recycled), processed chlorine free

This book has been published with the help of a grant from the Canadian
Federation for the Humanities and Social Sciences, through the Awards to
Scholarly Publications Program, using funds provided by the Social Sciences
and Humanities Research Council of Canada.

We acknowledge the support of the Canada Council for the Arts.

Nous remercions le Conseil des arts du Canada de son soutien.

Library and Archives Canada Cataloguing in Publication

Title: Under siege: Islamophobia and the 9/11 generation/Jasmin Zine.

Names: Zine, Jasmin, 1963– author.

Series: Advancing studies in religion; 12.

Description: Series statement: Advancing studies in religion; 12 |
Includes bibliographical references and index.

Identifiers: Canadiana (print) 20210363525 | Canadiana (ebook)
20210363541 | ISBN 9780228011194 (paper) | ISBN 9780228011187
(cloth) | ISBN 9780228012177 (ePDF) | ISBN 9780228012184 (ePUB)

Subjects: LCSH: Muslim youth—Canada. | LCSH: Muslim youth—Canada—
Interviews. | LCSH: Muslim youth—Canada—Ethnic identity. | LCSH:
Muslim youth—Canada—Social conditions. | LCSH: Islamophobia—
Canada.

Classification: LCC BP67.C3 Z56 2022 | DDC 305.23088/2970971—dc23

This book was typeset by Marquis Interscript in 10.5/13 Sabon.

This book is dedicated to my sons, Usama and Yusuf, who are part of the 9/11 generation and who inspired me to take on a study that unpacked the experiences they faced growing up during this fraught time. Their insights, support, encouragement, and love have been invaluable during this process and in my life.

Contents

Preface

The impetus for this project arose from three critical issues in my own life as a Muslim student, mother, and professor. I have been researching Muslim youth in Canada since the mid-1990s and was studying Islamophobia long before the Twin Towers fell on September 11, 2001. My personal and academic journey culminated in the writing of this book, which was borne of critical incidents and experiences that shape the political concerns that drive my research. Though this book is ethnographic, I am not a mere spectator in the lives of those who recounted their stories to me. I have many shared experiences with these research participants, and as a Muslim I am affected by the same conditions under examination in this study. Indeed, these circumstances have impacted my life, my children's lives, and my professional work in profound ways. While I was privileged to bear witness to the narratives of those whom I interviewed and learned from in this study, my testimony also informs part of the story.

Writing this book took me back to my own experiences as an undergraduate student at the University of Toronto in the late 1980s – a time which had an enduring influence on my personal, academic, and religious life. I joined the Muslim Students' Association (MSA) and became active in the Muslim subculture on campus. I was involved in organizing events such as Islam Awareness Week (a tradition that continues) to counter Islamophobia and the false stereotypes about Islam and Muslims as well as engaging in the social and spiritual activities of the group. During that time, I helped organize an MSA fundraiser for a charity called Human Concern International (HCI) to benefit orphans in Afghanistan living under Russian occupation. Several years later, HCI landed on a terrorism watch list because of ties to the Khadr family who was suspected to have links to Al-Qaeda. (HCI was later removed from the list without apology for false and unsubstantiated claims against them by the government.)

In the late 1980s, HCI and the Khadr family were involved in humanitarian work in Afghanistan and were well respected. Our MSA organized a major fundraising campaign via a multicultural bazaar and food fair for HCI to provide aid to Afghan families. There were booths of food, clothing, and artifacts for sale from India, Pakistan, Guyana, Morocco, and Somalia. The event was held in a Catholic school gymnasium. To ensure traffic coordination and safety for the event, we recruited Afghanistan refugee men, who were in Canada for medical aid and rehabilitation, to serve as a security patrol. They wore traditional Afghan clothing (long tunics, baggy pants, and turbans) and carried walkie-talkies. I imagine how this scene would play out today if a crowd of Muslims gathered in a Catholic school to raise funds for an organization previously on a terror watch list, with a patrol of Afghan men wearing traditional garments, with long beards, and carrying walkie-talkies, circling around the building. In the present climate of Islamophobic and Orientalist racist fears, this scene would surely have the Royal Canadian Mounted Police (RCMP) and the Canadian Security Intelligence Service (CSIS) converging on-site in full force! Pondering how this MSA event would be read differently today made me reflect on how Muslim youth must navigate in distinct ways the post-911 era of Islamophobia.

The second impetus behind my research was the experience of my two sons after 9/11. They were seven and eleven years old at the time. My younger son attended a full-time Islamic school, and on the day of 9/11 the school was on lockdown and had to be evacuated after bomb threats were received. When I arrived to pick up my son from school, men from the community had already gathered there and formed a security perimeter around the school and adjacent mosque. I realized then we were going to be collateral damage in this tragedy. My older son attended a public school and because his name is Usama (as in "Osama bin Laden") he was bullied, harassed, and threatened. Because of the negative views others held toward him, his sense of identity was impacted in destructive ways. It was soon clear how Muslims everywhere were bearing the brunt of collective guilt and punishment for actions committed by those who claimed to share their faith. Being regarded as an individual is a luxury not afforded to racialized communities painted with the same brush of negative judgments and stereotypes in ways that dominant White communities never have to face if someone who looks like them or has the same name, commits a criminal act. Later, my younger son, Yusuf, began an acting career and found himself being typecast and routinely called to audition for the role of "terrorist number 2." The ways my sons have had to contend with and resist the challenges they experienced as part of the 9/11 generation were an impetus for this study and are reflected in relevant places within the book.

Another catalyst for this book occurred in 2004, when I met a very keen male student who enrolled in my undergraduate Gender and Islam course at the University of Toronto. This student, who I will call Murad, would wait with me to take the bus to the university campus and had a notebook full of questions he wanted to ask me about Islam, politics, and social justice. Murad was very popular and active on campus. He began a group called Muslims for Social Justice to address a variety of social and political causes. So many of the young women in the MSA had crushes on Murad. I would overhear them giggling in the women's washroom and notice them swooning and writing his name in their notebooks. After a while Murad began asking me questions about a group called Hizb ut-Tahrir (HT). HT is an Islamist group that was active in the United Kingdom (UK) during that time. They sought political change in Muslim communities that would lead to a central ruling authority represented by a caliphate. Murad told me he had joined a group led by some Muslim professors and students who wanted to share this ideology with Muslim campus communities.

I later came to know that this was recruitment strategy used by HT in the UK, where they were eventually banned. This was not a group that condoned violence (unlike the HT offshoot Muhajiroon) but rather sought gradual and progressive changes within the Muslim community toward their goal of restoring the medieval caliphate system that once governed Muslim societies. They saw this as a return to a "golden age" that would unite Muslims under a common banner and provide moral and spiritual uplift and protection from outside military threats. They did not believe in nationalism or democratic politics that stemmed from Western ideas of popular sovereignty. I did not agree with this philosophy and was very surprised and concerned that Murad, who was a campus leader for social justice, would be drawn to such narrow, hardline political and theological views.

Later, when I started my tenure-track position in 2005, I was disappointed to find that the MSA at my university had been taken over by a group promoting HT philosophy. They were suspicious and unwelcoming of the Muslim faculty on campus who they regarded as "sellouts" because we did not espouse their version of Islam. While I did not have concerns about potential "radicalization" with respect to these youth (though I knew they were being surveilled by CSIS and the RCMP), I found their negative impact on campus culture problematic. They were insular and uninterested in connecting with wider campus community. They were not concerned with addressing Islamophobia and did not participate in a study the Canadian Federation of Students was conducting on anti-Muslim racism on university campuses. While groups like HT use Islamophobia and the global oppression of Muslims as a rallying cry to recruit followers, in practice they were very inward-looking and focused on morally policing other Muslims. The leaders of the group eventually graduated and moved on, and a more progressive leadership took the MSA in new and important directions. Yet, it always concerned me how Murad and these other university students could be drawn to such troubling ideologies.

These three experiences spanning almost thirty years are what shaped my interest in conducting research on the 9/11 generation and discovering more about how they have been impacted by the global and local conditions stemming from the "war on terror" and the post-9/11 iteration of Islamophobia. It is my hope to do justice to the voices of the youth and other participants in this study, as well as to bring full circle my own experiences of these circumstances. This book tells the stories of marginalized youth who have had limited space to divulge how the conditions ushered into the post-9/11 world have impacted their identities, choices, and futures. By sharing these stories and the resistance and resilience of Muslim youth, we can better understand Islamophobia as a system of oppression, develop the knowledge and tools to dismantle it, and create new ant-racist and decolonial legacies for future generations.

Acknowledgments

This ambitious research study relied on the support provided by many research assistants across Canada who worked with me along the way. I am indebted to their invaluable assistance in community outreach and accessing participants for this study, interviewing, attending events, note-taking, and transcription, as well as putting together annotated bibliographies and data bases.

First and foremost, this study owes a great deal to the tremendous support and invaluable contributions of Asma Bala. She worked closely with me as a research assistant during all phases of this study, and the fieldwork we undertook together benefited greatly from her intellectual observations, competency, and talent. Asma leveraged her strong community networks as part of the outreach for this project. She is well respected in the Muslim community, which was important in developing the trust necessary for participants to feel safe coming forward and sharing their stories. Together we spent countless hours driving to interviews and events and, during those drives, discussing and debriefing what we were learning. We sat with our notebooks and laptops in cafés, restaurants, at my university office, or in my home drinking chai and talking about the themes emerging in our fieldwork. I'm grateful to have had her company, dedication, and informative insights throughout this undertaking. We also co-authored a book chapter entitled "Faith and Activism: Muslim Students' Associations and Campus-Based Social Movements," in *Political Muslims*, edited by Tahir Abbas and Sadek Hamid (New York: Syracuse University Press, 2019), 52–74. Parts of that collaborative work appear in chapter 4 of this book, and I am grateful to Syracuse University Press for allowing excerpts of that chapter to be republished in this book. I have credited Asma's contribution to chapter 4. She was, and is, far more than a research assistant, and I am grateful to call her a dear friend and sister.

Along the six-year journey that brought this book to fruition, Sana Khalil, Humera Javed, Itrath Syed, Jacqueline Flatt, and Setti Kidane all provided research assistance. I relied on and benefited from their dedication and competent academic skills to make this project a success. They helped lighten the load in the otherwise daunting work that went into this study.

I would like to acknowledge the unwavering support and encouragement I received from Kyla Madden, senior editor with McGill-Queen's University Press. I brought the idea for this book to her several years ago, and ever since, her willingness to meet with me, read chapters, and provide thoughtful feedback was so important during the process of writing this book. I am thankful for her patience and professionalism throughout this journey. I am indebted to the support of the Social Sciences and Humanities Research Council (SSHRC) for providing the funding that made this study possible. I gratefully acknowledge permission from Boonaa Mohammed to print in the introduction several lines from his poem, "Terror Is," published online in 2015.

Finally, I am indebted to the more than 130 study participants from across Canada who shared their experiences with me and, ultimately, with the readers of this book. It is their courage and critical insights that guide this book. I am grateful that they entrusted me with their stories, and I hope I have done justice to them. As we mark the twentieth anniversary of 9/11 and its aftermath, which profoundly influenced the world that Muslim youth around the globe inherited, I hope this generation will be the architects of a better future.

UNDER SIEGE

Introduction

Islamophobia and the 9/11 Generation

Living "under siege" has become a reality for Muslims globally. Whether it is the ethnic cleansing and genocide of the Rohingya people in Myanmar, the persecution of the Uyghurs in China, the tyranny of Islamophobic Hindutva nationalism in India and Kashmir, the oppression of Palestinians, or the discrimination and securitization of Muslims in Western nations, living under siege is a by-product of global Islamophobia. The 9/11 attacks in the United States and the subsequent global war on terror have created a landscape of violence that is the inheritance of young Muslims whose lives are being shaped within and against these crises. The generation of Muslim youth who have come of age during these turbulent times have a unique legacy because they have not known a world before the aftermath and backlash surrounding these events. September 11 ushered in a period through which neo-imperial war was drawn along the global fault lines of race, religion, class, and nationality. The 9/11 generation bears daily witness to the violence and destruction exported to Muslim majority countries through US-led military campaigns, and in Western nations they are subject to domestic security policies that label them as potential terrorists and enemies of the state. They have grown up watching how the nameless, faceless masses "over there" live in militarized playgrounds and are reduced to moving targets for sharpshooters and carpet bombers while those "over here" in the West[1] are transformed from citizens to outlaws by virtue of their religion, ethnicity, and race.

In this fraught political terrain, the imperial politics of empire abroad along with stigmatizing domestic policies converge and set Muslim youth in the crosshairs of these ideological and very real battlegrounds. Some youth, primed by these conditions, are lured into radical transnational groups like Daesh,[2] while the majority are forced to bear the burden and repercussions of collective responsibility for the actions of a few. Muslim youth in the West have been labelled as an unwelcome foreign threat, and they find themselves in an ideological and political battle they did not create but are nonetheless entangled within. The Canadian Muslim poet Boonaa Mohammed shares this angst in his poem "Terror Is":[3]

> So, I guess maybe it's just Islam's turn to be the enemy
> But I don't want to be the enemy, it's hard enough just being me
> A black, African, son of a refugee Muslim living in a culture that
> is extremely hostile towards me

The predicament offered up in this poem is a salient one among diasporic Muslim youth in Western societies, who must contend with being positioned as alien, foreign, and dangerous outsiders to a land they call home.

This book explores the experiences of the 9/11 generation of Canadian Muslim youth who have come of age in these fraught times of global war and terror. Many studies map the currency of Islamophobia and anti-Muslim racism but not enough have focused on the toll these take on Muslim communities, especially youth. As Bayoumi (2009) observes, Muslim youth are constantly talked about but almost never heard from. This book centres Muslim youth voices as diverse interlocutors speaking to the social, cultural, and political challenges of growing up under the spectre of the war on terror and post-9/11 Islamophobia that affect their lives and the everyday choices they make. As young people, the 9/11 generation have lost their youthful claim to innocence and instead find their experience of coming of age is politicized and policed (see also Abdel-Fattah 2021; Bakali 2016; Ali 2014; Abbas 2011; Maira 2009, 2016; Sirin and Fine 2008). The 9/11 generation of Muslim youth have grown up under unique circumstances where their identities have become reconfigured as "radicals" and "jihadists" to serve as an iconic foil that makes the Western imperial project seem intelligible, reasonable, and just. These youth must live within the spaces of dissonance created through these renewed neo-colonial encounters. Like all Muslims, members of the 9/11 generation find themselves being collapsed into a singular, narrow, abject, and undifferentiated category that erases the vast diversity and heterogeneity among one-fifth of the world's population. Despite the narrow parameters within which they are viewed, there is a wide variety of registers through which Muslims live their lives. Yet all too often, this diversity is erased by sensationalized and stereotypical frames of reference.

So, what does it mean to be socialized into a world where your faith and identity are under siege? Sirin and Fine (2008, 1) refer to the dilemma facing the 9/11 generation of Muslim youth as the result of "growing up under the shadow of moral exclusion," where "overnight 'they,' Muslims, became the designated 'others' who had to be watched, detained, and sometimes deported in order to save 'us.'" Ahmad and Seddon (2012, 2) outline their concerns for the abject construction of Muslim youth identities: "The *Zeitgeist* of the current age sees young Muslims constitute part of the collective fears of Western liberal democratic societies, whether as a perceived 'fifth column' religious terrorists in the Western minority context, or as pro-democracy radicals in the frontlines of the 'Arab Spring' revolutions sweeping across the Middle East." And yet, as Abdel-Fattah (2021, 21) notes in her study of Australian Muslim youth coming of age in the war on terror, "[I]t became fairly obvious to me that Muslim youth don't rate being 'groomed by ISIS' as a concern in their lives." Within this age of global conflict and insurgency, Muslim youth are being coded into a variety of categories that have little to do with how they see themselves or their beliefs and values. There is limited space or opportunity for them to counter the dominant narratives that govern the distinctions between being regarded as either peaceful citizens or dangerous suspects.

Haliday in 2003 (cited in Abbas 2011, 138) notes that "issues such as the intrusion of the state into everyday life, legislation perceived as specifically targeting Muslims and the fact of external domination and strict immigration controls suggest that Muslim communities may feel that they are under constant threat." The pervasiveness of feeling "under constant threat" is conditioned by very real factors whereby global geopolitics have shaped the domestic landscape for Muslims, which has resulted in security policies, surveillance, targeting and harassment, and discrimination in all aspects of life from employment (Kazemipur 2014); schooling (J. Zine 2004, 2008; Sensoy and Stonebanks 2009; Bakali 2016); border crossings (Bahdi 2003; Hennebry and Momani 2013; Jamil 2017; Nagra 2017); immigration (Arat-Koç 2017); banking transactions (Nazim 2007); housing procurement (J. Zine 2009b); connections to mosques and Islamic organizations

(McDonough and Hoodfar 2009; McSorley 2021); and participation in public and civic life (Bullock and Nesbitt-Larking 2011; Bakht 2014). These conditions also lead to related states of mind among those affected by them. This affective conditioning occurs through an "emotional geopolitics" that acknowledges "the feelings, perceptions, views, subjectivities or bodies who experience the outcomes of geopolitical decisions and processes first hand during their everyday lives" (Pain 2009 cited in Hopkins 2011, 163). In other words, the war on terror has become a lived experience not just a geopolitical construct. This book is the first to explore the impact of these global and domestic conditions on how the 9/11 generation of Canadian Muslim youth navigate and make sense of their lives and the changing world around them.

"UNDER SIEGE" VERSUS "SIEGE MENTALITY"

The notion of living "under siege" is distinct from having a "siege mentality." For example, Razack (2008, 6) describes the siege mentality among ethnonationalists who fear the encroachment of difference: "In the case of the nation state we can immediately say what is born, or perhaps born again, is a national community organized increasingly as a fortress with rigid boundaries and borders that mark who belongs and who does not. The national subject of this securitized state understands himself or herself as being under siege." The idea of policing the boundaries of belonging and banishment within the nation out of a fear that foreign outsiders are taking over and undermining the way of life of "old-stock Canadians" is a common sentiment and basis for racist and Islamophobic conspiracy theories among far right, White nationalist groups.[4] In contrast, the idea of living under siege in the way it is taken up in this book is not about creating a fortress against imagined enemies; instead, it is about the precarities of living through real existential threats as marginalized youth. This is a predicament Muslim youth find themselves in that is not of their own making, and they must find ways to manoeuvre and challenge the fraught social and political conditions that have converged around them. They do so not as victims but rather as agents who resist these conditions.

THE LIMITS OF MULTICULTURALISM

Muslim cultural politics in Canada take shape within the backdrop of a contested notion and practice of multiculturalism. According to Haque (2012, 22), Canada's immigration policies and Multiculturalism

Act "locate the racialized immigrant on the boundaries of the nation and as constitutive elements of these borders." Multiculturalism then, demarcates spaces of belonging and exile as part of the "imagined community" of the nation (Anderson 1983). While multiculturalism offers the guarantee of social and cultural inclusion, it has been built upon and failed to overthrow historical legacies of White settler colonialism, racial exclusion, and inequality (see also Thobani 2007). The narcissism of the dominant culture regulates inclusion and how diverse cultural ways of life are inserted into Canada's stratified mosaic (Porter 1965). The diversity that is "celebrated" through multicultural festivals and cultural song, dance, and "ethnic" food fairs, is a performative act that secures Canada's standing as a benevolent nation.

Meanwhile, Indigenous, racial, and cultural inequality lurks behind the smokescreen. Sara Ahmed (2000, 103) notes that multiculturalism is a mechanism for the "management of the consequences of difference," which implies that difference needs to be "governed, contained, and made coherent through government policy." I refer to this White national overseeing of social and cultural diversity as a "disciplinary" form of multiculturalism, which keeps in check disruptive minoritized groups that deviate from dominant consensual norms and must be disciplined back into the grid of multicultural containment. Muslims are constructed as especially transgressive minorities in this formulation. Islam is often regarded as being at odds with liberal modernity and democratic values and unsuitable for allowing integration into secular pluralistic societies. This view underwrites liberal forms of Islamophobia where values of equity, diversity, and inclusion are espoused and celebrated, yet at the same time, policies and practices are enacted that target Muslims as suspect or "backward" minorities. Liberal Islamophobia arises when "Islamophilia," marked by cultural fascination and fetishism, meets Islamophobia. The paradox of these two contradictory impulses of fetishistic fascination and racial disavowal shapes the political and cultural terrain of multiculturalism. More than other extreme variants of Islamophobia, liberal Islamophobia does the work of normalizing anti-Muslim racism with greater legitimacy and institutional power.

Secular multiculturalism is viewed as a position of social "neutrality" and a universal civic value as opposed to an ideologically situated standpoint that in its draconian iterations subjugates religious life and limits public participation. Canada's combination of secularism and multiculturalism works in tandem to offer the illusion of equitable inclusion while each provides a camouflage for the other that obscures how they function to limit and exclude religious cultures. Ghassan Hage (2000) points out that multiculturalism was an offer of toler-ance that proceeded from unequal relations of power and thus could always be withdrawn, making the terms contingent on the managerial power of the White racial state.

Conversely, political conservatives and far right White nationalist groups attack multiculturalism for corrupting "Canadian values" by valorizing foreign parasitic cultures encroaching on the way of life of old-stock Canadians. Questions regarding the efficacy and limits of Canadian multiculturalism are also invoked in relation to the threat of "homegrown terrorism" that places Muslims, and especially Muslim youth, as the source of racial fears and angst. These notions are steeped in ideas of civilizational wars, not mere clashes (see Huntington 1996). Modern cultural eugenics use the code language of the "rule of law" and "our values" to demarcate the boundaries of the nation as a place for the supremacy of Judeo-Christian democracy. Religious minorities fall outside the normative parameters of these rigid boundaries and racial and religious hierarchies. Muslims are the emblem of this exis-tential and cultural crisis. In these world views, multiculturalism is seen has having run amok and allowing backward cultures to flourish in ways that oppress women and threaten the hegemony of Western lifestyles (Moller Okin 1999). Within this xenophobic rhetoric, multi-culturalism is the altar upon which Canadian culture, Judeo-Christian values, women's rights, and public safety are being sacrificed.

Other concerns revolve around how Canadian multiculturalism has not gone far enough, as opposed to having gone too far. Multiculturalism as a national policy and social ethic has left racisms and Islamophobia intact. Construction as the "enemy within" is an ontological category that further entrenches the tropes of racial and religious degeneracy ascribed to Muslims in the West, and shapes the way young Canadian Muslims frame their sense of identity and belonging within the national multicultural narrative.

WHO IS THE 9/11 GENERATION?

Research has demonstrated that generational markers are shaped by significant events and developments (Mackay 1997). During adoles-cence these experiences are formative, and while their impact on individuals cannot be essentialized or viewed reductively there are common characteristics. Bahr and Pendergast (2006, 69) suggest that "these shared experiences and conditions shape groups of people in particular ways that in turn shapes their thinking, values, and beliefs." For example, with those of the millennial generation, the advent of the internet and social media has had a significant impact on their development and on how they learn (Howe and Strauss 2000). Understanding the unique challenges of each generation provides some insight into what shapes their world views and common experiences.

According to a 2009 survey, the millennial generation (born between 1980 and 1996) cites the attacks on 9/11 as the most important influence shaping their attitudes and beliefs (Towns 2011). In describing the influences impacting millennials, Burstein (2013) identifies 9/11 as a defining moment for this generation. Bahr and Pendergast (2006, 70) cite the unique social, political, and technological developments that shape the millennial generation, including "internet chat lines, school violence, September 11, Bali bombings, terrorism, the war on Iraq and Kosovo." These developments and events characterize the conditions under which a large part of the world's population has come of age. In global regions such as Africa, the Middle East, and Asia, millennials make up a third to almost half of the population. There are 1.7 billion millennials worldwide, or one-quarter of the global population.

The 9/11 generation of Muslim millennials is a product of its times. When the fieldwork for this study began in 2009, the youth who took part in it were between the ages of eighteen and twenty-six years. This meant that during the time of the 9/11 attacks and their aftermath, these youth would have been between ten and eighteen years of age. These ages range from formative adolescent years into young adulthood. What is significant about their coming of age during this time, as Ali (2014, 1250) notes, is that "these young people experienced adolescence in a moment where the targeting of individuals associated with Islam increased dramatically."

Other research has confirmed the backlash Muslims faced after 9/11 has had a profound effect on young Muslims. For example, after surveying 120 Muslim university students in Toronto, Caidi and MacDonald (2008) found that 94 per cent of them "agreed" or "strongly agreed" with the statement, "I see a change in the way others view me since 9/11." Shahzad's study (2014) of the effects of the war on terror among 99 Canadian university students found that discourses of fear created anxiety among Muslim and non-Muslim students. Maira's (2016, 196) research on Muslim youth in the post-9/11 context of the United States asserted that "living with, accommodating, or resisting surveillance are part of the coming of age experiences of the 9/11 generation." The events of 9/11 and the aftermath of heightened Islamophobia and the war on terror have shaped the evolution of this generation of young people in ways they are often not even cognizant of. This blind spot is often the result of not knowing a world that existed prior to this catalytic moment and finding the circumstances they now face as normative experiences rather than as by-products of a global and domestic political shift.

In my own early boomer childhood memories, I recall seeing news reports on television about the Vietnam War. However, growing up in Canada, this terrible event did not impact my life, other than seeing disturbing images of body bags on the television screen. On the other hand, for Muslim youth who watched the horror of the Twin Towers falling on September 11, 2001, they soon discovered on September 12 – the very next day – they were immediately drawn into a new world order that affected how others saw them and how they would navigate growing up amid the backlash directed toward their communities. Overnight they were being held accountable to a collective guilt by association for crimes that people identified as their co-religionists were responsible for committing. Due to their age and limited experience, many of these adolescents did not know much about the world prior to this, so the experience of Islamophobic backlash soon became normalized for them. This is not to say that their rich and textured lives are entirely defined by these political conditions, but they have nonetheless had a profound effect on how they live their lives, navigate their identities, and imagine their futures. Capturing how the youth of this distinct generation are managing the circumstances they inherited and drawing attention to the blind spots that have at times normalized Islamophobia in their lives constitute an important focus of this book.

In *The Souls of Black Folk* ([1903] 1995), W.E.B. Du Bois asks the poignant question: "How does it feel to be a problem?" He recognizes that residing in a state of racial alterity creates an inverted gaze: "It is a peculiar sensation, this double-consciousness, this sense of always looking at one's self through the eyes of others, of measuring one's soul by the tape of a world that looks on in amused contempt and pity." Du Bois's analysis applies to how the 9/11 generation has been regarded with contempt, derision, and fear. Bayoumi (2009) argues that since 9/11, Muslims are the new "problem" (see also Aguilar 2018). In Canada, Muslims follow the line of other so-called problem groups beginning with Indigenous peoples and followed by immigrants such as the Chinese, Japanese, and South Asians, although Ukrainians, Germans, Irish, and Jews were also affected. This book draws attention to the way the 9/11 generation is grappling with Du Bois's question and how its members feel and react to being constructed as a problem in Canada.

ISLAMOPHOBIA: WHAT'S IN A NAME?

I provide an overview of how Islamophobia has been identified and defined in its contemporary formations and then supply the definition I have developed that offers a framework for the analysis in this book. Lorente (2010, 116) describes the difficulties of capturing the essence of what constitutes Islamophobia and the problems that lacking clarity holds:

> Although the concept is increasingly widespread, it seems especially hard to define in practice just what Islamophobia is, as it is often put on a par with other processes such as racism (anti-Maghrebi, anti-Muslim, anti-Arab, etc.), hostility to Islam and xenophobia, etc., and confused with or likened to terms such as "Maurophobia," "Moorophobia" or "Arabophobia." This has given way to a wavering definition, with no consensus as to either its definition or legal formulation, reaffirming both the emerging and changing social reality and the broad ignorance at different levels over what is taking place in our societies, regions and neighbourhoods, etc.

Scholars and policy-makers internationally have cited the need for a clear definition of the complex phenomenon of Islamophobia. The term itself has been highly contested (Sayyid 2014a). In breaking down the terminology as a "fear of Islam," it is a narrow and limiting notion. Lorente (2010, 120) argues that Islamophobia is a "grammatically incorrect" term "that would require the 150 years which the term 'anti-Semitism' needed to become grammatically acceptable."

To grasp a robust understanding of what Islamophobia is, it is important to clarify how this term has been defined and what meanings have been attached to it. The Runnymede Trust (1997) report on Islamophobia in the UK offered the first definition of Islamophobia. Twenty years later, the organizations followed up with an anniversary report entitled, *Islamophobia: Still a Challenge for Us All* (Elahi and

Khan 2017). The original Islamophobia report states that the term refers to three phenomena: (a) unfounded hostility toward Islam, (b) practical consequences of such hostility in unfair discrimination against Muslim individuals and communities, and (c) exclusion of Muslims from mainstream political and social affairs. The authors of the updated report (Elahi and Khan 2017) contend that in hindsight the focus on discrimination and exclusion from social and political affairs should be prioritized. Redefining Islamophobia in light of the social and policy context of Britain, they offer the following remit: "Islamophobia is any distinction, exclusion, or restriction towards, or preference against, Muslims (or those perceived to be Muslims) that has the purpose or effect of nullifying or impairing the recognition, enjoyment or exercise, on an equal footing, of human rights and fundamental freedoms in the political, economic, social, cultural or any other field of public life" (Elahi and Khan 2017, 7).

Here the revised Runnymede definition presumes there is an "equal footing" in the political, economic, social, cultural, and broader public sphere. This presupposition erases the structural inequities that make the idea of a level playing field impossible. Additionally, using the notion of "equality" versus "equity" is limiting with respect to the kinds of political outcomes these terms denote. The notion of "equality of opportunity" is founded on liberal myths of "meritocracy" and the individualizing of failure versus the reality of systemic barriers that marginalized groups face. Equality of opportunity cannot exist without an equality of condition. The term "equity," on the other hand, acknowledges the systemic underpinnings of inequality and proposes the redress of these conditions according to the needs of historically disadvantaged groups.

In Canada, the Ontario Human Rights Commission (2005, 10) offers the following definition of Islamophobia: "A contemporary and emerging form of racism in Canada has been termed 'Islamophobia.' Islamophobia can be described as stereotypes, bias or acts of hostility towards individual Muslims or followers of Islam in general. In addition to individual acts of intolerance and racial profiling, Islamophobia leads to viewing Muslims as a greater security threat on an institutional, systemic and societal level."[5]

Defining Islamophobia as "a contemporary and emerging form of racism" is a limiting notion. Islamophobia is not "emerging." It has existed in various iterations since the first Muslim community was ostracized, harassed, and vilified for its beliefs and has continued into other historical periods like the Crusades, the expulsion of the Moors in Spain, and into colonial modernity and the imperial present. Racism has antecedents that reach back into the Middle Ages yet developed as a system of classification in the modern period (Goldberg 1993). Given this historical trajectory, it can be argued that Islamophobia predates modern forms of racism. Furthermore, the attempts to link the definition of Islamophobia to notions of Muslims as security threats as primary definitional markers in the OHRC example, fail to allow room for understanding how Muslims represent the existential threat of civilizational danger through popularized notions of "creeping sharia," for example. Both the Runnymede and OHRC definitions do not fully allow for an understanding of Islamophobia as a dynamic phenomenon and process that is shored up by discursive apparatuses. A broader understanding of Islamophobia must capture the socio-logical dynamic through which it operates.

problems w/ both definitions

The definitional debates surrounding Islamophobia are important to consolidate its meaning and intelligibility and because language and discourse are constitutive of social realities as post-structuralists contend. How we define and construct social phenomena impacts what interventions can take place. For example, reducing Islamophobia to a form of "intolerance" or "hate," as is so often seen, constructs it as an interpersonal problem as opposed to a structural and systemic one, since the act of "intolerance" operates within the purview of individuals rather than as a function of the state. The interventions that follow from this understanding are therefore limited to the realm of individual relations as opposed to interrogating and challenging state practices. Moreover, the goal of being "tolerated" is also not an enviable one and amounts to the lowest common denominator within social and cultural encounters.

limits of tolerance / approach

From a socio-psychological standpoint, the notion of Islamophobia is often loosely translated as an "attitude of fear, mistrust, or hatred of Islam and its adherents." However, this definition presents a narrow conceptual framework and does not account for the social, structural, and ideological dimensions through which forms of oppression are operationalized and enacted. Far from being based on "ignorance," Islamophobic attitudes are part of a rational system of power and domination that manifests as individual, ideological, and systemic forms of discrimination and oppression. The idea that discrimination, whether based on race, class, gender, sexuality, ability, or religion, stems from simple ignorance allows those engaged in oppressive acts

social /
racial
hierarchies

and policies to claim a space of innocence. It also does not account for the various political projects maintained through social and racial hierarchies, where embedded political interests ensure the reproduction of these oppressions. By labelling Islamophobia as an essentially "irrational" fear, this conception denies the logic and rationality of social dominance and oppression. These systems operate as multiple interlocking oppressions and relations of power that reproduce and embed Islamophobia into various social and institutional structures.

ISLAMOPHOBIA AS A SYSTEM OF OPPRESSION

author's
definition

I propose that Islamophobia is best captured as: *a fear and hatred of Islam and Muslims[6] (and those perceived as Muslims)[7] that translate into individual actions and ideological and systemic forms of oppression that support the logic and rationale of specific power relations* (J. Zine 2004). This broader definition outlines the sociology of Islamophobia as a dynamic and pervasive form of oppression that is embedded in structures of power.

The "individual actions" in this dynamic are manifestations of Islamophobia that include acts like vandalism, name-calling, exclusion, harassment, microaggressions, violence, and hate crimes. For example, a report by the Toronto Police Service (2001) revealed that there was a 66 per cent increase in hate crimes in 2001 after the 9/11 attacks in the US. In recent years, Statistics Canada found hate crimes against Muslims in Canada grew 253 per cent from 2012 to 2015 (Minsky 2017). The number of anti-Muslim incidents reported to police rose from 45 in 2012, to 159 by 2015. Testimonies of 181 Muslim women living in various cities across Canada found that at least one attack per week took place against mosques across the country from September 2001 to June 2002; sixteen of these were bomb threats (Helly 2004, 28). These actions led to social-psychological effects and trauma (Awaad 2015; Rousseau et al. 2015).

253% increase in hate crimes 2012-2015

Canadian Muslims have been profoundly impacted by the collective trauma of Islamophobic violence and terror following two mass murders in 2017 and 2021 respectively. A terror attack in London, Ontario, on 6 June 2021 killed four members of a Pakistani Muslim family out on an evening stroll in their neighbourhood. Police called this deadly incident an Islamophobic hate crime and stated that the Afzaal family, hit by a speeding truck, were targeted because of their Muslim faith. A nine-year-old boy survived the attack but was left hospitalized with serious injuries. This was the second mass murder of Canadian Muslims in four years, following the shooting in a Quebec mosque on 29 January 2017, where six Muslim men were killed after their evening prayers. These tragedies underscore the deadly consequences of Islamophobia and the threat of White nationalist terror. This violence underscores the urgency for unpacking the dynamics of Islamophobia and examining the breeding ground for such acts (J. Zine 2021).

Individual actions are the most prominent and visible phenomena in the Islamophobia dynamic. We can imagine these acts as the tip of an iceberg and hidden below the surface are the ideologies that serve to justify and rationalize these actions and the systemic practices through which Islamophobia is reproduced. There are ubiquitous ideologies and tropes that serve to demonize and vilify Islam and Muslims. These include stereotypes like Muslims are terrorists who engage in *taqiyya*[8] and are really "wolves in sheep's clothing," who want to install creeping sharia laws that will undermine Western society and civilization. Other stereotypes relegate Muslim women to being backward and oppressed, without agency or freedom. Muslims are interpolated into discourses, such as being the bearers of "barbaric cultural practices" that conjure images of bearded maniacal men and submissive women in burkas hell-bent on the destruction of feminism and the West.

These Orientalist tropes popularized in colonial contexts have been coded into Western fears and fantasies about the "Islamic peril" and are retrieved and redeployed from this archive in new imperial moments (see also Karim 2003). Kumar (2012) warns that such myths about Islam become common sense ideas that shape the public imaginary. These notions become hegemonic as they are filtered through the institutions of civil society such as media (television, film, social media) and education, and are embedded in pop culture through widespread circulation on the internet. These discourses are often uncritically absorbed, taken on as truths, and rarely debunked through counter-narratives. Allen (2010, 190) identifies vilifying ideologies as a facet of Islamophobia that is similar in theory, function, and purpose to racism and that perpetuates negatively evaluated meanings about Muslims and Islam through "shared languages and conceptual maps" that shape and sustain negative social consensus (see also Sheehi 2011; Semati 2012). Orientalist ideologies shape Islamophobic imaginaries and provide the rationale for systemic practices through which Islamophobia becomes institutionally embedded and reproduced.

Bazian (2015, 162) notes that while Islamophobic ideologues "attempt to classify who belongs to the civilized world" versus who is the "demonized and ostracized global other," there is a deeper level whereby Islamophobia becomes "a rationalization of the existing domestic and global racial stratification, economic power hierarchies, and open-ended militarism." As Bazian observes, Islamophobic ideologies have material consequences in the way they shape, inform, and authorize global militarism as well as domestic policies relating to immigration, security, and social policies. In this way, Islamophobia provides a rationale for systemic practices such as racial and religious profiling and surveillance, state policies governing religious attire (i.e., hijab/niqab bans), as well as authorizing institutional discrimination in education, social services, healthcare, and law enforcement. Canadian security policies targeting Muslims include, for example, the Anti-terrorism Act (Patel 2012), Security Certificates (Flatt 2012), and the "No-Fly List" (Jamil 2017). Bahdi (2003) remarks that after 9/11 racial profiling focused more on Arabs and Muslims and that surveillance spilled over into areas such as banking and employment and Muslim charities (McSorley 2021), as well as increased scrutiny at Canadian airports. Hennebry and Momani (2013) have also pointed out that Canadian security policies and legal frameworks have specifically targeted Arab and Muslim Canadians. They note that racism and security collude in these measures: "Once securitization measures are implemented, racialization becomes legally entrenched, made normal and morally acceptable as a necessary tool to protect the nation and its citizens from potential 'terrorists,' criminals and /or 'undesirables'" (Hennebry and Momani 2013, 7).

In addition to security policies, other Canadian social policies exemplify systemic forms of Islamophobia. These practices form the basis of liberal Islamophobia, in which on the one hand, governments promote the values of diversity, equity, inclusion, and multiculturalism but on the other enact anti-Muslim policies. These actions span across the political spectrum in Canada. From Conservative MP Kellie Leitch's proposal for an RCMP tip line to report "barbaric cultural practices against women and girls," to pushing for bans against the niqab at federal citizenship ceremonies and among civil servants, these social policies and proposals promote gendered Islamophobic ideologies in the name of rescuing and protecting Muslim women from their supposed backward and misogynist faith. Policies in Quebec have also focused on policing and regulating Muslim women's dress in the name of preserving secular values and francophone culture. These systemic practices are underwritten by long-standing Orientalist tropes and ideologies that find renewed currency in the Canadian public policy.

Often the term "anti-Muslim racism" is preferred over Islamophobia, as it is seen to better capture the phenomenon of discrimination against Muslims and solves the problem that critics of Islamophobia hold by separating out criticism of Islam. I argue that anti-Muslim racism is a manifestation of Islamophobia, which is evident through the violence, hatred, and discrimination enacted against Muslim bodies, but since these acts rely upon the demonization of Islam to sustain and reproduce its racial logic, one does not exist without the other. Islam and any markers, referents, and adherence to it comprise a predominant focus of social and political disapproval, legal regulation, and cultural concern. The historical and ontological specificity of Islamophobia as a form of oppression must be considered in the ways that both religion and race are invoked (J. Zine 2017). Grosfoguel and Mielants (2006, 4) describe Islamophobia as a form of cultural racism, arguing that religion has a dominant role in cultural racist discourses: "The contemporary tropes about 'uncivilized,' 'barbarian,' 'savage,' 'primitive,' 'underdeveloped,' 'authoritarian,' and 'terrorist' inferior people are today concentrated in the 'other's' religious practices and beliefs." Therefore, the confluences of race and religion need to be understood in tandem. In Western nations, Islamophobia is underwritten by racial and imperial logics as well as religious bigotry. In other nations, different forms of Islamophobic ethnonationalisms are in play that promote religious persecution.

Global manifestations of Islamophobia are growing and include Buddhist Islamophobia in Myanmar against the Rohingya, Islamophobia in China against the Uyghurs, Hindu nationalist Islamophobia in India and Kashmir, and the Islamophobic oppression of Palestinians by the Israeli state. These forms of violent, state-led, ethnonational Islamophobia operate differently from how we view Islamophobia in Western nations. Islamophobia also exists in Muslim majority countries, where it is embedded in systems of power supported by postcolonial elites and secularization policies and practices (see Bayrakli and Hafez 2019). Understanding Islamophobia in a global context requires a more complex analytical and historical tracing of its genealogy and roots in different forms of religious and racial oppression. It also requires a broad definition that can encompass and unpack its resonance and dynamics in these diverse settings.

The "racialization of religion" is a related factor in discerning how Islamophobia is constituted. Through this process, racial characteristics are ascribed to religious categories, and racial phenotypes are coded as religious markers (Joshi 2006). Meer (2012, 5), for example, notes that "the category of race was co-constituted with religion, and our resurrection of this genealogy implicates the formation of race in the racialization of religious subjects." This is an important acknowledgment of how religious and racial discriminations are aligned rather than being conflated. Following these understandings, highlighting how race, religion, and culture have shaped public policy and opinion in Canada is important in comprehending the social-political landscape of this study.

ISLAMOPHOBIA AND QUEBEC'S ETHNONATIONALISM: THE QUEBEC MOSQUE ATTACK

The date 29 January 2017 will go down in Canada's history as the day of the worst mass murder to take place in a house of worship, when six Muslim men were shot dead in a Quebec mosque. The victims were Ibrahima Barry, thirty-nine; Mamadou Tanou Barry, forty-two; Khaled Belkacemi, sixty; Abdelkrim Hassane, forty-one; Azzedine Soufiane, fifty-seven; and Aboubaker Thabti, forty-four. These men came to Canada from Morocco, Algeria, and Guinea. Nineteen other worshippers were injured, including Aymen Derbali, who was paralyzed in an attempt to stop the attack.[9] Alexandre Bissonnette, an armed White nationalist terrorist, went on a shooting rampage in the Islamic Cultural Centre in Laval, Quebec, just after evening prayers. Media reports indicated Bissonnette, a twenty-seven-year-old anthropology student from Université Laval, had browsed websites linked to Robert Spencer, a prominent anti-Muslim activist; David Duke, the former Ku Klux Klan leader; Dylann Roof, a White supremacist terrorist who gunned down nine African American worshippers at a South Carolina church; and Marc Lépine, the shooter in Montreal's 1989 École Polytechnique massacre. He also made over 800 online searches of former US president Donald Trump.

Bissonnette later confessed to police that he had been motivated by Prime Minister Justin Trudeau's message of welcome to refugees,[10] following Donald Trump's travel ban on seven Muslim majority countries. Bissonnette told police, "I was watching TV and I learned that the Canadian government was going to take more refugees who couldn't go to the United States, and they were coming here ... I saw that and I, like, lost my mind. I don't want us to become like Europe. I don't want them to kill my parents, my family ... I had to do something, I couldn't do nothing. It was something that tortured me" (Cecco 2018).

The first suspect in the Quebec shooting was a Moroccan man. He was in the mosque during the attack and called police, who then misidentified him as a suspect. This rush to judgment demonstrates how easily and routinely Muslims are associated with criminality and terror, even when they are the victims. Alarmingly, at the same Quebec mosque where the attack occurred, a pig's head with a sign that read "Bon Appétit" was left at the door a year before (Magder 2016).

After the mosque shooting, Motion 103 was tabled by Liberal MP Iqra Khalid to address Islamophobia, systemic racism, and religious discrimination, and to implement measures to research, document, and challenge these concerns. This proposal was met with virulent Islamophobic rhetoric and hate. MP Khalid received more than 50,000 emails in response to Motion 103, many of them with overt racist, sexist, and Islamophobic content, including direct threats. All of this came as an affront to Muslims who had barely had time to grieve the horror of the massacre before dealing with the onslaught of Islamophobia and anti-Muslim racism. After four years of community-led campaigns that called for the commemoration of this tragedy and concrete measures to combat the Islamophobia that led to it,[11] the federal government announced in 2021 that 29 January will be designated as a National Day of Remembrance and Action on Islamophobia.

REASONABLE ACCOMMODATION

In the religious and political landscape of Canada, Ramji (2008, 104) notes that for non-believers and non-religious people 9/11 was an event that seemed to prove that "religion causes nothing but trouble." Such concerns are heightened in Quebec, where secularism has deep roots grounded in the Quiet Revolution of the 1960s, which shifted the social and political foundations of society toward secularization and separatism. In 2007, public hearings were held across the province to address issues such as wearing the hijab in martial arts, accommodation of prayers and provision for halal and kosher food in public and private institutions, and the designation of female staff to cater to Muslim or orthodox Jewish women in healthcare facilities. These

circumstances were tested by the balance between upholding the duty
to accommodate religious diversity as enshrined in the Canadian
Charter of Rights and Freedoms and preserving the distinct nature
and secularism of Québécois society.

In their report on Reasonable Accommodation in Quebec based
on the inquiry, Bouchard and Taylor (2008b, 121) conclude that
Canadian multiculturalism "emphasizes diversity at the expense of
continuity" and therefore is an unsuitable model for Quebec – a sentiment
they note most of the interveners expressed at the public consultations.
The inquiry concluded that the model of "interculturalism" was pref-
erable for Quebecers since "interculturalism fosters the edification of
a common identity through interaction between citizens of all origins"
(Bouchard and Taylor 2008a, 88). However, by asserting the "edification of a common identity" as a hallmark of interculturalism, the
report assumes there is a level playing field for cultural encounters to
take place and does not account for the power relations between
dominant and subaltern communities. Not situating this process
within the histories and legacies of subordination with respect to race,
class, ethnicity, religion, language, and culture denies the imbalances
of power and privilege hidden beneath the rhetoric of inclusion. In
what way does achieving this common identity erase all other diverse
ways of being? How does this idea serve as a code for assimilation
to francophone culture within a White settler colonial context? Along
with liberal multiculturalism, the discourse of interculturalism depoliti-
cizes race through a colour-blind politics of denial. For example, as
Hennebry and Momani (2013) point out, while the Reasonable
Accommodation debates targeted many minorities, they focused most
prominently on Arab Canadians and Muslims who were questioned
regarding their loyalty to the country.

POLITICS OF SARTORIAL NATIONALISM
AND COERCED UNVEILING

Gender is also sacrificed on the altar of Quebec's interculturalism,
whereby policies that regulate, police, and banish Muslim women's
religious attire from the public sphere are implemented in the name
of secular "neutrality." Elsewhere I have argued that these policies
enact a form of "sartorial nationalism" in which veiled Muslim women
are rendered as illiberal and "unimaginable" as citizens. Citizenship
and national belonging become determined sartorially, as the nation

is not only circumscribed by dominant cultural values and beliefs (that veiling is seen to undermine) but also is configured through the kinds of dress that signify belonging and allegiance to these same values (J. Zine 2012a). Coerced unveiling policies and practices are based on the problematic ways Muslim women's religious attire has been regarded within the racial project of secularism as a sign of anti-modern and anti-democratic religious sensibilities. Muslim women are viewed as subservient to religious patriarchy and devoid of the agency and political maturity to make choices about their body (rights other Canadian women enjoy), and thereby require secular state intervention. Natasha Bakht (2015, 419–20) laments these regressive laws: "In the 21st century, the Western world is at an astonishing historical moment, when women's clothes are still the subject of legislation (Beaman 2013, 725), judicial, and public approbation. Women who wear the niqab or the full-face veil have borne the brunt of oppressive government tactics internationally to limit their choice of clothing."

The introduction of Bill 94 in 2010 by Quebec's Liberal government sought to ban the niqab from civic spaces, even though it was estimated that between twenty-four and ninety women in the entire province wore this form of religious attire at that time (Patriquin and Gillis 2010). The pervasive fear offset by the small number of women who actually wear the niqab signals a deeper cultural fear and the need to shore up the boundaries of national belonging to exclude the foreign cultures that threaten its cohesion and "sameness." Haque (2010, 84) points to the elephant in the room by asking, "How did Muslim women become the litmus test of tolerance and civilization within and beyond the nation?" Muslims reside within the imagined space of the Canadian nation as the "anti-citizen" (J. Zine 2012a), and gender plays a key role in demarcating and policing the divide between the liberal White settler majority and illiberal Muslim minorities. The Hérouxville "citizen's code" was an example of shoring up the boundaries against the cultural pollution of Islam and Muslims (see J. Zine 2009). Hage (2003) reminds us of how "paranoid nationalism" and the construction of embodied otherness form the discursive context upon which the nation is consolidated as a space of White supremacy.

Bill 62 on "religious neutrality," passed in the Quebec National Assembly in 2015, obliged citizens to uncover their faces while giving and receiving state services. This legislation effectively targeted Muslim women who wear the niqab. In 2019, Bill 21 was introduced as "An act respecting the laicity of the state,"[12] which banned public workers and those in positions of authority from wearing religious symbols. In line with Quebec's secularist politics, public opinion in the province revealed negative views of Islam and Muslims. In 2009, an Angus Reid poll found that 68 per cent of Quebecers held an unfavourable opinion of Islam. Responding to the same question in 2013, the views in Quebec remained steady at 69 per cent (Angus Reid Institute 2013). The trend continued as a 2015 survey, ordered by the Quebec Human Rights Commission, found that nearly half of Quebecers had an "unfavourable" view of religion (Noël 2015). However, there was an uneven split in their evaluations: while only 5.5 per cent of Quebecers expressed their dislike for the Christian cross, 48.9 per cent said they were uncomfortable with Muslim veils. A 2016 Leger poll also found a steady decline in francophone views of Islam since 2012, with 48 per cent of Quebec respondents holding negative views (Canadian Press 2016).

In the rest of Canada, where 46 per cent held an unfavourable view of Islam in 2009, that figure rose to 54 per cent in 2013 (Geddes 2013). The survey also revealed that many Canadians who do not object to other forms of religious clothing draw the line at Muslim women's niqab. Ninety per cent of Quebecers and 62 per cent of the population in the rest of the country said that women who wear the niqab should not be allowed in public sector workplaces. A survey published in March 2015 by Ipsos found that 68 per cent of respondents disagreed with allowing Muslim women to wear niqab or burka during citizenship ceremonies, and 72 per cent "agreed" that the burka or niqab are "symbols of oppression and rooted in a culture that is anti-women." Later, a 2017 Angus Reid survey found that 46 per cent of Canadians view Islam and clothing associated with the religion unfavourably compared to how they view other religions like Christianity and Buddhism. In terms of wearing religious dress in public, 88 per cent of those surveyed supported a person wearing the nun's habit or a turban (77 per cent) compared to those wearing a niqab (32 per cent) or a burka (29 per cent). While negative attitudes toward Muslim women who wear Islamic attire exist across Canada, Quebec has institutionalized gendered Islamophobia and codified anti-veiling into their provincial policies and practices.

The 2017 Angus Reid survey also measured public responses in Quebec to Bill 62, referred to as Quebec's "Religious Neutrality Bill," which prohibits anyone wearing face coverings from receiving government services. Over 62 per cent of those surveyed said they "strongly support" this bill, while only 4 per cent said they "strongly oppose" it.

Another 2017 Angus Reid survey revealed that in response to the prompt that "a woman visiting a government office in a 'niqab' should be ..." 70 per cent of those polled inside Quebec responded "prohibited" compared to 40 per cent of those in the rest of Canada, while 8 per cent of those in Quebec responded "welcome" compared to 28 per cent in the rest of Canada. Twenty-three per cent of people polled from Quebec responded "discouraged while tolerated," compared to 31 per cent in the rest of Canada. The poll suggests that while most Quebecers (65 per cent) believe wearing religious symbols in public should be banned, 66 per cent believe such a ban should apply to educators, 76 per cent believe religious symbols should not be worn by persons in authority, and 67 per cent believe such a ban should apply to all public servants.

However, the survey revealed that a higher number of people in Canada, including Quebec, are beginning to view Islam in a more positive light. For instance, Quebecers who say they regard Islam favourably more than doubled since 2009, a jump from 15 per cent to 32 per cent. More Quebecers are also seeing Sikhism (32 per cent) and Hinduism (50 per cent) more positively. It is notable that the survey was conducted two weeks after the Quebec mosque shooting. This may have played some role in softening public opinion.[13] As for the rest of Canada, the survey noted that one in three Canadians viewed Islam favourably, an increase from 2013, when only one-quarter of Canadians viewed Islam in a positive light. Christianity was regarded the most favourable religion among 68 per cent of the survey respondents.

Few studies assess the impact of Islamophobic public policies. Hassan et al. (2016) conducted a study on the psychological impact of the Quebec Charter of Values (Bill 60) on francophone students at the Université du Québec à Montréal. The bill stoked xenophobic and Islamophobic sentiments under the guise of safeguarding French values of secularism and *laïcité*. Out of a sample of 441 students, the researchers found almost a third reported experiencing or witnessing discrimination after the charter was introduced. The numbers were higher for immigrants and members of minority groups. The Quebec Charter of Values included articles that required employees and public services users to provide and receive services with their "face uncovered," and it prohibited activities and practices in childcare and schools "such as dietary practices stemming from a religious precept" (Nadeau and Helly 2016).[14] These secular laws police and restrict religious freedom and have been challenged by civil rights organizations for their violation of the Canadian Charter of Rights and Freedoms.[15] Quebec's ethnonationalism is a major driver in legislating fear and institutionalizing Islamophobia in Canada.

THE ISLAMOPHOBIA INDUSTRY

What distinguishes Islamophobia from other systems of oppression is that there is an industry behind purveying anti-Muslim hate. An influential report in the US titled *Fear Inc.: The Roots of the Islamophobia Network in America*, by Ali et al. (2011, 9), was the first to shine a light on "the Islamophobia network of so-called experts, academics, institutions, grassroots organizations, media outlets, and donors who manufacture, produce, distribute, and mainstream an irrational fear of Islam and Muslims." Lean's (2017) study titled *Islamophobia Industry* further exposes the ideologies and tactics of the proponents of Islamophobia in the US from both the right and left political spectrum, religious and secular groups, as well as politicians and media personalities whose propaganda contributes to politicizing and legislating fear of Muslims. These studies were able to identify the key elements of the Islamophobia industry and identify major donors financing the promotion of anti-Muslim hate and propaganda in the United States.

According to a report by the Council of American-Islamic Relations (CAIR) and University of California, Berkeley's Center for Race and Gender, there is a $208 million small, tightly networked group of donors, organizations, and misinformation experts designed to advance certain political interests (Kazem 2016). In their updated report *Hijacked by Hate*, CAIR's (2019) research found that in the United States a staggering 1,096 charitable institutions financed at least thirty-nine Islamophobia Network groups between 2014 and 2016 through Donor Advised Funds. These foundations donated a wide range of sums from $20 million up to $32.4 million. The report also documented that between 2014 and 2016, these thirty-nine anti-Muslim organizations had access to at least $1.5 billion through their collective organizational financial capacity.[16] The financial resources at the disposal of the Islamophobia Network are staggering and demonstrate how Islamophobia monetizes anti-Muslim hate.

The Islamophobia industry provides the ideological underpinnings that underwrite the individual, ideological, and systemic social dynamics described earlier (Abadi 2018; Bazian 2015; Saylor 2014). Ingraining fear and moral panic (Cohen [1972] 2014) about Muslims allows for hate crimes as well as draconian security policies and racial profiling to be seen as legitimate and necessary to preserving public safety (Jamil and Rousseau 2012; Razack 2008; Thobani 2007; Bahdi 2003; Khalema and Wannas 2003). There are a wide variety of discourses circulated through the individuals and organizations connected to the Islamophobia industry, including representing Muslims as the "fifth column," "Islamofacism," "creeping sharia," "Muslim invaders," and "wolves in sheeps' clothing (*taqiyya*)," to name a few. As discussed previously, these ideologies feed into the dynamic of Islamophobia by justifying individual actions like hate crimes, vandalism, harassment, and violence as well as proving the rationale for draconian security measures that target Muslims. The Islamophobia industry instrumentalizes fear and hate through the narratives of religious and racial degeneracy.

Massoumi, Mills, and Miller (2017) refer to the "five pillars of Islamophobia" as being the institutions and machinery of the state; the far right, the counter-jihad movement; neo-conservatives; transnational Zionist groups; and the pro-war left and the new atheist movement. Along similar lines, in Canada, the Islamophobia industry is comprised of individual ideologues, media outlets, White nationalist groups, Zionist Jewish and Christian organizations, Muslim dissidents, think tanks, and political figures. Across Canada as of 2019, there are 300 White nationalist groups up from 130 in 2015 (Habib 2019). Promoting Islamophobia is a core mandate for some of these Canadian-based groups, such as Patriotic Europeans Against the Islamisation of the West (PEGIDA), Soldiers of Odin, Canadian Infidels, Worldwide Coalition Against Islam, Rise Canada, Northern Guard, ID Canada, Proud Boys, Cultural Action Party, Yellow Vests, Canadian Nationalist Party, Blood and Honour, Combat 18, Students for Western Civilization, and the Three Percenters. All these groups have engaged in public rhetoric against Islam and Muslims, and their views are prominent in their social media posts. Along with the Islamophobic group La Meute, Nadeau and Helly (2016, 2) cite the rise of "extreme right parties" (such as Génération identitaire, PEGIDA, English Defence League) indicating "the emergence of an extreme right 'sensibility' in the Province of Quebec."

While these groups can be regarded as the "foot soldiers" who take their Islamophobic hate to the street in overt ways, there are "soft power" groups (comprised of Zionist Jewish and Christians organizations) within the Islamophobia industry that purvey Islamophobic ideologues under the guise of promoting a "Judeo-Christian democracy," "Canadian values," "free speech," and "the rule of law" and thereby engage in a "liberal washing" of White nationalism (J. Zine 2019). These ideological purveyors espouse conspiracy theories about Muslims as a Trojan Horse for groups like Hamas and the Muslim brotherhood who they see as having an agenda of global domination. These ideas are also echoed through the Canadian far right media outlet Rebel Media headed by Ezra Levant and launched the career of Islamophobic influencers such as Faith Goldy and Lauren Southern. Other unlikely Islamophobic ideologues include self-proclaimed "Muslim dissidents" that include prominent public figures like Tarek Fatah and Raheel Raza among others. The dissidents play the "insider role" of validating negative views of Islam and significantly contribute to fomenting and legitimizing Islamophobic hate.

Political figures also contribute to purveying Islamophobia as part of their election campaigns. For example, former Canadian prime minister Stephen Harper publicly stated in 2011 that "Islamicism [*sic*] is the biggest threat to Canada" (CBC News 2011). At a military swearing-in ceremony, Harper invoked the civilizational discourse of "us and them" in the following statement: "Their alleged target was Canada, Canadian institutions, the Canadian economy, the Canadian people. We are a target because of who we are and how we live, our society, our diversity and our values – values such as freedom, democracy and the rule of law" (Chase 2006). This rhetoric portrays Muslims as illiberal, anti-democratic subjects who are irreconcilable with "civilization and modernity," language reminiscent of the idioms of colonial racism. Conservative and far right politicians along with right-wing think tanks circulate and authorize Islamophobia as a political currency, legitimizing the discursive apparatus of the Islamophobia industry and rationalizing the securitization of Muslims as a form of systemic oppression. These networks operating within the Canadian landscape play a key role in the circulation of Islamophobic propaganda.

RESEARCH METHODS AND FIELDWORK

Conducting research on Muslim communities in a post-9/11 context can be risky business. As Tuhiwai-Smith (1999, 5) points out, "[R]esearch is not an innocent or distant academic exercise but an activity that has something at stake and that occurs in a set of political and social conditions." During times of war and terror, conducting research on targeted communities presents a variety of challenges. Three primary concerns that became evident during this study speak to the politics and ethics of research on marginalized Muslim communities in the West.

The first concern relates to how post-9/11 security policies might potentially impact the ability to maintain research ethics and confidentiality should one's research become subject to government scrutiny. After 9/11, the Anti-terrorism Act known as Bill C-36 was introduced in Canada and raised fears surrounding the potential confiscation of research data by government officials should anyone in our participant pool be deemed a "person of interest." Given that Muslims became suspects simply by virtue of their religious affiliation and racial identities and that there was heightened scrutiny levelled against the community, these concerns were not unwarranted. The newly securitized conditions post-9/11 raised questions for ethnographers as to what we could reasonably promise our participants when it came to providing anonymity and confidentiality.

Ali (2018, 434) notes the perils of researching 9/11 Muslim youth, where the "carceral context of surveillance mediate the subjectivities of all participants in the research process." Some of Ali's participants were reticent to speak in specific spaces or be recorded for fear of the premises being bugged or having their words misconstrued in a climate of Islamophobic fear. Despite being a Muslim researcher and facilitator who participated in community events, Ali (2016) indicates that he was not immune to distrust where the motives of his research and presence in the community were at times rendered as suspect. Part of the experience of living under siege is the internalization of external surveillance (see chapter 5). This creates a paranoia that spies may be infiltrating Muslim communities in the guise of safe and friendly community insiders. This distrust represents a loss for intra-community engagement and dialogue, which are under the constant shadow of suspicion and internalized fear. For Muslim researchers, these securitized conditions can potentially prohibit honest and open conversation with their youth participants.

Ali (2016, 87–8) highlights such fraught context in this reflection: "Ibrahim, whom I knew more than two years, stated, 'At the end of the day, I don't know if you work with the NYPD or FBI; I have to trust, but I really don't know … and you don't know about me either.' While trust is central to developing political communities and identities, young Muslims simply did not know whom they could or could not trust. But it was clear to the youth that the US government did not trust them." Ali's experience as a Muslim researcher doing fieldwork among the 9/11 generation in the United States reads as a cautionary tale of the way that global geopolitics and domestic security concerns shape, inform, and at times threaten the research context.

While I was not regarded with this same suspicion among my participants (perhaps because I was an older female?), I was nonetheless cognizant of the need to ensure trust, safety, and accountability among the youth I was interviewing. The fieldwork for this study began a couple of years after the 2006 arrests of seventeen youth and one adult on terror-related charges in what was dubbed the "Toronto 18" case (see chapter 6). During the arrests and the trials that followed, Muslim youth were the focus of security investigations and often sensationalized media attention in Canada. At this time of heightened scrutiny and surveillance, I felt it prudent to introduce extra measures to anonymize the data to safeguard the identity of the research participants. All participants' real names were only kept on their paper consent forms, and all electronic references to individual participants were anonymized by codes and pseudonyms due to securitization concerns. The effects of these new security policies upon our ability to conduct research in an ethical and confidential manner was not clear at the outset of the fieldwork, and while there were no problems over the six-year span of the study, I was still mindful of exercising an extra level of caution and care to protect the youth who participated.

The second concern that emerged in the course of research involves academic colonialism and opportunistic research. Now that Muslims are a "hot topic," Muslim experiences are not just being commodified as academic currency but cannibalized in the form of what bell hooks calls "eating the other." Muslims are viewed through the ambivalent nexus of desire and disavowal: there is the Islamophilic desire to consume the exotica and sensationalism of Muslim experiences along with the dialectical Islamophobic impulse to disavow this otherness. In discussing this phenomenon, hooks (1992, 39) writes: "The overriding fear is that cultural, ethnic, and racial differences will be continually commodified and offered up as new dishes to enhance the white palate – that the Other will be eaten, consumed, and forgotten." Muslims become the paradoxical objects of Orientalist fascination and humanist pity through academic as well as pop cultural discourses and archives that are constructed for the edification of Western audiences (Taylor and Zine 2014). Oprah's Book Club exemplifies how narratives of abject Muslimness in the form of novels and memoirs, such as

Kabul Beauty School, The Kite Runner, and *Reading Lolita in Tehran: A Memoir in Books,* are uncritically read as windows into strange and unintelligible worlds of exotic fascination and religious and cultural debauchery that cultivate what Burwell (2014, 133) describes as a "[t]oo quick enthusiasm for the other." The fetishistic gaze directed at Muslim experiences reproduces colonial desires, subjectivities, and relations of power. These representational practices underscore the need for the decolonizing of research methods to decentre what Tuhiwai-Smith (1999, 59) calls "research through imperial eyes." This requires attention to the issues that marginalized communities prioritize rather than a voyeuristic approach to research that reproduces an Orientalist gaze while making claims of allyship.

A third concern that arises for Muslim researchers studying Muslim communities stems from being situated as a "native informant" who is charged with translating their societies' experiences to the outside world as academic tour guides, subaltern emissaries, and cultural ambassadors. Commenting on how, as a Muslim researcher, Khan (2005, 2023) became both *ascribed* and *inscribed* within this positioning, she writes: "I too have been recruited into this role. Literary, cultural, and political pressures over here position me as a unitary subject, a third-world native informant (re)producing the voice of alterity." When situated in the West, the Muslim researcher/native informant must negotiate a complex political terrain, knowing what we write and "reveal" about our communities can feed into racist and Islamophobic narratives. These considerations come into play when I write about "radicalization" since what I reveal can be read by some on the one hand as confirmation of the worst Islamophobic fears or on the other hand be dismissed as apologetics. A third possibility, as Khan warns, is that our research is "coopted by and appropriated within liberal discourses so that we become as Trinh reminds us, someone's private zoo" (Trinh 1989, 82; Khan 2005). Khan's observation takes us back to my previously stated concern regarding the consumption and appropriation of subaltern narratives as a Western Islamophilic desire that satiates a salacious and voyeuristic neo-imperial impulse.

PARTICIPANTS AND FIELDWORK

The qualitative fieldwork for this study spanned a period of six years, from 2009 to 2015, and involved 135 participants from across Canada that included Muslim youth between the ages of eighteen and twenty-six as well as youth workers and religious leaders. Most of the youth were university students (undergraduate and postgraduate), although some attended vocational community colleges, a few just graduated high school, and others were working and not connected to educational sites. The participants represented a cross-section of the Canadian Muslim community and came from various socio-economic backgrounds.

Information about the study along with an invitation to participate were circulated electronically through MSA and through community networks in the Greater Toronto Area and other parts of Southern Ontario, Ottawa, Montreal, Vancouver, and New Brunswick. Participants self-selected in taking part in the study and there was some use of snowball sampling, where prospective participants were referred. Youth workers and religious leaders were identified through community contacts and selected based on their involvement in relevant work such as youth initiative projects in marginalized neighbourhoods, youth support helplines, and working with community social service agencies.

Interviews were conducted in university settings, coffee shops, mosques, libraries, offices, community centres, and at a youth conference. Individual interviews and focus groups lasted from one to two hours and covered a lot of ground. Each youth participant answered twenty-eight questions during the personal interview or focus group session. Youth workers and religious leaders were asked ten questions. The interviews were transcribed and coded for data analysis using NVivo software. Direct quotes have been edited for clarity and brevity while maintaining the full intent of the speaker's words and character of their speech. To ensure validity and conduct member checks, a subset of participants was invited to follow-up sessions during 2016–17 to provide feedback on the first round of preliminary data analysis. This allowed for a measure of collaborative theorizing whereby participants were able to be co-constructors of the meanings being drawn from their experiences. Overall, some participants were more vocal than others and provided more feedback. Unfortunately, given the vast amount of data collected, not all the participants' contributions could be represented in this book; however, every attempt was made to include as many voices as possible and to paraphrase more general views shared among them.

The participants involved in this study were predominantly Muslims from Sunni and Shia backgrounds. Sunnis are the largest and most predominant Muslim sectarian group in Canada. With the help of research assistants, we conducted targeted outreach to youth from the Shia community to ensure wider representation. There were no participants from minority sectarian groups such as the Ismaili or Ahmadiyya. This was not by intention or by design but a product of who self-selected to take part in the study. Admittedly, however, a more targeted outreach to these communities would have broadened the sample.

The participants were comprised of the following twenty-three nationalities: South Asian (Pakistani, Indian, Bangladeshi, Gujarati, Sri Lankan, Punjabi); African (Somali, Eritrean, Ethiopian, East African, Nigerian); Middle Eastern/North African Arab (Iraqi, Moroccan, Tunisian, Egyptian, Palestinian); Asian (Afghan, Iranian, Turkish); Eastern European (Albanian, Macedonian); Caribbean (Guyanese); and "Canadian"[17] (African Canadian, White converts). Many of the participants were Canadian born, whereas others were immigrants or international students. These additional social markers are identified where relevant. The ethno-racial diversity of the sample allowed for the examination of a multiplicity of experiences as well as underscored the commonalities among diverse Muslims when it comes to experiencing Islamophobia. The intersectional experiences are referenced and integrated into the analysis as they were narrated and shared by the participants, although they were not specifically asked to respond to questions from their ethno-racial location. It was left to participants' discretion to share the particularities of their experiences along racial or ethnic lines.

Not only did participants self-identify as Muslims, but it is safe to say that being Muslim was important to them. Overall, participants tended to be religiously oriented though in varying degrees. This was not intentional but simply a reflection of the youth who were attracted to the study. Not all youth were practising Islam in the same way (or at all), but they felt some stake in their identities as Muslims. For many Muslims in the West, it was 9/11 that created the circumstances in which they were forced to reckon with their Muslimness (see also Caidi and MacDonald 2008). They had to confront their identity in new ways, since overnight their religious identity became a category by which they were negatively defined by others (see chapter 2). The post-9/11 era ushered in a moment of identity consciousness where being Muslim held consequences with profound effects for how you would be evaluated and treated. This is not to say that Islamophobia was non-existent prior to this time, but the aftermath of 9/11 signalled a shift in the intensity of discrimination at all levels.

The salience of one's religious identification prior to the Twin Towers falling would have an impact on the degree to which the backlash would hit home, yet being non-religious also did not offer immunity from negative attention and scrutiny and the attendant social and psychological impacts. The youth who chose to participate in this study wanted to share their stories and contribute to unpacking the circumstances they faced and the impacts on their lives and opportunities as young Muslims.

The gender balance was relatively even in the sample, and the voices of the participants reflect strong representation from those who identified as female as well as male.[18] Islamophobia is intersectional, and the gendered implications were important to consider and examine. While gendered social identities are multiple and fluid, gendered Islamophobia (J. Zine 2006a) is examined in this study to identify the ways Muslim women are differentially impacted. Gendered identities and gender relations were also prominent themes when examining the internal dynamics of Muslim student groups and campus culture. The participants were able to reflect upon both the internal and external ways their gendered identities were constructed, negotiated, and challenged.

As a Muslim ethnographer, I have been researching Muslim youth in Canada since the mid-1990s. I have been a vocal community advocate and public intellectual. My reputation in the Muslim community helped to garner trust and elicit candour among the participants in this study. As a mother of two sons who are part of the 9/11 generation and have dealt with the consequences of this identity,[19] I was deeply attuned to the information the youth participants shared and the meanings they attached to their experiences. The research assistants who helped in identifying contacts and conducting interviews in Toronto and Southern Ontario, Ottawa, Montreal, and Vancouver were also young, female, and Muslim and shared an inter-subjective understanding with the participants. These connections through faith, community, and similar ethno-racial identities and experiences with Islamophobia were helpful during interviews so that participants may have felt less inclined to "perform" for the researchers, telling them what they thought they wanted to hear.

The fact that everyone involved in the fieldwork also had "skin in the game" allowed for the participants to feel comfortable with confidentiality, despite the securitization concerns that are part of their lived experience. For example, even in a safe setting among other

Muslims, there is a slight hesitancy to say certain comments aloud. At times nervous laughter erupted in the group. But there was also a sense of not having to explain or justify one's views or experience. At other times, there was open laughter and inside jokes that created a sense of familiarity and provided comedic relief amid discussing difficult and heavy topics. However, I acknowledge that despite my "insider" positionality, the fact that I was connected to a university also elevated my status in ways that created a power imbalance. I had the sole authority to structure, order, and represent the participants' voices and experiences. I recognize this role as a responsibility and public trust.

MAPPING THE BOOK

This book unpacks the dynamics of Islamophobia as a system of oppression and examines its impact on the 9/11 generation of Canadian Muslim youth. The narratives of youth participants are centred throughout the book: their voices and experiences drive and shape the way this inquiry is structured and framed. Each chapter situates the narrative analysis within important theoretical groundings to connect the qualitative research to broader sets of ideas and implications that arise from them and presents different horizons from which to view the experiences of the 9/11 generation. Covering topics such as Muslim youth identities, securitization, radicalization, campus culture in an age of empire, and subaltern Muslim counterpublics and resistance, this book provides a unique and comprehensive examination into the complex realities of Muslim youth in a post-9/11 world.

Chapter 2, "Identity, Citizenship, and Belonging in an Age of Islamophobia," addresses and examines the challenges of post-9/11 identities for Muslim youth. How do the Muslim youth of the 9/11 generation negotiate their identities during times when the politics of war and terror shape popular understandings of who they are and how others perceive them? How do these discourses constitute Muslim youth as post-9/11 subjects, and how do they respond to this ontological positioning? How are the affective registers of Islamophobia configured? This chapter focuses on how Muslim youth connect to their faith during a time when it has been vilified in media, politics, and pop culture, and examines how they respond to the collective labelling and guilt that has been ascribed to them because of the violent actions of a few of their co-religionists. Muslim youth identities have become politicized in ways that other youth do not have to face, which makes the Muslim 9/11 generation unique. Chapter 2 explores these challenges and how youth are navigating and responding to these conditions.

Chapter 3, "The 9/11 Generation and the Dynamics of Islamophobia," examines the individual, ideological, and systemic dimensions of Islamophobia through the narratives and experiences of Muslim youth. Their stories are an entry point to unpacking these dimensions of Islamophobia and illustrate how these conditions manifest in their daily lives as well as how broader systemic factors shape their realities. This chapter also provides an analysis of "gendered Islamophobia" (J. Zine 2006a) based on how visibly marked Muslim women experience Islamophobia at the intersection of their religious identity and gender. Muslim women, especially those who wear religious attire, face discrimination based on their faith, gender, racialization, and ethnicity. Gendered Islamophobia is marked by the historical legacies of Orientalist representation that maintain currency in contemporary imperial politics where Muslim women are cast as imperilled and in need of Western rescue and rehabilitation (J. Zine 2006a; Razack 2008; Abu-Lughod 2013). This chapter provides a journey through the interlocking dynamics of Islamophobia and how it has affected Muslim youth in different facets of their lives.

For the past fifty years, Muslim students have organized on campuses across North America. MSAs offer important spaces for developing Islamic subcultures on campus where youth find community, camaraderie, and opportunities for activism as well as religious guidance and support (Mir 2014; Zine and Bala 2019). Chapter 4, "Campus Culture in an Age of Islamophobia and Empire: Muslim Youth Counterpublics," highlights the role of what I refer to as "Muslim youth counterpublics." My earlier research examined MSAs in high schools (J. Zine 2000, 2001) and the role these groups played in helping students negotiate their religious identities within secular, Eurocentric environments. In this chapter, I examine how MSAs operate as a subculture in university campuses as social movements and counterpublics that challenge Islamophobia in an age of imperial politics and domestic security concerns, as well as how they connect Muslim youth with national and transnational struggles. The participants' narratives also allow for an exploration of the internal dynamics of these groups in relation to gender and sectarian concerns.

According to Hatem Bazian (2018, 11), "All that is needed is Islamophobia and the most draconian policies are sanctioned and democracy itself becomes a vehicle for securitization." Chapter 5,

"Islamophobia and the Security Industrial Complex," links the phenomenon of Islamophobia and securitization, which as Bazian notes, are inextricably tied within the governing apparatus of democratic states. Drawing on the analyses of Foucault (1991), Bourdieu (1997), Agamben (2005), Bigo (2008), and Cohen ([1972] 2014), I propose a framework for a "security industrial complex" as a network of interconnected institutions, technologies, economies, and policies through which state and non-state actors operate within contemporary surveillance regimes. I argue that these conditions have created a "securitized habitus" into which Muslim youth are socialized. Through the experiences of the 9/11 generation, a deeper analysis of these panoptic times is possible through their first-hand accounts. Their narratives shape new understandings of how surveillance is structured and racialized in ways that target Muslim communities, especially youth, as contemporary "folk devils" (Cohen [1972] 2014). Muslim youth have been identified as security threats and potential jihadists, which has led to practices of racial and religious profiling. Racial forms of securitization link race and the racialization of religion to the security industrial complex as the basis upon which threats to public safety are determined and safeguarded against. The narratives presented in this chapter speak to how racial and religious surveillance impacts the lives of the 9/11 generation and how the panoptic gaze is internalized.

Chapter 6, "Being Cast as the Bogeyman: Muslim Youth on 'Radicalization,'" expands on the securitization of Muslim youth to examine how they have been cast as the bogeyman in the post-9/11 imaginary. This chapter begins with a discussion of radicalization and the contested drivers believed to account for the existence of these extremist movements. The aims in this chapter are to better understand how Muslim youth make sense of these movements; examine how the collective negative labelling affects them, and examine the dialectical relationship between Islamophobia and radicalization. The narrative analysis in this chapter features Muslim youth discussing their views on radicalization and how they have been impacted by it. Centring youth voices here allows them to serve as critical interlocutors on issues they have been implicated in but are rarely given a space to respond to.

Finally, chapter 7, "Muslim Counterpublics: The Arts and Anti-colonial Public Pedagogy," focuses on how youth engage in resistance through the arts and cultural production. According to Hopkins (2011, 166), Muslim youth are "not simply accepting the global-national-local transmission of negative discourses about their religion and are instead actively responding to this through everyday resistances, creative dialogues and challenges to the status quo." This chapter explores how Muslim youth cultural producers are countering the clichéd images of Islamophobic media representation, featuring interviews with Muslim spoken word artists, theatre actors, comedians, and poets who challenge this messaging through their artistic interventions. It was important to conclude this book with a reflection on the politics and modalities of resistance that Muslim youth employ as part of an anti-colonial public pedagogy. These youth are not victims or captives of their circumstances, rather they are actively engaged in counter-storytelling and creating new narratives that work against the pervasive stereotypes about them.

2

Identity, Citizenship, and Belonging in an Age of Islamophobia

UNDER SIEGE: POST-9/11 IDENTITIES

The 9/11 generation of Muslim youth constitute a unique category since their identities and subjectivities are shaped within and against a climate of Islamophobia in various national contexts and within the global geopolitical arena. Most are unaware of what the world was like before the social, political, and cultural structures that emerged in the aftermath of the 9/11 attacks transformed Muslims into perceived threats in many Western nations. This is not to say that Islamophobia in the West was merely a by-product of 9/11, but rather that this moment marked a new iteration of anti-Muslim racism that found expression in domestic immigration and security policies and gained currency through justifying imperial wars abroad. New formations of Orientalist racial logics have codified these ontologies of racial and religious difference in ways that serve neo-imperial goals. Muslim youth must navigate and contest the framing of their faith and identities within this fraught context as well as challenge the political and discursive modalities of power that shape the ways they are represented and treated.

Identities are formed at the nexus of discourse, subjectivity, and power. They are produced through a complex interaction with prevailing discursive paradigms or what Foucault (1991) refers to as "regimes of truth" that enact forms of social discipline and conformity. National discourses, for example, tell us about who "belongs" to the nation through the sets of ideas and norms promoted by government and various institutions within civil society that allow us to distinguish cultural insiders versus outsiders or citizens versus outlaws. According to Althusser (1971), the ideologies embedded within major state apparatuses and social and political institutions constitute individual subjectivities through the practice of interpellation or being "hailed" into discourse.

I like to illustrate this practice using Fanon's (1967, 112) example in *Black Skin, White Masks* where a White child sees him and is frightened: "Mama see the Negro!" he says. In that moment Fanon recognizes himself as interpellated into a racial discourse where a White child's pronouncement hails him into a history and embodiment of racial oppression: "I was responsible at the same time for my body, for my race, for my ancestors. I subjected myself to an objective examination, I discovered my blackness, my ethnic characteristics; and I was battered down by tom-toms, cannibalism, intellectual deficiency, fetishism, racial defects, slave ships and above all else, above all 'sho good eatin'.'" The demoralization and estrangement Fanon describes in response to the child's utterance of fear and fascination is a profound example of how subaltern identities are interpellated into ideologies of dread and degeneracy, which then become constitutive of these racialized ontologies. To further the connection that Foucault (1994) draws between discourse, power, and subject, Mahmood (2005, 188) makes an insightful intervention in pointing out the work that discursive practices perform in "making possible particular kinds of subjects." It is important to keep in mind that through the complex social, political, and discursive constitution of identity and subjectivity, particular kinds of subject positions are not only produced but also challenged and contested.

Identities are also formed relationally through the self/other binary and are therefore mutually constituted within personal and societal relations of power. In other words, as we construct self we simultaneously construct other. Stuart Hall (1997, 48) aptly describes this relational dynamic as "seeing the self as it is inscribed in the gaze of the other," which harks back to Du Bois's formulation of double-consciousness noted in this book's introduction. These dialectical articulations of identity take place interpersonally and are embedded in the larger hierarchical structures of power in society. For example, Taylor (1992) describes a politics of recognition and misrecognition within multicultural societies. Recognition of subaltern identities in the public sphere involves the demand for equality, dignity, and the equalization of rights and entitlements. Taylor (1992, 25) notes that in the absence of this recognition, a misrecognition occurs whereby "a person or group of people can suffer real damage, real distortion, if the people or society around them mirror back to them a confining or demeaning or contemptable picture of themselves. Nonrecognition or misrecognition can inflict harm, can be a form of oppression, imprisoning someone in a false, distorted and reduced mode of being."

For Muslims in the West, this dialectical encounter through which self/other is constituted takes place within larger national and international geopolitical contexts. Islam and Muslimness are coded with ideological markers related to persistent Orientalist fears and fantasies of zealotry, violence, and racial and religious degeneracy. The discursive power of these ideological imprints shapes the Muslim presence in the West and the context within which Muslim children and youth must come to identify themselves and others within and against these limiting tropes. The process of negotiating agency and managing the discourses that define you is not easy for youth constantly under siege by Islamophobic narratives that have gained renewed currency through the ongoing war on terror and domestic security policies. The relations of power governing this exchange are inherently asymmetrical. In other words, when Muslims are constructed as terrorists or as illiberal religious minorities incompatible with secular modernity, this has negative implications ranging from discriminating encounters in the public sphere to social policies that attempt to discipline, manage, and culturally rehabilitate them. However, if Muslims view the dominant culture as xenophobic, racist, and Islamophobic, this has no bearing on changing or impacting these realities. These cultural and institutional asymmetries support the dominant formations of power and privilege.

ON BEING MUSLIM

Unlike many Muslims who identify as "cultural" and not religious, the participants in this study were drawn to the research because of their investment in an Islamic identity and seeing themselves as emissaries of Islam dedicated to presenting a positive counter-narrative to the way Muslim identities have been demonized in the post-9/11 context. Irrespective of how Muslims articulate their faith, they must all contend with the impact of anti-Muslim racism. The question of Islamic identity and what being a Muslim means for the 9/11 generation was a starting point for youth interviews. Are their feelings toward a core religious identity and Muslimness impacted by Islamophobia and the ongoing war on terror? Is it possible for Muslim youth to hold the essence of religious identity apart from the political tensions that define Islam within the context of global imperialism and reactionary ideologies? How does their conception of faith and identity animate their sense of purpose and inform how they navigate their lives as Muslim Canadians? The questions were left open-ended to allow participants to infuse their own meaning into the ontology of Muslim identity.

Sociologically, Muslim identities reside between the epistemic and ontological, the textual and the temporal, that is, between the textual meaning and modalities of being derived from the Quran, Sunna, and Hadith[1] and how they are lived and enacted within various temporal, cultural, and political milieux. The interplay of these epistemological and ontological underpinnings and the tensions that arise from negotiating these in different settings drive the dialectical process of Islamic identity formation. The theological boundaries of Islam governing how Islam is lived and practised have adapted to changing times and conditions over the last 1,400 years. While grounded in certain timeless principles, Islam is not static in its practice and application and is subject to ongoing hermeneutic and exegetical examination, including more recently feminist interpretations (Wadud 1999; Barlas 2002). Similarly, Muslim identities are equally fluid, intersectional, and adaptive to changing temporal, cultural, and geographic conditions.

The narratives that follow unpack the complexities of how post-9/11 identities are shaped and formed within these social, cultural, and political arrangements and the ways Muslim youth are responding to, engaging with, and resisting how they are positioned within them. In the discussion that follows, it becomes evident that how Muslim youth view and construct their religious identity cannot be extricated or disentangled from the political and discursive relations of power in which they have been socialized and constituted as part of the 9/11 generation.

THE BURDEN OF REPRESENTATION AND RESPONSIBILITY

"Because if you're Muslim, you're taking the burden of the whole Muslim world."

                                                            Ateeka, student

Ateeka, a Bengali student from New Brunswick, expressed a sentiment that echoes the concerns of many other participants who also spoke to the burden of representing the 1.5 billion people worldwide who share their religious identification. Bearing the collective guilt and responsibility for 9/11 and all other incidents of terror enacted by those who claim an affiliation with Islam makes profound demands on Muslim identities that become essentialized and reduced to negative categories of ascribed danger and suspicion. These narrow ontological spaces are constituted and referenced through historically rooted Orientalist tropes that leave little room for personal autonomy. As a result of this social and political positioning, Muslims find ways to forge and enact alternate narratives that work against these limiting discourses (see chapter 7). These narrative strategies are configured within the affective registers of Islamophobia, which shape the feelings, sensibilities, and dispositions of Muslims within the emotional geopolitics of the post-9/11 world.

Publicly representing Islam and serving as an "image corrective" by exhibiting positive behaviours and actions inculcates a sense of duty and a burden of responsibility. This responsibility is invoked whenever Muslims are called upon to publicly condemn violence and terrorism carried out by their co-religionists (or be accused of moral and political culpability) but is also internalized and enacted through behaving and acting (consciously and unconsciously) in ways that reflect positively on Islam. For some, the burden of responsibility involves the duty to perform *dawah* (teaching others about Islam) by modelling good Islamic behaviour. For others it may manifest as greater self-awareness of their public identity as Muslims and how they can dismantle stereotypes through their words and actions. This sense of responsibility was often religiously motivated to promote positive public perceptions of Islam and challenge the widespread misconceptions and Islamophobic propaganda that often dominated public attitudes.

GOOD MUSLIM/BAD MUSLIM

The nexus of representation and responsibility also plays out through the "good Muslim/bad Muslim" tropes identified by Mamdani (2004, 24). This binary became a means of categorizing the characteristics ascribed to "good Muslims" as being "modern secular and westernized" while "bad Muslims" are "doctrinal, anti-modern and virulent." These tropes gain currency through political rhetoric and media discourse and have left an imprint not only on the public imaginary, but also on how Muslims have come to see themselves and shape their actions and responses. Throughout this study, Muslim youth spoke of the burden

of responsibility they shouldered to serve as a corrective to the popularized maligned views of Islam and to distance themselves from a
securitized agenda where their identities are cast as suspect citizens
(Nagra 2017, see chapter 5).

Karima, a student of Algerian and French background in Montreal,
felt the collective responsibility to perform the "good Muslim" archetype
limited her sense of autonomy and individuality:

> The biggest thing now is that I had to justify that Muslims are kind.
> I'd have to show people that we do smile, we do have fun! I felt
> that the whole image of the Muslim community fell upon me
> and that when I was walking down the street, I had to represent
> the whole community because I know everybody is going
> to judge me. That's a huge challenge also of a lot of the youth
> because I feel we have to justify ourselves – that we have
> to differentiate ourselves from the 9/11 criminals.

Karima found that being a "public ambassador of Islam" filtered
into to her classroom experiences:

> Somebody made a presentation once in class about 9/11, and I put
> my hand up and I said, "I just want to clarify that we don't support
> this as a Muslim community, this is a minority." And the response
> I got was very interesting: "Don't worry, we don't think you're
> a terrorist." I said, "I know you don't," but what was going on
> in my head was that I know the people that know me personally
> don't think I am, but do they think that of the rest of the Muslim
> community? I feel that's a challenge on me to represent the whole
> community and to make sure they don't think that.

Pushing back against the tendency to be the "exception to the rule"
and counter the stereotypes held against all Muslims poses a challenge
and ignites a sense of social and political responsibility commonly
cited by the youth in this study.

Mohammed, an Arab international student in Southern Ontario,
saw the role of an emissary of Islam as part of a collective social
responsibility and a mantle that Muslim youth needed to adopt to
redress negative stereotypes:

> I think it's a responsibility to convey the right message to broader
> society, to understand that you are a representative to society

and whatever actions you do can have both positive and negative consequences. Being a Muslim within the last ten years has dynamically changed. Every action that you do is broken down into bits and pieces and sometimes you feel like after 2001, Muslims have somewhat redefined themselves in a careful way and have undergone a whole examination because we're trying to picture ourselves as the good guys. Probably it wasn't like it was for Muslims years ago.

The post-9/11 phase of Islamophobia created a significant shift for Muslims in Western nations and created a new reality for the youth who have come of age during this time. Miguel, a Latin American student from Montreal, felt the obligation to represent Islam through manners, speech, and comportment was a way to fulfill the Prophetic example and a duty incumbent upon Muslims to portray religious virtues, conduct, and *adab* (etiquette):

If we only stay in our own little ghettos, people will always be excluded from our principles and values, which are beautiful and the real essence of our belief. If we expose that more to the world, we will have shifts in terms of the negative image we have. For instance, in the Metro if you see somebody just threw something on the floor you could go pick it up and throw it in the garbage. If people see that you are Muslim, they will be like, "Wow!" We shouldn't underestimate small gestures. If you see a lady that has a hard time carrying her bag up the stairs, you should, as a Muslim, have the obligation to help her. Small gestures like these on an individual basis can make a big difference. The Prophet was one man and he created a huge revolution. So, we should always be at our best in everything we do and remember that as soon as we step out of our homes, we are Muslims. Your body language is really important: how you smile, walk, talk. Just to monitor yourself on a constant basis is very important. We should always remember that we are responsible for the image of Islam.

As Miguel notes, engaging in charity and good works is central to Islam and is therefore an important foundation for building Islamic character and identity. When these acts occur in the public sphere, they also serve the purpose of domesticating Muslim identity within a framework of good civic citizenship. This helps work against the ways Muslims are otherwise negatively cast and perceived.

It is interesting to note that I found this ethic of public charity evident in my earlier studies on Muslim youth and identity before 9/11 (J. Zine 2008). The youth I interviewed at that time remarked that while the motives behind their good deeds, like giving up their seats for the elderly, were spiritual, a useful corollary effect was that such acts might also counter negative stereotypes. Using public charity as a conscious practice to mitigate against Islamophobia predates the 9/11 context and reminds us that Islamophobia has been a long-standing factor in the way Muslim youth navigate their social and political environment. Combatting negative attitudes about Muslims by modelling good behaviour, performing acts of good citizenship, maintaining ethical conduct, and being approachable, are ways that Muslim youth navigate Islamophobia (see also Maira 2012) and avoid being cast as "bad Muslims."

Zareena, a Turkish student from Vancouver, echoed similar sentiments regarding the need to monitor her behaviour and actions so that she can support the Muslim image corrective: "Well it's already obvious that I'm a Muslim because of the way that I dress; I wear the scarf and all that. But I try to identify myself through my actions as well: be careful how I talk, not really act all crazy, try to watch my language so people can see that Muslims are respectful." Bushra, a South Asian student from Southern Ontario, expressed a similar view, noting the need for self-censorship to avoid backlash: "Everything you do, you think of your religion first and how it would impact your religion. Like the way you act. You censor yourself, so that people don't see Islam negatively." In this way Muslim youth present themselves in a "public relations" role by ensuring their actions do not tarnish the image of Islam.

Roksana, an Iranian Shia student from Toronto, found the burden of representation too much at times, and this made her reticent about sharing her Muslim identity, especially because she did not fit people's image of a "typical" Muslim: "I hate telling people that I'm Muslim. I hate the reactions I get from people. I hate when people say things like, 'Oh, no way! I would have never guessed' … like they make me feel inadequate. They make me feel like not only I'm a bad Muslim because they would have never thought I was Muslim, but I feel like they think I'm just bullshitting them when I try telling them that my religion isn't what FOX News brings it out to be."

Members of the 9/11 generation are forced to defend their faith against attacks and to distance themselves from negative stereotypes. Roksana explains that this makes her feel as though she is always in a defence mode: "I try to show them through my identity that not only is my religion about peace but that I myself am a confrontation-hating, peace-loving kind of person and that universal values of social justice mean a great deal to me, but at the same time when I try to explain that to other people, I feel like I'm always on the defensive. I feel like my entire life has become just defending something I even don't understand myself."

Muslim youth are forced into being the ambassadors and protectors of the image of Islam often at the same point in their lives when they are trying to negotiate their identities and understand the faith for themselves. This stage of emerging personal and spiritual development is complicated by the Islamophobic contexts that surround them. The prevalence of anti-Muslim racism constrains their identity development by forcing them to engage within the discursive parameters shaped by Islamophobia. It therefore becomes impossible to separate the discourse of Islamophobia from the articulation of Muslimness. Muslim youth identities are shaped through engaging with Islamophobic tropes, either by resisting and challenging or distancing from them. The imperative to perform and represent Islam positively is internalized as a burden of responsibility that many Muslim youth described as part of a social and political role they fulfill, both consciously and unconsciously, to distinguish themselves as "good Muslims" as opposed to being feared, vilified, and surveilled as "bad Muslims."

Ziad and Mohammed, South Asian students from Southern Ontario, described how post-9/11 representational politics have led to critical introspection and a conscious re-examination of faith within the Muslim community:

> **Ziad:** I'm trying to clarify that message, trying to eliminate all types of propaganda and negative images. We have changed over the past years. We had to become more aware. We had to become more conscious and a lot of us have really returned back to the roots of religion and we've identified ourselves and we've evaluated ourselves. Who am I? I am a Muslim. I have the duty, I have a responsibility, so there has been a change.

> **Mohammed:** I'd have to say that there's been a surge of a lot of Muslims trying to understand who they are just because they want to defend it. And I feel the Muslims today, they are trying to go back to the fundamentals and try[ing] to understand Islam from its own perspective and not from what society thinks.

Other youth saw themselves being placed in a perpetual "*dawah* mode," having to educate others about Islam and at the same time having their own identity and agency constrained by being seen as a representative of their faith, family, and community. Lamya and Suheir, Palestinian students from Southern Ontario who wear hijab and have their Islamic identity visible, described how they must carry the collective responsibility that stems from their individual actions:

Lamya: You're constantly in *dawah* mode. You're constantly aware of your actions and how your actions affect others. Whether it's your family, or even yourself, your own self-image. I also think it's confinement in the sense that you're constantly fighting stereotypes.

Suheir: I think being Muslim is like a role model. Islam is everything to me. Islam is my life and being a Muslim is a reflection of Islam. It's an identity thing. Being a hijabi[2] in the West, we attract a lot of attention, and we need to show others Islam by what we do and how we act, and whether we, how we interact at school, at work, with others.

For Muslims, like other racialized and marginalized communities, regard as an individual is never a given. Our actions and the choices we make have repercussions for others who share our racial and religious affiliation, and the actions of others from our community in turn impact how we are treated and evaluated. Individuality is a luxury not readily afforded marginalized communities, rather judgments about individual group members are based on the perception of the group as a collective. This allows for a standardization of assumptions. The actions of groups like ISIS/Daesh and Al-Qaeda have nothing to do with the vast majority of Muslims worldwide, but all Muslims are called into account for the actions of these extremist groups. Consequently, all Muslims must resist labels, marginalization, and discrimination.

These negative associations can also spark fear and angst. After ten youth in Quebec were arrested in 2015 on suspicion of planning to join a jihadist group (Russell 2015), Zabeda, a Shia Muslim from Vancouver, expressed how this collective labelling affected her: "Personally, I feel nervous. I feel scared. When I saw that Montreal case, I was scared that people would associate this with me. And it made me nervous."

Others also spoke of the psychological burden of Islamophobia. Sofia, a Somali student in Toronto, described how the internalized oppression, negative essentialism, and self-surveillance took its toll on her ability to act as agentic subject: "When you are in public and you're wearing the hijab, you are extremely aware of every action that you take. If you are in a bad mood and you are like scowling at everybody, right? You are Muslim. It's not just me having a bad day – I'm 'the Muslim girl.' I don't represent just myself anymore." Collective pejorative labelling has a direct effect on how Muslims must navigate public space, and visibly marked Muslim women bear the brunt of this burdensome public scrutiny.

INTERSECTIONAL IDENTITIES

All the youth interviewed spoke of the present Islamophobic context and global forms of imperialism and militarized conflict, and many were involved in various forms of political engagement and critique through their activism on and off campus. (See chapter 4 for a discussion on campus-based activism.) Mehrun, a South Asian student from Vancouver who studied in Manitoba, spoke about being the "token" in her law school and being called upon to speak to issues simply by virtue of her identity:

> I've been propelled into this role that I didn't necessarily choose, which is just the token Brown Muslim girl in law school. So, that's one way. I find that a lot of people turn to me and end up talking to me about things that are happening in the media, to do with Islam, to do with Pakistan. And even if we are studying legal issues, like the niqab case that's at the Supreme Court right now, just by virtue of being a Muslim, even though I am not a woman who identifies with the niqab or the hijab, I find myself talking a lot about it.

From honour killing and niqab controversies to global terrorism, Canadian Muslim youth are called upon in their university classrooms and in the wider public sphere to explain, account for, and provide a disclaimer against these issues that have no bearing upon them other than by virtue of their ethnicity, race, and religious identity.

Awad, an international student from Nigeria, experienced instances of misidentification whereby people were surprised that he was Black and Muslim: "Mostly a lot of people do not believe that I'm a Muslim when they see me. What should a Muslim look like? Generally, I understand that they see me as a Black person, and they don't generally assume that a Black person is Muslim." The vast ethno-racial diversity of Muslims is often reduced to specific essentialized markers. Since 9/11, Muslimness has been linked more to Brown bodies than Black, due the association of Islam with the Middle East and the large number of South Asian Muslims in Canada. Within the ethno-racial diversity of Canadian Muslim youth, many therefore become either overdetermined based on their negatively ascribed racial and religious identity or are not seen as Muslim at all. Both circumstances call for the reassertion of identity as a corrective to popular misapprehensions. Black Muslims must contend with the erasure of their Muslimness and the saliency of anti-Blackness within the wider society as well as in the Muslim community (see McCloud 1994; Jackson 2005).

Muslim women face specific challenges when it comes to engaging a sense of belonging within the nation as well as navigating the patriarchal structures of the community. Aisha, a South Asian student from Vancouver, described the double surveillance Muslim women experience in society at large but also within "mosqued" communities where they are judged according to conservative religious and cultural norms:

> As a Muslim woman, sometimes when you go into space like
> a mosque, there is also surveillance. It is a different kind of
> surveillance than what's outside in public space, it's kind
> of gendered surveillance of what you are wearing, who you
> are talking to, especially if you are young, especially if you are
> not married, especially if you are involved in the mosque.
> In my ideal world you could just belong to a community that
> you want to belong to and there wouldn't be these conditions
> for belonging, right?

Aisha's concerns address the precarities of belonging when we occupy spaces in the larger society, as well as in our community, where belonging is always contingent. This is especially true for youth searching for places where they can belong, fit in, and call home. Residing within liminal spaces, Muslim women must also contend with double surveillance: racial surveillance within the nation and patriarchal and religious surveillance in more conservative sectors of the community.

Lamya, who is of Palestinian and Sudanese origin, spoke about the need to promote to others her "neo-feminist" views through asserting her voice and identity in order to challenge sexism within the Muslim community and Islamophobia outside of it: "I always feel that I have to prove myself. I have to affect women, talk, speak out for women, and always be the one talking in class, because they better not have that stereotype about Muslim women! I feel like I always have to educate people, even within the Muslim community. I guess my identity is a bit aggressive in that way because I always feel like I'm fighting an uphill battle and there's wins and there's losses."

Projecting her identity as a forthright and outspoken Muslim woman, Lamya shatters stereotypes of Muslim women as reticent and demure. Muslim women, like all other women, have diverse dispositions and identities that are held in tension with the narrow, Orientalist paradigms that stigmatize them. Yet, what is significant here is the ontological choices that Lamya makes to correct the epistemological closure that Orientalism has placed on Muslim womanhood. She is aware that to be an advocate for herself and to be what she termed a "feminist rights crusader" requires her to work against the Islamophobic tide of pejorative representations of Muslim women. In describing the pedagogical role her identity performs both inside and outside the community, Lamya is gesturing to the difficulties that Muslim women face in having to negotiate on the one hand Orientalism and Islamophobia, and on the other hand fundamentalism and patriarchal religious conservatism (see J. Zine 2006b). This is especially challenging when one form of oppression (religious fundamentalism) feeds into the construction of the other (Islamophobia). As a result, when Muslim women openly discuss sexism in the Muslim community it feeds into racism and Islamophobia outside of it by supporting bigoted views that Muslim men are barbaric and misogynist. Muslim women are challenged with managing these competing tensions.

Muslim men also spoke about the extrinsic markers of their identity such as sporting a beard, which is considered a Sunna practice based on the emulation of the Prophet Muhammad or their "Brownness" which in the racial logics of the post-9/11 context is part of the "profile" used to surveil and mark Muslim male bodies as potential terrorist threats. "Blackness" as a racialized category negatively signifies certain types of criminality, which intersect with the experiences of Black Muslims (especially men who bear the brunt of scrutiny in securitized racialization) and can also invoke identification with terrorism such as the case of "disappearing Somali youth" or becoming foreign fighters with Al-Shabab (see chapter 5). Being "Brown" as a racialized category is a common descriptor used to mark and label Muslim men and collapse them into a unified category of "Middle Eastern terrorists." While most Muslims are not from the Middle East, the essentialism of Islamophobic archetypes creates this racial fiction.

Zahir, a South Asian student from Montreal and representative of a Canadian Muslim human rights organization, commented on navigating his identity as Brown and male identified: "I think if Muslim men are visible or Brown, have facial hair that makes them appear as if they are Muslims, then there are challenges. It's not to the same degree as women who wear hijab but men who keep the beard or look Muslim are looked [upon] as male chauvinists not respectful of women or maybe having some terrorist sympathies." Being viewed as male chauvinists and misogynists is another layer of pathology ascribed to Brown Muslim male bodies. Abdel-Fattah (2021, 182) describes the way these notions become attached to marginalized identities as the "racial stickiness" of abject identification.

Several of the study participants were converts to Islam and described how they were first drawn to the faith and how it shaped their identity. White converts represent a growing part of the community of Muslims in Canada and were also represented in this study. White Muslim women who wear hijab have been victims of Islamophobic hate and exclusion while also branded "race traitors" by other White people, especially in the growing climate of White nationalism in Canada. In a study on Muslim converts in Canada, Flower and Birkett (2014, 1) observe that since 2001 the Muslim population in Canada has been increasing due to religious conversions by non-Muslim Canadians: "The growth in Islamic conversions has coincided with a period of increased Islamic missionary activity, and (somewhat paradoxically) a rise in negative media coverage on Muslims and Islam following the attacks by Islamic extremists on September 11, 2001." These findings based on Statistics Canada's (2011) Survey on Religion in Canada may seem counterintuitive given that more people were converting to Islam at a time when the war on terror brought home images of radical jihadists, and the Toronto 18 case galvanized the trope of "homegrown terror," disrupting the peaceful image of Canada. With heightened Islamophobia and anti-Muslim sentiments on the rise in Canada, the co-terminus growth of non-Muslim Canadians converting to Islam seems paradoxical. However, the increased attention upon Islam also led to greater curiosity among some Canadians, which opened the door to their explorations of the faith and eventual conversion.

Khalid, an African American student now living in Canada, converted to Islam in the United States after 9/11. He admitted to knowing little about Islam prior to 9/11, and what he was aware of was based on common stereotypes: "I didn't even know that Islam existed. I'd heard of it, but it was like 'those foreigners,' like those 'Buddhist thingies.' Those people 'over there.' I started asking my [Muslim] friends, 'What's up with these terrorist guys?' And they wanted to defend Islam. They started talking, saying, 'I'm doing this because of Islam, look. I'm giving more to charity,' wanting to show people that this is Islam; or wanting to pray in public and show people their faith. That was the learning aspect for me."

Witnessing Islam in action among his Muslim friends, Khalid was able to discern the actions of "the believers" (the majority of those who proclaim their faith to be Islam) from the actions of terrorists that were inconsistent with the faith. He also noted that his friends in the non-Muslim African American community sympathized with the plight of Muslims, regarding them as "underdogs" after 9/11, and as marginalized youth, they could relate to them. Khalid saw African American youth connecting to Muslims through hip hop culture (see also Alim 2005; Aidi 2014), which was making Islam more mainstream in his social circle as opposed to being something foreign and unintelligible.

POST-9/11 ONTOLOGIES

"If you overlap an environment that is hostile towards a certain group of people with the normal issues faced by youth, you've got a really big problem. [September 11] became a defining moment for many Muslim youth. For those who came to Canada after or slightly before, there is no existence before 9/11."

Safeeya, teacher

As previously discussed, the moniker of the 9/11 generation is significant in the way that Muslim youth identities have been impacted by the context of the war on terror. Their identities are formed within the political and discursive aftermath of 9/11 as well as the global conditions that led to it. The identities of the 9/11 generation are therefore shaped by the context of imperialism, militarism, and Islamophobia. In one way or another, globally Muslim youth are implicated by these forces as part of the fabric from which they must fashion a sense of identity, belonging, and citizenship within their nations and through their connection to the broader *ummah*.[3] The world view and ontological positioning of Canadian youth are bound within these dynamics in complex ways, whether or not they immediately recognize how they are affected. This becomes evident in the way they assimilate the context of surveillance and securitization as part of their "normal" milieu (see chapter 5).

Samiya, a South Asian student from Montreal, discussed the existential crisis that 9/11 and its aftermath posed for Muslim youth who had to become more critically introspective and assert a more outward civic identity:

> One of the biggest challenges in the aftermath of 9/11, is it forced us to re-examine our role and position within our society. For those of us who never considered ourselves all that different, we were forced to become conscious of and realize that now we're in the limelight and now that the focus is on us, what were we doing? What are we doing in our towns, in our cities, in our homes? I don't mean in the sense of, "Oh I don't want to appear all sketchy and suspicious." But all of a sudden there was a renewed sense of citizenship and thinking of what it means to be a citizen in our particular context. That was a huge challenge specifically to the Muslim youth. It became this issue of who am I as a Muslim in the context of my citizenship and my country?

Questions of citizenship became more salient for Muslim youth whose sense of belonging as Canadians was being challenged while they were subjected to greater scrutiny and interest.

Samiya had been interviewed during a community-based forum on Muslim youth and civic engagement, which was created to keep Muslim youth away from potential forms of radicalization. This forum was based on the logic that if Muslim youth are productive citizens, they will be less alienated and less likely to be attracted to activities that threaten public safety. "Countering Violent Extremism" (CVE) programs like this involve a problematic set of assumptions about Muslim youth as "anti-citizens" who need cultural reform and civic rehabilitation to avoid the trajectory of radicalization. This limiting narrative also disregards the contributions that Muslim youth make in their schools, communities, and universities through social engagement activities, humanitarian work, and social justice activism. Nevertheless, Muslim youth must constantly confront the "jihadist bogeyman" that haunts how they are perceived and treated (see chapter 6).

In addition to identities being fluid, hybrid, variegated, and inter-sectional, they are also relationally constituted. Proximity or distance from social value is determined by racial logics. How we are seen by others affects our self-image and becomes part of the ontological repository we draw upon to position ourselves within the world around us. Mohammed described how "internalized Islamophobia" was part of his coming of age after 9/11: "I feel that a lot of Muslim youth, in the last ten years find that they're just growing up listening to the 'war on terror' over and over again and it almost make[s] you question yourself and what's going on." The war on terror propaganda impacts Muslim youth in ways that are consciously recognized as well as unconsciously assimilated.

In addressing the concerns of internalized oppression among con-temporary Muslim youth, Miguel recalled the time of the *sahaba,* or companions of the Prophet Muhammed in seventh-century Arabia, who he felt would have better weathered the negative stigmas and been more unwavering in their faith. He felt that the image of Islam as noble faith differs greatly from common Islamophobic conceptions that dominate the media and Western public imaginary. He felt that too many Muslims were internalizing propaganda and allowing it to infiltrate their sense of identity instead of engaging in a "politics of refusal":

Today, a lot of people unfortunately still see Islam as being a religion of terrorists or of people with shady backgrounds or appearances. It's really an issue of identity. We are unfortunately not as proud to be Muslims because we tend to believe the media, what they say and how they portray to us. We play a huge role also in the bad image that we have. Instead of standing up and saying, "No, this is not who we are," we just accept that image and we don't do anything. By doing so we are not moving the cause forward. It all comes down to an issue of inferiority complex.

For Miguel, Muslims are complicit in reproducing negative para-digms when they allow them to hinder their sense of pride and internalize inferiority.

Layla, a Moroccan student from Montreal, and Anela, a Somali student from Toronto, engaged in the kind of politics of refusal and ontological resistance that Miguel advocated:

Layla: The terrorist alerts don't touch me, because I consider them as actions aimed at sullying the image of Islam like it has been done for years. It became normal for me. However, after 9/11, my Muslim identity is more awake. I have since that day strengthened my Muslim identity, which for me was more important than I thought now that we are bombarded with allegations.

Anela: It gives you motivation to be who you are because you know nobody is gonna accept you as who you are except yourself, so you have to be a strong Muslim. You can't bow down to what other people say. A lot of people crumble under that pressure, but some people just solidify [their identity].

Many other participants felt similarly about how the post-9/11 context has fortified their faith and identity and made these more "awake" amid the normalization of Islamophobia. This resurgence of religious identification in the face of pervasive Islamophobic representations and policies is one of the manifestations of how identities under siege are being reimagined and redeployed as both oppositional and affirmative. In other words, challenging the Islamophobic status quo occurs through opposing negative archetypes and at the same time affirming Islam and Muslim identity as liberating, powerful, and sustaining. This is achieved by refusing to capitulate to the ideologies of hate and demonization that can result in diminished pride.

The 9/11 effect on identity also impacted group solidarities among Muslims. Samir, a Shia East African youth from Vancouver, saw that group cohesion was in some ways solidified in the aftermath of 9/11: "I think 9/11 in terms of our group identity it did strengthen it in some regards, because when faced with the backlash from the rest of society we are forced to retreat back to our own communities. So, in that sense it increased our community cohesion."

Heba, a South Asian student from Southern Ontario, spoke similarly of the critical introspection that the Muslim community in North America underwent after 9/11 and the productive tensions that emerged. She felt that until then Muslims had a sense of complacency about their faith, but then 9/11 and the war on terror heightened public attention and scrutiny on Islam, which initiated a space for inquiry, introspection, and furthering intra-community dialogue. "When people started asking questions, that's when we started reflecting on what we stand for and kind of made us question about who we are and what we believe in. There is definitely a lot more activity going on in the Islamic world because of 9/11. It really made us think of getting more dialogues and debates going." Heba acknowledged the importance of Islamic conferences, such as the annual Reviving the Islamic Spirit in Toronto, in creating a space for community dialogue and debate that in her words, "Gets us moving and thinking about who we are so we can answer back to the world. Because right now, we do feel threatened ... we're in a shaky position." Having community-based spaces of support and camaraderie during times of trauma and collective angst is important for strategizing and organizing as well as for healing and spiritual renewal.

INVESTMENT IN AND ESTRANGEMENT FROM MUSLIM IDENTITY

Youth workers and community activists spoke of a crisis of identity that many youth face. Mustafa, an African American religious leader, chaplain, and youth worker from New York City discussed some of the dynamics he had witnessed among youth south of the border. "Well, what I've noticed is that the challenges confronting the youth in the post-911 context have garnered two very opposite responses. On one hand, I've found that many Muslim youth have gotten much closer to their practice of Islam and their identification as Muslims, while [on the other hand] because of the frequent abuses they've suffered as a result of their identification as Muslims, many have assimilated so much into the mainstream identity that it's hard to identify them as Muslims."

These dual manifestations of the 9/11 identity complex as resulting in either *investment* in or *estrangement* from Islam were evident in specific examples Mustafa provided. "Since 9/11, many Muslim students, young people, are calling themselves names that they weren't before 9/11. By the same token there are as many Muslim youth, especially the sisters who are wearing hijab where they weren't wearing it before. The way that Muslims and Islam are being challenged, they've taken this as a personal challenge, a personal affront and they have outwardly expressed their dedication to their faith."

Whether through the anglicization of their names where Osama becomes "Sam" or Mohammed becomes "Moe" or by other means, Muslim identities are being camouflaged in various ways to avoid being connected to a vilified identity. Whether applying for jobs, housing, or other opportunities a Muslim name can elicit prejudice, discrimination, and differential treatment. This retreat from Muslim identity represents estrangement as well as cultural self-preservation, where identifying as Muslim has negative consequences. Mythen, Walklate, and Khan (2009, 749) note similar findings in their study of British Pakistani youth. The discrimination these youth faced caused some to "play down their Muslimness at the level of surface appearance" and instead sport western clothes and speak English rather than wearing hijab or other forms of Islamic attire. Similarly, Ahmed and Muhammad (2019) found that among Black American Muslim youth the discrimination and microaggressions they experience can in some instances lead them to dissociate with Islam and the Muslim community altogether. Abdel-Fattah's (2021, 200) study noted similar trends among Australian youth who "felt the need to tame their Muslimness to strategically erase and conceal their identities."

Conversely, the existential challenge of being Muslim in the post-9/11 context has led to some youth investing in their identity in more pronounced ways as a means of defiance to the negative perceptions of Islam. Becoming more outwardly dedicated to their faith by adopting the hijab for example, was for some women a way to avoid capitulating to Islamophobic narratives. Whether through camouflage and denial of identity or through a fidelity to religious tradition by sporting visible markers of faith, Muslim youth have developed complex and contradictory moves to negotiate their identities. These dynamics involve either affirming or denying their Muslimness, depending on the circumstances they face. For example, anti-Arab Islamophobia created affinities with Karima's Arab identity that she did not otherwise feel. Whenever anyone would discriminate against Arabs, she would automatically be motivated to defend them. Islamophobia has created the conditions for some young Muslims to invest selectively in their identity when they feel under siege, even though otherwise it may not be a strong part of how they identify themselves. Even if they are marginally affiliated with their ethnic, racial, cultural, or religious identity, they are still impacted by the negative association attached to it.

Marwa, a Tunisian Muslim human rights activist in Ottawa, spoke of how the crisis of identity that Muslim youth face is both existential and spiritual:

> Of course, there are questions about identity. Who are they?
> Are they Muslim? Are they Canadian? Are they both? Do they
> have the same identity as their parents? How can they live this

identity inside and outside their community? A lot of it revolves around this crisis of identity. There are also problems from the outside like Islamophobia. Islamophobia is more of an issue because it hinders the journey to find themselves. Everyone, when they are young, [is] trying to figure out who they are. For many years I've seen Muslim youth who didn't wear hijab, then became really religious, then wore niqab, then stopped wearing hijab altogether, then came out that they were gay. They're going through all these different things.

The confusion that all youth face around "finding themselves" and their place in society is compounded for Muslim youth, who must also address the challenges they endure in a society where their identities are demonized alongside often an internal struggle to find their place within the fold of Islam. These youth are pulled in a tug-of-war with the competing forces of secular society and religious conformity.

As Marwa points out, there are various youth subcultures that serve as reference groups. These range from secular to religiously focused subcultures they encounter in schools, society, or through social media and popular culture. In some cases, these groups may be connected to Islamic youth subcultures in their schools or universities (see chapter 4) and may be from a range of theological leanings. Many youth reject the traditional religious pathways and only have peripheral links with their communities or engage with Muslim identity as more of a cultural identity rather than a religious one. Regardless of their orientation to Islam and their religious commitment, all youth who are identifiable as Muslim either through their name or country of origin, or through more overt markers such as Islamic dress, must contend with the repercussions of Islamophobia and anti-Muslim racism. Coming of age in the post-9/11 context has meant that they are not in control of the meanings that others attach to their bodies.

CONTINGENCIES OF CITIZENSHIP AND INTEGRATION

The participants reinforced a strong sense of being Canadian, though many felt that their acceptance within the nation was not necessarily guaranteed. Zabeda expressed this contingent sense of identity: "I think I see myself as a Canadian, I don't find any conflict between these two identities. But the problem is that other people do, they do see me as, you know, 'you can be either Muslim or you could be Canadian.

You can't be both.'" There is a distinction between the formal relationship to the state that citizenship ascribes versus belonging within the
nation as an aforementioned "imagined community" (Anderson 1983).
Citizenship involves rights and responsibilities, while membership in
a nation is determined socially and culturally by the standards of the
dominant community. The extent to which marginalized ethno-racial
communities are considered part of a nation depends upon whether
the dominant society and culture deem them worthy of being included
(Hage 2000; Thobani 2007).

Bannerji (2000, 65) expands on this argument: "So, if we prob-
lematize the notion of 'Canada' through the introjection of the idea
of belonging, we are left with the paradox of both belonging and non-
belonging simultaneously. As a population, we non-whites and women
(in particular, non-white women) are living in a specific territory. We
are part of its economy, subject to its laws and members of its civil
society. And yet we are not part of its self-definition as 'Canada'
because we are not Canadians." Bannerji reminds us that identities
are relative and relational. Socially devalued identities may be exiled
from national belonging while remaining legal citizens by virtue
of how dominant group members perceive them. This underscores
the difference between citizenship and national belonging as a contingent condition for Muslims, who are often viewed as suspect citizens
(see also Nagra 2017).

Asking the question about whether Muslim and Canadian identities
are compatible was part of the political rhetoric after 9/11. Cases like
the Toronto 18 and the bid for sharia law arbitration in Ontario raised
questions as to whether Muslims were able to reconcile their faith
within a secular liberal democracy or whether they were irreconcilable
as Canadians, having customs, beliefs, and traditions that were regarded
as illiberal and anti-democratic. Contesting these notions, Mahvish,
an Iranian Shia student from Toronto, felt that her identities and
values as a Muslim and Canadian were completely in sync: "I don't
know what being a Canadian means if it didn't allow me to be myself
and I don't know what being Muslim would be if it didn't allow me
to be Canadian. So, the two are not mutually exclusive. Canadian
values like inclusivity, democracy, equality, peace, all of those really
beautiful aspects of our Canadian heritage are totally compatible with
aspects of my really beautiful Muslim heritage. That just doesn't happen
to be making it to the sound bites on the news right now."

Muslim youth who grow up in Canada can feel attachment to their
Canadian identity as well as their Muslim identity without difficulty,

reconciling what many like Mahvish see as complementary social locations. However, the prevalence of Islamophobia can make Muslims feel like outsiders who hold views deemed fundamentally incompatible with "Canadian values." Policies such as the Zero Tolerance for Barbaric Cultural Practices Act[4] and the Charter of Values in Quebec are predicated on notions of religious degeneracy, which must be guarded against to preserve Canadian values of freedom and democracy.

Saleha, a South Asian student from Vancouver, felt alienated by these policies and public misperceptions:

> I could give you a gazillion stories of times where I was just going through my everyday business and suddenly, you know, I felt targeted specifically because I was Muslim. I was held accountable for anything that anybody who claims association with Islam ever did. So that is difficult to grow up with, right? I already felt like racial minority in my school, then on top of that your religion is attributed to all of these horrible things and you are constantly defending yourself. So how are you supposed to develop a sense of positive self-identity or self-esteem or connection to Canada when you are constantly being told that you can't be a Canadian Muslim and that these two things are incompatible?

Saleha's story reveals the multiple and intersecting forms of oppression that Muslim youth face based on their ethno-racial identity as well as religious affiliation. This can produce a sense of existential angst and impede self-esteem, as well as cause youth to question their ties to the nation.

Addressing what she felt were unfounded concerns about the Muslim presence in Canada, Anisa, a Somali student from Toronto, referred to the Quranic verse that emphasizes human diversity as a naturalized and divinely ordained condition through which we come to know of others: "Islam teaches us to be mindful of where we live and to be loyal to the country that we live in. Because in the Quran it is said, 'We put you into nations and tribes so you may get to know one another.' So obviously I'm going to be loyal to Canada because I'm a Canadian."

All the youth interviewed validated both their Muslim and Canadian identities but also acknowledged the tensions between the two. In my earlier research on Muslim youth in Canada (J. Zine 2000, 2001, 2008), I identified a "double culture syndrome" whereby Muslim youth from religiously observant immigrant and second-generation families are forced to contend with the competing cultural demands between their home and school as well as society at large. Pressures to conform to dominant values and mores in Canada (such as those regarding dating, premarital sex, drug and alcohol use) conflict with more traditional Islamic beliefs and practices and lead to contradictory demands for different sets of lifestyle choices. Muslim youth navigate these tensions in a variety of ways, and in some cases end up leading double lives to conform to the competing expectations they face. Others from less religious families or those who have chosen secular lifestyles, may not have the same challenge of cultural adaptation but must still deal with the limiting misperceptions of Muslims as a monolithic group.

Other youth found being Muslim in Canada allowed them to have the cultural and discursive space to construct Muslim identities without the oversight of traditional religious authorities. Tariq, a South Asian student from Montreal, found being Muslim in Canada optimized the religious pathways available to him:

> I think, being a Muslim in Canada is probably more compatible than being Muslim in some Muslim countries. Whereas in other countries you're born into it and you are forced and entrenched. But here, you have the ability to learn about it and to make the choice if you want to undertake it, if you don't, we have these rules and laws that protect you from any backlash you may in theory get from your family. I find that being a Muslim here is actually easier than it is in other parts of the world. It's more accepting and more open, and I think that's what Islam promotes; it doesn't push the idea of being forced into anything.

Tariq felt that secular democracies like Canada enabled greater religious possibilities more so than in some Muslim countries with more rigid and authoritarian practices. He found that the pressure of religious conformity was less pronounced in Canada's Muslim diaspora.

Others spoke of a tug-of-war between their Canadian identity and their ethnicity. Most youth used hyphenated descriptors of their religious, ethnic, and national/Canadian identity when locating themselves; Muslim identity came first and then their ethno-racial origin and Canadian identity. But when their countries of origin were under attack, they identified more with that nationality, and when their Canadianness was challenged, they asserted their right to be recognized as part of the nation. Some acknowledged that they enthusiastically rooted for Canadian teams in international competitions, but when Canada became involved in the battlefields in Afghanistan their patriotism waned. All of them had an appreciation of and genuine allegiance to Canada, though not necessarily when it came to its policies and politics.

Marwan, a Moroccan student from Montreal, spoke of the hegemony of a Québécois identity over that of a Canadian one, arguing that in White francophone Quebec "many people consider themselves more Quebecer than Canadian." He felt that Québécois and Canadian identities were referenced by specific cultural markers like "what kind of food you eat in the morning, going to watch hockey, how you dress." For Marwan, conformity with the status quo cultural practices determined the contours of belonging within Québécois society and simultaneously excluded those who refused to adapt.

Naima, an Iraqi student from Montreal, felt a strong connection to her Canadian identity, having been born and raised in Canada. She loved living in Montreal and felt there was freedom of expression in the city, but she was also cognizant of how negative media representations led to widespread fear and distrust of Muslims:

> No matter what happens they make a synonym of a Muslim
> being a terrorist. I wish that would stop. Also, the Québécois
> here have this fear that we want to turn Quebec into Saudi
> Arabia or something. If they could understand us more, they
> would give it a rest. We are not the type that impose what we
> want on others. In Islam, you don't go and make people Muslim.
> You just have to present yourself as a "good one" and whoever
> wants to become one will come to you. That is God's job,
> not our job. Our job is just to be good ourselves and that's it.
> I guess if everyone understood that about the real Islam,
> they would not be like that anymore.

Naima was aware of the specificities of Québécois Islamophobia as a fear of cultural loss and the erosion of secularism as the cornerstone of Quebec's identity should the Muslim presence become too pronounced or embedded.

Integration is seen as the responsibility of newcomers with little regard for the barriers that limit or preclude acceptance and inclusion. Instead of viewing integration as a fluid reciprocal exchange, immigrants, newcomers, and other marginalized communities must find ways to adapt, conform, and accommodate their lifestyles. Oppression and systemic discrimination are not factored into the xenophobic equations that shore up the integrity of White nationalism in this "adapt or perish" paradigm. Yunus, a Somali student from Toronto, challenged the one-way street of integration in relation to dominant fears of un-integrated and maladapted Muslim youth becoming radicalized: "We call it multiculturalism, but we forget that it works for some people but not for everybody. We were talking about integration before, some of these youths are starting to follow more radicalized ways of not being integrated. The responsibility of the integration is not only on the back[s] of these youth, there is a responsibility on society itself."

Lack of integration, most often a by-product of alienation, raises questions about how society, and not just individuals, is maladaptive, leading to barriers in social integration and cohesion. Samir acknowledged the need for integration, including more politicized engagement: "We don't live in a communal world anymore. We live in a cosmopolitan, universal world where we have the responsibility to integrate and to interact with other people in society. And I think first and foremost is the issue of integration into places where we live and that includes integration politically."

Furthering integration into the wider public sphere, including media and professional vocations, is a way of mainstreaming the Muslim presence in Canada, which has already made prominent headway through the development of Muslim institutions, schools, community organizations, social services, businesses, and political representation in all levels of government. South Asians, the largest and most established community, have shown greater gains in most areas while other immigrant and refugee groups are still evolving and growing their community presence. For example, Sakina, a Somali student from Toronto, discussed the developments in her community:

I identify with the Muslim community. I identify with the African community, specifically the East African community, and I guess we have our own strengths. Most of us from the East African community are more recent immigrants here in the last twenty-five years or so; we haven't been able to make the kind of substantial dent that other communities who've been here longer [have] been able to make, but we're going at a good pace and I see a lot of progress. A lot of the youth are just now growing up and going to university, so I guess our legacy is to be seen in a couple of years or so.

In addition to the challenges of integration, Muslims with transnational ties must navigate the ruptures created by geopolitical conflicts, which unsettle the connections between ancestral homelands and new diasporas. Simone, an African Canadian youth worker in Ottawa, raised concerns about the young female refugee youth population that she worked with and the kinds of resettlement stress they had to contend with, in addition to other kinds of trauma they were experiencing:

A lot of the girls I work with are refugees and have a specific reality, which isn't commonly shared by the entire Muslim community: issues of having suffered post-traumatic stress; having witnessed war and conflicts; having parents [who] witnessed war and conflicts; poverty issues because most of them still live in poverty; living in housing communities where there is a cycle of poverty. Also, a lot of girls that live there are sort of trapped between two worlds because their parents come from one culture and Canada is another culture. They don't really know where they are gonna live. Right after high school or even one year from now, they don't know where they are going to be living. They might be living in Canada, they might be living in a different part of Canada, they might be going back home, or they might be going to another country. Because of citizenship issues or economic reasons, a lot of them are constantly in transit. That's another factor with the girls I work with, home is always in transit. Their sense of identity is always in transit.

For refugee communities dealing with the loss of and dislocation from their home, living within cycles of poverty and cultural dissonance leads to ontological instability and unsettled identities. The unique set of social and political circumstances that underwrite the experiences of the 9/11 generation of Muslim youth is further explored in the next chapter, which discusses the dynamics, manifestations, and impacts of Islamophobia.

3

The 9/11 Generation and the Dynamics of Islamophobia

As discussed in the introduction of this book, Islamophobia is best understood as a *fear and hatred of Islam and Muslims (and those perceived as Muslims) that translate into individual actions and ideological and systemic forms of oppression that support the logic and rationale of specific power relations.* Put simply, individual actions like vandalism and name-calling are supported by widespread ideas like "Muslims are terrorists," and these ideologies find expression in systemic practices such as racial profiling. Picture this construct as an iceberg, where individual actions are what become visible above the water, while the ideologies and systemic practices lie below the surface underpinning, supporting, and sustaining the structure.

The ideological apparatuses supporting the purveyance of Islamophobic narratives via mainstream media and a growing Islamophobia industry justify and legitimate the individual manifestations of Islamophobia as well as the systemic practices that allow for their reproduction. The discursive dimension of Islamophobia creates the alibi of "Muslim peril," which authorizes restrictive and draconian state policies targeting Muslims as well as legitimating the ongoing war on terror and global militarism. What is central to this framework is that at every level – individual, ideological, and systemic – the relations of power that underwrite this dynamic support historically constituted racial logics. As a system of oppression, Islamophobia is embedded within formations of power that create the discursive, structural, and legal context of subordination that Muslims face. In Canada these conditions are rooted within the racial power structures built from White settler colonialism and are reinforced through contemporary global circuits of imperial racial formations enacted by the post-9/11 war on terror. Using this paradigm as a framework of analysis, this chapter explores the individual, ideological, and systemic dynamics of Islamophobia and anti-Muslim racism and the impact of these forms of oppression on the 9/11 generation of Muslim youth. The intersectional aspects of anti-Muslim racism are also addressed by examining how gendered forms of Islamophobia differentially impact Muslim women.

INDIVIDUAL ACTIONS: THE IMPACT OF 9/11

Individual actions, referring to interpersonal forms of Islamophobia, can range from daily microaggressions to hate crimes. They can also be directed at symbols of the Islamic presence, such as mosques or Islamic schools, through vandalism or issuing threats. While participants in this study did not raise cyberbullying as a concern, it is a new frontier for Islamophobic harassment (CAIR 2017). Sometimes these actions are overt and at other times, they are more subtle and harder to identify, name, and challenge. The Muslim youth I interviewed described experiencing Islamophobia along a wide-ranging spectrum. Schools and workplaces along with public spaces like parks or the transit system were common sites for interpersonal acts of Islamophobia to occur. For most of them, it was the 9/11 attacks that ushered in heightened tensions and made them subject to overt and subtle forms of anti-Muslim racism.

The youth in this study were in middle school or high school at the time of the attacks on the World Trade Centre in New York City, and much of their recollections of this tragedy as well as the backlash they experienced transpired through individual encounters within these settings. Ateeka reflected on her experience as an immigrant student attempting to integrate into her Calgary high school during the aftermath of 9/11 and having to deal with bullying and harassment that eventually led to her removing her hijab.

> After September 11, things kind of got worse. My friend who I knew at school got beaten up there every other day. I got pushed into a locker. It was really hard for me to go to school for a couple of weeks because I was so embarrassed of my religion. I was scared to say that I was Muslim, so I took it [hijab] off. After that I haven't worn it because it had such an effect on me. Because when someone just beats you up because of who you are, then you think that everything will be different when you take it off.

The internalization of Islamophobia is evident here in Ateeka's words when she admits being "embarrassed of my religion" after 9/11. Taking on the collective guilt levelled against all Muslims for the tragic acts perpetrated by a few misguided extremists on 9/11 resulted in her fear of attending school in the aftermath of this tragedy and ultimately led to her removing her hijab because it was making her a walking target of hate, harassment, bullying, and violence.

Ateeka was aware that the backlash against her was provoked by Islamophobia and not purely racial animus because she noted, "[T]hat didn't happen to the Indian kids who are not Muslims. You know the Punjabi students, that didn't happen to them. They were called Paki ... They were called names, but they weren't pushed into lockers." Many Sikhs and Hindus have been mistaken for Muslims and become victims of Islamophobic harassment and violence; however, in this case Ateeka differentiates between the racial harassment of other South Asian students versus the Islamophobic attacks against visibly Muslim ones. She went on to note how over time, the incidents were less frequent and by the time she entered university in New Brunswick on the east coast of Canada, she felt less judged. She found that people were becoming more aware that only a minority of Muslims engage in violent forms of extremism, and this did not have any bearing on her.

Rania, Canadian born with Egyptian parents, had moved to the United States with her family prior to the 9/11 attacks. She, like most students, was in school during the time information about the attacks became public. In many cases, students and teachers were watching the horrific destruction live on television sets in hushed classrooms. Rania recounts what happened in her class after they viewed the televised attacks:

> The day of September 11 we are watching the Twin Towers falling, and I remember my grade seven World Cultures teacher came and pointed her finger in my face and said, "Tell your people to stop attacking Americans!" ... I was a very sarcastic child, and I was always made fun of because I wore hijab since grade three, so as my defence mechanism, I wouldn't cry. I would always just say something sarcastic. So, I remember I was really on the defensive, because I was very emotional, and I was like, "Hand me a phone, and I'll call my uncle Bin Laden!"

By the time she was in middle school, Rania had already developed her defensive sarcasm against daily Islamophobic microaggressions. The teacher's verbal assault made it clear where Rania stood in the "us versus them" binary, which triggered the student's defensive attempt at humour. While the teacher was not fired or even reprimanded for singling out Rania and demanding that Muslims en masse be held to account for the 9/11 attacks, Rania was suspended for her outburst.

Faiza, in Vancouver, watched the collapse of the Twin Towers just before heading out to her classroom. She recounts her experience that day and the panic she felt as she hoped the perpetrators were not Muslim, knowing what this would mean for her community if they were:

> I remember when 9/11 happened, I was in grade ten. I watched the planes hit the Twin Towers and then I was in shock! I went to class and everybody was following the news. Our teacher didn't even teach that day. He just left the TV on for everybody to watch. And they were talking about who could have done something like that. And the whole time, I remember I was thinking, "Please let it be anybody but a guy with a turban! Please!" And then, Osama bin Laden's face shows up and I'm like, "Dang!" I was so worried! I was thinking, that's it, it's going to be hell for us.

Thinking, "Please let it be anybody but a guy with a turban!" is a common response for Muslims to a terrorist attack. While "white exceptionalism" (J. Zine 2017) allows a space of innocence for the actions of White terrorists to not be transferred to others of their racial group, this is never the case for Muslims and other racially marginalized groups routinely held to account for the actions of people who happen to resemble them or share the same faith.

In another school-based incident, Rania's classwork on Palestine was censored by the teacher and principal:

> I remember that same year, we had current event projects that we had to present to our history classes. That was the year that I became very politically active, very interested in world issues, so I remember I did a presentation on Palestine. I had a huge typed presentation and I had pictures of babies with bullet holes in their chests and mothers carrying their dead child[ren]. I wanted to pass them around my class because

nobody else would ever listen to me if they didn't have [these pictures], so I was going to make my classmates care. I remember I was so excited. I would show the people sitting next to me at my table and I would run up and show my teacher. Before my history class presentation, the principal sat me down on a picnic bench outside and said, "I heard you have a current events presentation, what is it?" And I thought, "Oh my God, somebody told the principal that I'm so smart, and I'm gonna do the presentation for him!" So, I ran into the class and pulled out the pictures and showed him. I was giving him the presentation and thinking, "Oh man, I'm so smart!" He stopped me and sat me down and said, "I talked to your teacher and she really doesn't want you to give this presentation. It'll really upset your classmates. But she will give you 100 per cent on your presentation." And he's talking to me as he's rolling up my papers. And I thought, "I don't want 100 per cent, you can give me a zero if I don't present, but that's ridiculous." Time after time, things like that would happen. I didn't understand. I just knew that I was upset that he rolled up my papers. That's where my grade seven mind kind of stopped.

Although there may have been concerns over the graphic nature of the images that Rania was planning to show or simply because of the perceived "controversial" nature of the Palestinian struggle, she was not given an explanation as to why she could not share her project with the class.

I was struck by her statement that she needed to show these graphic images of suffering and dead children so that she could "make her classmates care." Butler (2009) reminds us how only certain bodies are deemed of value when they perish or are worthy of universal and unconditional grief. These distinctions are often drawn along racial lines of empathy. As Rania continued to be singled out for differential treatment by the teacher, Rania's parents eventually interceded and threated legal action against the school for discrimination, after which the teacher was placed on probation. Rania notes that by then it was too little, too late to repair the damage already done to her psyche, spirit, and sense of belonging within the school.

Mahvish described the irony of receiving verbal assaults and even death threats after 9/11, following a panel discussion on religious tolerance that she participated in: "I put on a religious tolerance panel after 9/11 in my grade [twelve] year of high school and actually received death threats and I was called a 'cult follower' and a 'brain-washer,' a 'liar' all kinds of things ... 'heretic' ... everything ... and [was] basically told that I'd be condemned to hell, and it wasn't only from Christians." Being pacifiers of public sentiment through mounting interfaith dialogues and public talks affirming the peaceful nature of Islam in contrast to the violent imagery of Daesh and Al-Qaeda was not a buffer against bigotry for Mahvish.

Dealing with individual acts of Islamophobia such as daily micro-aggressions and bullying, as well as racial and religious profiling, takes a toll on the emotional well-being of children and youth, as Idil, a Somali youth worker, explained: "I have done a research project about Somali youth and one of the things that came up a lot was the stress factors. Thirteen- and fourteen-year-old[s] are stressed and they are oversleeping or overeating. It is strange. They do feel different and they are picked on because of their race, religion, or culture. The relationship with depression and anxiety comes with the stress these youth are going through in grade eight or nine." Other studies confirm Idil's findings about the difficulties Muslim children and youth in the West face, coping with stress and hostility arising from the negative treatment they experience (Peek 2003, 2011; Sirin and Fine 2007; Rousseau et al. 2015; Elkassem et al. 2018; Tahseen, S.R. Ahmed, and S. Ahmed 2019). For Somali and other Black Muslim youth, Islamophobic bullying is compounded by anti-Black racism, leaving a variegated imprint of historically rooted forms of oppression on their psyche.

Hate crimes and threats targeted at mosques and Islamic schools have created a sense of unease in places where people should feel safe. Sakina described what she witnessed in Toronto: "People have scribbled graffiti on walls ... people have thrown stuff at Muslims, who are going to prayer. So yeah, it's kind of medieval." Naima attended an Islamic school in Montreal and remembered how in the aftermath of 9/11 her school had closed for a few days due to the security concerns from threats they received. The principal warned the students to be careful on their way home and cautioned them to be vigilant against possible personal attacks. In the days that followed there were incidents of vandalism and graffiti at the school. Some physical altercations occurred when Islamic school students were targeted by youth from public schools while riding public transportation.

Physical violence was not as commonly reported, but some youth had troubling stories to share. Sikander, a South Asian student from Ontario, described some experiences that he and his friends encountered:

"I know guys who've been roughed up by cops, some were beaten. My brother's friends were left bruised up when roughed up against a wall. One said that he'd been kneed in the gut too. But you won't hear of this. We don't report these things. No big deal. Even I was roughed up a couple of times. No big deal. Embrace it, it helps to learn your place. Ain't needing no lawyer or teacher to tell us that." Sikander's flippant attitude spoke volumes as he described the physical assaults as a matter of course in a society where marginalized bodies are disciplined into submission. The reluctance to speak about these violent incidents inhibits the collection of hate crime data as he points out, making it difficult to determine the prevalence of such acts.

Individual acts of Islamophobia and anti-Muslim racism ranged from overt practices such as name-calling and exclusion to perceptions of fear and hatred conveyed in more tacit ways. In the preface, I recounted my son Usama's experience in middle school after 9/11, where he was bullied, harassed, and teased because of his name. Other youth spoke of similar incidents they personally faced or those of family and friends as their Muslim names became sources of fear and derision. Arif, a South Asian Shia Muslim from British Columbia, found that confronted over time with these "jokes" he developed a way of responding and coping by turning the comments back at people: "When I was younger, I was reluctant to say I was Muslim. It's easier now when people are joking around and stuff, you can just joke back with them. You don't take it personally, or like even if it is somewhat of an offence, you kind of throw it back at them so they look bad. Through experience you learn how to do it." Muslim youth can develop a "thick skin" against taunts and bullying and what others might see as innocuous "jokes," but this resilience comes at a price to their own sense of self and belonging. As Arif points out, at times it is easier to not divulge one's Muslim identity in the first place.

Shaila, a South Asian student from Toronto, was called a "Paki" and received hate messages on social media. Mahvish also described experiences she, her family members, and community faced in the aftermath of 9/11 and since: "I got called a dirty effing Paki and I'm not a Paki. I went shopping with my grandmother who wears a hijab and the cashier refused to serve her and that was after 9/11. Besides what has happened to me at the border and the airport every single time I travel, especially to the US. So yeah, definitely I've noticed that. Have I noticed anything in particular against Muslims in my community? I would say just intense hostility ... suspicion ... fear."

The individual actions of harassment, exclusion, and hate crimes perpetrated against Muslims rely on the demonization of Islam, which is the basis upon which such acts are conceived, gain currency, and ultimately secure their justification and legitimacy. Saleha commented on how she connected racism and Islamophobia in tandem with other interlocking forms of oppression that are often elided through the essentialization of Muslim identities:

> I think Islamophobia is parallel to racism and it intersects in a lot of ways. Muslim identities have been racialized in particular ways when you see who is represented on TV and what kind of roles they play. Most of the time it is Arabs, right? So, people tend to think that all Arabs are Muslims and all Muslims are Arab. And they kind of forget about other kinds of Muslims even though those are of larger proportions, for example, South Asian Muslims. I think that sometimes it is a bit confusing what's happening when you experience something. Is it racism? Is it Islamophobia? Is it both? Is it sexism? Or is it something else completely, right?

Attempting to disentangle racism and Islamophobia is difficult because they are interrelated. Certain aspects of oppression are at times more salient than others, and it can be difficult for people experiencing intersectional forms of discrimination to discern which specific factors are at play.

Karima, an Algerian/French Canadian student from Montreal, discussed how her mixed racial identity allowed her to "pass" as White, which made racism less of a concern for her, but her identity as a Muslim woman, evident from her hijab and clothing, made Islamophobia more pronounced in her experiences:

> I haven't had any overt comments, it's more prejudice about religious minorities. Whenever I walk into a store whenever I do something, if I am scared of discrimination it's not based on my race, it's based on religion. It's probably because of my veil, but I don't want to put that as the issue because sometimes you can believe everything is because of the veil when someone might have just had a bad day or someone just might not like you. That's the problem with religious/racial profiling is that you start to question everything. Are they profiling me? Are they not?

Karima raises an important issue that when confronted with suspicion, surveillance, or other differential treatment it is impossible not to connect these to one's religious or racial identity. Even if, as Karima suggests, it might just be a case of a person "having a bad day," the possibility of racism or Islamophobia cannot be ruled out. This kind of differential treatment that White or racially ambiguous Muslims experience speaks to the racialization of religion discussed previously, whereby racial characteristics are ascribed to religious categories and their followers.

Islamophobia is underwritten by essentialist ideologies, which are continually reproduced and reconstituted in new ways that purvey and project Orientalist fears and racial anxieties. The circulation of these ideas rationalizes Islamophobic hate and acts of discrimination and violence. The following section examines the ideological under-pinnings of Islamophobia through the experiences of Muslim youth who are set in the crosshairs of these discourses and the destructive practices they authorize and inspire.

IDEOLOGIES

A project spearheaded by the University of Leeds examined dominant European narratives about Islamophobia from eight then EU member nations (France, Germany, Belgium, the Czech Republic, Hungary, Portugal, Greece, and the UK). Uncovering the discursive formations of Islamophobia is essential in mapping its national genealogies and in developing critical responses rooted in specific historical and cultural contexts. According to one of the working papers from this project on European Human Rights Law:

> These narratives were found to fix Muslims collectively as, in descending order of prevalence, a threat to security, unassimilable, a demographic threat, an Islamisation threat, a threat to local, national and European identity, as responsible for the oppression of women, as essentially different and violent, as incomplete citizens and as a risk to the majority, and essentially homophobic. A worsening environment of Islamophobia was identified with respect to media content, political discourse and experiences of discrimination, indicating the new and increasingly acceptable hostility against Muslims in many spheres of everyday life. (Trispiotis 2017, 6)

The findings of this study revealed some of the deep-seated ideological foundations of Islamophobia, which have a common resonance across various nations. The study also demonstrated how the discursive practices and narratives of Islamophobia connect to the normalization of discrimination against Muslims.

In Canada, Islamophobic narratives have filtered through media and influenced Canadian cultural politics. For example, in 2006, after the arrests of seventeen Muslim youth and one adult on terror-related charges (see chapter 5), the front page of a prominent national publication, *Maclean's* magazine, read, "Why the Future Belongs to Islam" with a feature article by Mark Steyn. The caption below the title reads, "The Muslim world has youth, numbers and global ambitions. The West is growing old and enfeebled and lacks the will to rebuff those who would supplant it. It's the end of the world as we know it." This apocalyptic view is underwritten by the fear of a Muslim future in a world dominated by radicalized Muslim youth. In this widely read article, Steyn encapsulates various tropes that create moral panic about the Muslim presence in Canada and in Western nations globally.[1] These narratives speak to the demographic threat of Muslim overpopulation, creeping sharia, and jihadist terrorism:

> On the Continent and elsewhere in the West, native populations are aging and fading and being supplanted remorselessly by a young Muslim demographic. Time for the obligatory "of courses":
> *of course*, not all Muslims are terrorists – though enough are hot for jihad to provide an impressive support network of mosques from Vienna to Stockholm to Toronto to Seattle. *Of course*, not all Muslims support terrorists – though enough of them share their basic objectives (the wish to live under Islamic law in Europe and North America) to function wittingly or otherwise as the "good cop" end of an Islamic good cop/bad cop routine. But, at the very minimum, this fast-moving demographic transformation provides a huge comfort zone for the jihad to move around in. (Steyn 2006, n.p.)

These Islamophobic discourses stoke racial fears about Muslims as imperilling Western nations whether through a demographic takeover as a bio-political threat (see also Bracke and Aguilar 2020); sources of "civilizational danger" through a "stealth jihad" to hijack Western societies with barbaric sharia laws; or promoting political Islam and violent jihadism. These ideologies create existential fears and moral panics that align Muslims with death (i.e., through outpacing the White population and leading to "White genocide," potential jihadist terror attacks, or the death of culture as Western civilization is imperilled by a "triumphalist" Islam).

According to media critic Sam Keen (2008), "We first kill people with our minds, before we kill them with weapons. Whatever the conflict, the enemy is always the destroyer. We're on God's side; they're barbaric. We're good, they're evil. War gives us a feeling of moral clarity that we lack at other times." Keen's reading of the power of the media is akin to a "sympathetic magic" where the destructive rhetorical practices become a rehearsal for actual violence like prehistoric cave drawings of hunting were preparation for a successful kill. Laying the discursive groundwork for the construction of abject difference plays into the sociological dynamics of Islamophobia by providing the alibi and justification for violence and systemic oppression.

Jiwani and Dessner (2016, 36) surveyed Canadian news media from 2010 to 2013 to examine the representation of Muslim youth and found that "Muslim youth are cast not only as an enemy within the nation state, but also as a contaminating force that must be disciplined or ejected from the body politic. They are, in short, barbarians in and of the land." Participants in this study provided further examples of how mainstream media pathologizes Muslims and supports the grand narrative of the jihadist bogeyman. For example, Zabeda and Zahir contrasted the treatment of Anders Breivik, the White Christian terrorist in Norway, versus Michael Zehaf-Bibeau, the Parliament Hill shooter in Ottawa, or the Toronto 18:

> **Zabeda:** If a Muslim breaks the law the media should not jump to blame it on a religion. If there's a terrorist act, if somebody does something really stupid and crazy then maybe they have psychological problems. It does not necessarily have to be about religion. Like the terrorist guy in Norway, right? He killed so many innocent people and they said he had psychological problems. Had it been a Muslim person, it would be like, "He's a terrorist!" That's it, end of story, right? But there's more to that, there is more to people.

> **Zahir:** If you are White you are simply an individual and you are separate from the rest of the society. Whereas, if you are Muslim you are linked to the whole community. Concerning Islamophobia, it's a daily thing. A lot of work needs to be done

to have accurate reporting in the media and to have Canadians at large understand that Muslims are not terrorists blowing up each other, or wife beaters.

As astute consumers of media, Muslim youth are cognizant of the double standards evident in reporting on Islam and Muslims.

According to a study from the University of Alabama (Kearns, Betus, and Lemieux 2019), researchers found that terrorist attacks committed by Muslim extremists receive 357 per cent more US press coverage than those committed by non-Muslims. Terrorist attacks committed by non-Muslims (or where the religion was unknown) received an average of 15 headlines, while those committed by Muslim extremists received 105 headlines. The study notes that "[t]he disparity in media coverage is particularly out of sync with the reality given that white and right-wing terrorists carried out nearly two times as many terrorist attacks as Muslim extremists between 2008 and 2016."[2] The disproportionate attention given to terrorism committed by Muslims versus other groups – especially White supremacist groups – operating in the US fuels the moral panic against Muslims and promotes Islamophobia in the public imaginary. Media discourses that fixate on Muslim terrorism heighten the public's fear and perceptions of threat, and provide the ideological justification for racial profiling and security policies that target Muslims (see chapter 5).

Saleha spoke to how these misconceptions are fomented by the media and affect the representation of Muslims as a continuation of colonial era tropes evident long before 9/11:

I remember life before September 11, and I remember there were a lot of misconceptions. I remember watching TV and seeing Arab terrorists. So, it is not just that "boom," September 11 happened and everything changed! If you look at old Hollywood and colonial era travel narratives, you see the way that Muslims, the Middle East or Arabs, Afghans, in particular, have been always kind of characterized as backwards, barbaric, uncivilized, violent, misogynistic. And Muslim women have been always silenced, have been the veiled figure in the background who have no voice. They need to be liberated and have no agency. You don't see positive representation of Muslims. Then whenever you do you see Muslims, it remains in negative ways that position the West as superior and dominant versus the East.

The positional superiority of the West (Said 1979) is shored up by
the currency of Orientalist tropes that have underwritten the global
war on terror and have continued to impact the lives of Muslims who
live under the spectre of these narrow ideological frames.

Youth in the study that is the basis for this book encountered
Islamophobic ideologies and sentiments throughout their daily lives.
Negative media representations of Islam and Muslims filtered into
their encounters in schools, at work, or in public. Shaila, a South Asian
student from Toronto, described a pervasive feeling of being judged
based on media representations of Islam that others negatively and
indiscriminately associate with all Muslims: "In a post-9/11 world
definitely everybody has become a lot more defensive, especially since
after that Muslims and Islam have surfaced in a bad light. They don't
really understand what Islam is so they're just gonna judge you based
on what the media has brought to light." For many, common understandings of Islam and Muslims are drawn from mainstream media
where reporting is often salacious and sensationalized (Karim 2003;
Alsultany 2012; Jiwani 2016, 2017, 2019). Abdel-Fattah (2021, 164)
describes these motifs and tropes as being part of "the inventories of
ideologies" that shape the political, social, and discursive terrain
Muslim youth must navigate. The lack of general knowledge regarding
Islam makes it easier for more stereotypical constructions to become
uncritically absorbed and hegemonic.

Zabeda described the pre-9/11 public as being "uninformed" while
the post-9/11 public is "misinformed" largely by the "Fox News version
of everything." Farheen, a South Asian Shia student from Vancouver,
found the ignorance regarding Islam to be wilful and dangerous:

> I was watching Anderson Cooper and they had a group of
> American Muslims that were on the show and a lady in the
> audience was like, "Ever since 9/11, I have researched about
> Islam, your prophet is like this or that …" So, Anderson asked
> her, "Have you read the Quran?" And she is like, "I have read
> some passages." So, he's like, "So you haven't read the whole
> Quran?" And then she's like, "Just passages." So, he is like,
> "You googled it." It was obvious that she was not well informed.
> They have their own misconceptions and don't want to let it go.

The weaponizing of the Quran through decontextualized and abstracted
passages is a strategy to situate Islam as an immanent and inherent

danger to Western societies and part of a well-orchestrated repertoire of Islamophobic fearmongering. Muslims are forced to be the corrective to the misinformation about Islam or they are expected to play the role of an interlocutor in global political affairs or Islamic theology by virtue of their religious affiliation.

Being asked to respond to the random inquiries of strangers, acquaintances, teachers, and professors is a common experience for Muslims. Rummana, a South Asian Shia student from British Columbia, described how she was called upon to be a political and religious "expert" any time Muslims were depicted in the media:

> Every time something happens in the media they come to you like the informed insider, they expect you to have the answers to everything, to be well versed on jurisprudence, all one hundred versions of it, and have a working knowledge of all Middle Eastern politics. If you don't have the answer, then something is wrong with you. They have these weird ways of sizing you up. This guy in my class made a comment like, "Well what do you know, all Muslim women in the Middle East are the property of their men." Because there is one incident that happened somewhere far off in the Middle East, and suddenly I am supposed to have the answer for that.

Being positioned as experts on Middle East politics or religious jurisprudence by curious strangers or classmates often forces youth into defensive roles on issues they are not experienced with or otherwise inclined to comment upon.

Saleha recounted being asked about political context in Afghanistan because it was assumed that as a Muslim, she would have some insight on the rise of the Taliban: "People start conversations, 'What do you think about this?' And you're like, 'Well I am not Afghan, so why are you like asking me,' right? And why have I been held accountable for all those things, right? So that is what I found after September 11. That happens in the classroom too. A professor will just bring up examples that will be completely unrelated and then look at me [*laughs*]."

Saleha found the representation of peacekeeping Canadians in Afghanistan holding "barbarian" Muslims at bay reinforced Islamophobic ideologies: "The official Canadian identity [is] as a peacekeeping nation that is completely innocent and goes out and helps. Any violence the Canadian forces do it is legitimate because, you know, we are trying to help those people who have just lost every part of humanity and are completely violent or whatever." The juxtaposition of these narratives of noble soldiers and barbarian extremists has been a way to secure the boundaries of the savage and civilized within the geopolitical imperial order.

A popular Islamophobic ideology is the "sharia bogeyman." Saleha recalled being in grade nine, a couple of years after 9/11, when the implementation of sharia[3] law in family arbitration in Ontario was being debated amid a backdrop of Islamophobic rhetoric and sensationalism (see J. Zine 2012b). A teacher asked her to account for the community's views on the subject: "I was leaving the class and was the last to leave. I was packing my stuff, and my science teacher asked me, 'Saleha can I ask you a question?' And I was like, 'Okay.' And she was like, 'Do Canadian Muslims want sharia?' And I was like, 'What?!' And she was like, 'Because that's when they chop people's hands off, right?'" The notion that Muslims are subversively promoting a creeping sharia that threatens the freedom of Western culture is a pervasive narrative among the alt-right and White nationalists who promote Islamophobia. Saleha's example shows that even schoolchildren will be asked to account for Islamophobic propaganda.

Zareena noted how the constant reiteration of negative tropes feeds moral panics and leaves a negative impression that Muslims are constantly burdened with having to dismantle: "It is just drilled into people's brains that a Muslim is an extremist and they hate everyone. And their goal is to kill everyone. And that just makes us look bad and then a person, who is not a Muslim, gets to know you properly, they are like, 'Oh, wow, your religion is actually really peaceful.'" The social and emotional toll of the discursive labour involved in constantly justifying one's faith adds additional stress, anxiety, and an epistemic battle fatigue to the lives of Muslims (see also Elkassem et al. 2018).

Keen (1988, 19) warned of a "consensual paranoia" that is bred in a culture of war through which an enemy is imagined and archetypally reproduced: "Consensual paranoia – the pathology of the normal person who is a member of a war-justifying society – forms the template from which all the images of the enemy are created. By studying the logic of paranoia, we can see why certain archetypes of the enemy must necessarily recur, no matter what the historical circumstances." These reiterative constructs feed into the creation of moral panics and then circulate with impunity in ways that justify draconian security and immigration practices targeting Muslims. Once the conditions have been ideologically primed, they create an alibi for heightening practices of securitization and regulating Muslim bodies within the state and public sphere (see chapter 5).

SYSTEMIC PRACTICES

Negative ideologies about Muslims inform the systemic and structural conditions they face, whether in educational settings (Schmidt 2002; Van Driel 2004; Collet 2007; Mir 2014); healthcare (Samari 2016); housing (J. Zine 2009); policing and law (Bahdi 2003; Razack 2008; Bakht 2014; Beydoun 2018); immigration (Kazemipur 2014); and poverty and employment (Khattab, Miaari, and Mohamed-Ali 2019). The systemic dimension of Islamophobia operates through a variety of institutional sites, including state policies and practices. Post-9/11 forms of governmentality targeting Muslims include the systemic practices of racial and religious surveillance and securitization. (The securitization of Muslims is discussed at length in chapter 5.) Muslim youth also described other kinds of systemic bias and barriers they have experienced or observed and how these impacted them. As young people who were considering their future employment, workplace discrimination was a pervasive concern as was systemic bias in the delivery of social services and educational programs. Systemic discrimination allows for the reproduction of Islamophobia as it becomes embedded in institutional practices.

Saleha was worried about how the demonization of Islam and Muslims was tied to the reproduction of racialized poverty, as well as how it affected institutional practices within social services or healthcare: "I am concerned about the impact of what it's like growing up in an environment where there's a lot of vilification of Muslims, and young people are caught in that sort of discourse. Warfare of Canadian identity, right? Which is using Muslims as this essentialized yet nebulous enemy. I'm also concerned about how that connects to the racialization of poverty and the ways that Muslims access health services and social services."

As a graduate student in social work, Saleha raised important concerns about how the demonization of Islam can further exacerbate the racialized poverty many Muslims experience as well as adversely impact their ability to access healthcare and social services in an environment free from bigotry. My research on Muslims experiencing poverty and homelessness in Canada after 9/11 bears out Saleha's concerns. Due to the backlash after 9/11, fewer Muslims were accessing social services, while some landlords openly refused to rent to them (J. Zine 2009). Within that volatile political climate, Islamophobia became a barrier to accessing safe and affordable housing.

Educational institutions were also settings where Muslims were subjected to biased practices. Yumna, an Egyptian student from Montreal who wore hijab, described an encounter with a French school where she had enrolled in a course. She was ridiculed for her language skills and denied a place in their program after insisting she come to an interview in person so the interviewer could "first look at her." Yumna found the experience demoralizing and humiliating and felt the teacher's manner and attitude had more to do with her religious attire than her language skills. Yumna's story is one example of how racial and religious profiling occurs in educational settings, not just at borders.

Canada's immigration policies have been historically grounded in practices of racial exclusion. Amira, a student from Ottawa of Arab descent, cited concerns over former prime minister Stephen Harper's rhetoric that she feared might have negative implications for the reunification of her family: "The fact that we have a majority Conservative government and Harper seems to think that 'Islamicism' is the number one threat could be really dangerous! I think there will be a lot of policies that would encourage racial profiling. My dad wanted to bring his parents from Switzerland, now there is very little chance with the Harper government." A politics of distraction uses fear and moral panic to justify and legitimate public safety policies that serve to fortify a racialized security state. As a youth worker, Idil cited the need for Muslim youth to be aware of their rights in a climate where racial profiling and surveillance are predicated upon Islamophobic narratives. Developing a political literacy around state policies is part of the knowledge and skill set that the 9/11 generation develops as a rite of passage.

EMPLOYMENT AND SYSTEMIC BIAS

A key systemic concern for many participants of the study was the ways Islamophobia hinders employment opportunities. Asserting a Muslim identity in the public sphere can lead to pragmatic concerns about discrimination in the workplace, schools, and other institutions. Zafar, a South Asian youth advocate in Toronto, talked about the challenges for Muslim men who choose to wear religious attire such as a *topi* (hat) or political symbols like a kaffiyeh (Palestinian scarf) while on the job hunt: "There's guys who'll be wearing the traditional outfit and say, 'We're gonna go out and get jobs.' In the workforce you have the right to wear what you feel comfortable with religiously, but in the time we live in it's like, 'Buddy, good luck getting a job!'"

Zafar volunteered in a youth organization that served a low-income community with newcomers from Afghanistan and East Africa. He was concerned about how overt expressions of religiosity subjected Muslims to systemic discrimination: "There are specific challenges for people who visibly express their religion, like having to disassociate themselves [from] their faith to fit in. Because of the post 9/11 climate, they're hesitant to express their religious identity." Muslim identity and identification with Islam can be a hindrance for workplace advancement, education, and in other sectors of society where Islamophobic assumptions guide interactions and shape public discourse.

Zulfikar, a South Asian student from Montreal, emigrated from Dubai after 9/11 and found that while he did not face overt racism, his family was affected by the consequences of Islamophobia. "My dad once had a few people come to his gas station who refused to get gas from him. He told them that it is not his gas, and that it belonged to a 'White person,' but they refused to get it and they just left." Anti-Muslim messaging is often purveyed in this manner of exclusion and boycott. Zulfikar's father's attempt to assure customers that the gas belonged to a "White person" was his way of deflecting the negative attention he was receiving. Xenophobia and Islamophobia are intertwined in many of the scenarios of workplace discrimination that participants shared.

Rummana addressed the experience of being regarded as a backward "third-world" immigrant in her workplace: "In one of my work environments, I missed taking a fifteen-minute break and the supervisor turned to me and she said, 'You are working in Canada now, you get breaks, you don't have to work eighteen-hour shifts, if you want to do that go back to your third-world country.' Which, ironically enough, is my research topic – I study labour laws in the Middle East. I wanted to start spewing off the actual policies. But then I thought, 'You know what? Forget it.'" Being confronted with xenophobic attitudes by her supervisor placed Rummana in a precarious power relationship where challenging the demeaning way she was treated could have impacted her job security.

Mahvish spoke of her decision to drop "Mohammed" from her name to camouflage her identity while she was job-hunting: "I found that on job applications I get call-backs way more. People are afraid of us and what people don't understand they fear, and what they fear they hate. I don't feel very popular since 9/11." She described witnessing an encounter at work involving a Muslim customer, which accentuated how Muslims are constantly subjects of suspicion and unfounded scrutiny: "I worked at Costco for a while and I had a Muslim convenience store owner come in and buy $1,000 worth of chocolate bars. The police came in and he was detained because of how suspicious that transaction was as a Kwik-e-Mart owner. So, we're afraid and we're defensive."

Yusra also took stock of the systemic bias that she and other Muslims face based on racial and religious discrimination: "There is still an imbalance within the Canadian society in terms of the jobs that you can get, in terms of payment, in terms of how you're looked at within the workplace and what qualifications you have to show compared to males, especially white males ... [T]hose sort[s] of things still exist and they're difficult to get around." The racially stratified workplace poses barriers for Muslim and other racialized communities seeking equitable opportunities within unequal structures. For the 9/11 generation, Islamophobia plays a salient role in shaping their workplace experiences along with other facets of their lives.

Understanding Islamophobia as a system of oppression allows for a holistic analysis of its dynamics. The narratives demonstrate how Islamophobic ideologies inform individual actions that single out Muslims for exclusion and discriminatory treatment as well as feed into biased systemic practices. This interplay of individual, ideological, and systemic practices forms the matrix of Islamophobic oppression.

GENDERED ISLAMOPHOBIA AND MUSLIM WOMEN

The intersectional dimensions of Islamophobia include the way gender mediates and shapes the experience of anti-Muslim racism. Ongoing Orientalist tropes shape the discursive terrain through which Muslim women's lives come to be known and in effect "knowable." These discourses bear the imprint of either colonial representations of backward, oppressed women who are subservient to religious patriarchy, or the fetishized imagery of exotic, seductive, mysterious women enticing imperial fantasies, curiosities, and desires. Muslim women have come to be known through these contradictory narratives in the neo-imperial present (Yegenoglu 1998; Taylor and Zine 2014). The proliferation of limiting representations that once served to justify the civilizing imperatives of colonial missions in Muslim lands (i.e., Spivak's [1988] formulation of "saving brown women from brown men") now serve in similar ways to shore up the need for imperial wars against Muslims in the war on terror.

The political and discursive work these narratives accomplish maintains the saliency and currency of these tropes. (J. Zine 2006a; Razack 2009). Gendered Islamophobic discourses have material consequences in Muslim women's lives, translating into individual and systemic forms of oppression. Since 9/11 and after any act of violence linked to extremist Muslim groups, Muslim women visibly marked with Islamic attire are the most vulnerable targets of physical hate crimes and harassment (Perry 2014). They have also borne the brunt of policies to ban the hijab or niqab where coerced "unveiling" is used as a means of showing fidelity and allegiance to the secular liberal state through forms of "sartorial nationalism," as discussed previously (J. Zine 2012a). The intersection of gender and Islamophobia is important to fully understanding the scope and effect of Islamophobia as a variegated system of oppression that exists on various social, cultural, and political axes.

Saleha saw liberal multiculturalism contributing to contemporary formations of gendered Islamophobia: "Muslim women's bodies have been kind of manipulated in this discourse of multiculturalism. We are going to save Muslim women from barbaric cultural practices like FGM, forced marriage, niqab, honour killings. We're going to do it by stopping those cultural practices in Canada and banning them, right? Versus looking at what grassroots movements are happening in those communities and what women have always been doing. The reaction from the community is that people get more isolated and more cut off from supports."

Saleha's concerns reference Moller Okin's (1999) argument that "multiculturalism is bad for women" by allowing illiberal minorities to run amok with traditions that subordinate and violate women's bodies and rights. Liberal forms of Islamophobia are more easily normalized than extreme or far right expressions of anti-Muslim animus. Ideas like those Moller Okin promotes allows xenophobia and religious discrimination to be mapped into social policies through the "state of exception" (Agamben 2005) created by heightened fear and moral panics. Saleha went on to critique the "psychological warfare" levelled against the practice of veiling:

> The psychological aspect of colonialism means you attack those aspects of culture and knowledge that are important to a people and then you introduce Western practices or colonial practices as superior. So, there is that psychological warfare part of colonialism. So, if you attach the veil to oppression and then the next part is attaching Western women's dress to freedom, right? And then you have the slow progression, okay first we unveil them, and then we get them to adopt "our" Western or colonial standards and then people get cut off from their history, their identity, their sense of self, belonging, and community.

Saleha raises similar concerns that Fanon (1965) outlined in a chapter titled "Algeria Unveiled" in *A Dying Colonialism* where colonial attitudes toward the veil were based on notions of Muslim degeneracy that required Western cultural norms to intervene as a corrective.

The ongoing desire to rescue and save Muslim women is now widely challenged (see Abu-Lughod 2013), yet the imprint of these colonial legacies exists in the framing of Western state policies targeting Muslim women's religious attire and compromising their agency. The presumption that women's emancipation resides within Western liberalism rehabilitating Islam and Muslims from pre-modern values, beliefs, and inherent misogyny is predicated on notions of the positional superiority of Eurocentric ideals and values over Islamic ones. Mahmood (2003) critiques the hegemony of liberalism as the only modality of thought or philosophical tradition capable of providing justice, especially when so many campaigns of systematic violence have been waged on its watch. Nonetheless, Muslims are still evaluated on the grid of liberal conformity as the primary measure of civility and democratic capacities.

NEGATIVE REPRESENTATIONS AND AGENCY

As Taylor and Zine (2014, 7) observe, "Representational practices that code Muslim women as foreign, abject and unintelligible filter into a racially inscribed western imaginary where they reside as signifiers

of racial and cultural contamination or as ideological outlaws."
Muslim women grapple with these abject discursive frames in their
everyday lives. Sofia described how she was met with exotic Orientalist
fascination at the intersection of her identities as a Black Muslim
woman: "It's mixed responses I've gotten ... partly Black female,
partly a hijabi ... so there's the whole the oppressed female thing
which consistently comes up, like, 'Did your mom or did your dad
make you wear it?' More often than not, due to political climate,
you're either the 'exotic' or 'the Oriental.'" The political context weighs
heavily upon how Sofia is perceived as either an oppressed woman
or an object of exotic curiosity.

Saleha went further to describe a wider typology in the representation
of Muslim women in the West:

> So, the narrative of a Muslim man is that they are violent and
> misogynistic, they hate Canada, and are completely anti-Western,
> etc., etc. But the narrative about Muslim women is that there
> are two kinds of women. There are the Muslim women who are
> voiceless, oppressed, subjugated, in need of liberation. And there
> is the second kind of Muslim women who are the compatriots
> of those terrorist Muslim men who are trying to undermine
> the West, in the West, by maintaining their barbaric cultural
> practices and whatever, right? So, you basically keep getting
> shifted between those two groups. Depending on how someone
> sees you, they might address you in a different way. They might
> give you this whole sympathy, like, "Oh you probably aren't
> allowed to do this, this, and this." And I am like, "Yeah, actually,
> I am!" And they are like, "Wow!" It blows their mind. Or when I
> actually have an opinion, they are like, "Whoa, you must be
> one of those dangerous Muslims!"

There is a specific way in which Islamophobia registers gender as the
abject difference that situates Islam and Muslims in tension with
the West, civilization, and modernity. Muslim women's bodies have
come to mark that divide. As Saleha contended, when these misconceptions do not conform to the realities of Muslim women (who
cannot be reduced to these narrow and limiting tropes), there is a sense
of surprise that they do not in fact confirm the stereotype.

Faiza, a Shia Muslim from Vancouver, also described how her
identity as a hijabi Muslim was overdetermined by the meaning others

imposed on her body, which forced her to monitor her behaviour to work against the negative, essentialist stereotypes about Muslim women. She explains her experience of "driving while hijabi": "In Kuwait I was driving like a maniac like everybody else. But here I can't drive like that because it is not a maniac driving, it's a 'Muslim maniac' driving! So, when I'm driving here, I always follow the rules because I know that if I break a rule then they will be like, 'This hijabi doesn't know how to drive!'" Common Orientalist tropes about Muslim women as reticent and absent from the public sphere coupled with the authoritarian state sanctions against women driving in Saudi Arabia inform gendered stereotypes. These narrow archetypes reduce Muslim women's identities into shallow and outmoded clichés such as walking ten paces behind men, or being oppressed by militant Muslim men. These tropes affect how Muslim women and girls are treated and shape the terrain upon which they must construct oppositional identities to challenge demeaning Islamophobic perceptions.

Many women spoke of the patronizing assumptions people often made about them as Muslim women who, despite being born in Canada, are foreigners within the nation. Rummana shared the difference in her experiences after donning the hijab:

> Having gone from not wearing hijab to wearing hijab you see the complete night and day difference in the way that you get treated. The second they find out that you have some sort of educational background they're almost surprised, like you can actually do that! Like it's something that's unfamiliar to people from "my civilization." Even just the fact that you can speak English. I have people coming up to me all the time being like, "Hi, how are you?"... Like, slowly, trying to articulate. And English is my first language! I can speak it just fine. I read, write, and speak English pretty well! So, it is little things like that just get under your skin!

In my own experience as a former hijabi, I recall an undergraduate professor remarking that he was "very surprised" when I spoke out in his anthropology class (as I recall I challenged his limited framing of the concept of "jihad"). He said in front of the class that he thought I would be "very shy and demure." This was the first time I realized how gendered Islamophobia was a container waiting for my identity to be poured into it.

Zeenat, a South Asian MA student from Toronto, shared similar concerns about how her body was misread and perceived by others: "Some people may see me and assume that I am less capable or less intelligent than I really am. But then reality hits. I can open my mouth and speak in English and I tell them about what I do, so I really enjoy the reactions I get when people are proven wrong!" For Zeenat there was a moment of satisfaction when she defied the confining stereotypes about her identity. Rupturing stereotypes goes with the territory for Muslims trying to navigate their identities within Western nations where Islamophobia dictates the hegemonic understandings of Islam and Muslims.

Bushra spoke to the dissonance that the activism of the women in her high school MSA created for those who viewed Muslim women as passive rather than political activists:

I feel like, being a hijabi, I deconstruct some of the stereotypes. I try to get involved in political movements. We did an event for Somalia and it was actually a great success and it was driven pretty much by girls in hijab and a lot of people came. A lot of White people. They were pretty impressed by it, because they don't expect us to be in the front doing something which was run completely by women. So, it gives you motivation. Like I need to do this so that people realize that we're not just quietly sitting here. We have a voice and we are willing to speak up!

Subverting the limitations of gendered Orientalism to Muslim women's agency requires emotional labour and discursive redress. Muslim women must contend with and challenge hegemonic stereotypes and the gendered forms of social and cultural surveillance they face on a daily basis. They are initiated into this political labour often at a young age. Because of this, the 9/11 generation of Muslim women have a unique set of social, political, and cultural challenges to navigate and negotiate along their path to adulthood.

BULLYING AND HARASSMENT

Canadian Muslim women have experienced physical violence as well as harassment and threats. An eighteen-year-old Muslim girl was assaulted on public transit in Vancouver by a man uttering death threats, racial, Islamophobic, and sexual slurs. He grabbed her by her head scarf and tried to shove her head into his crotch. He then hit her across the face. Only one bystander intervened on the crowded train (Johnston and Ip 2017). After the London, Ontario, terror attack that killed four members of a Pakistani Muslim family in 2021, there was an uptick in violent hate crimes targeting racialized Muslim women in Western Canada that included being attacked at knifepoint (Snowden 2021). Such incidents take a toll on the psychosocial well-being of Muslims, especially women. In a study on PTSD among Muslims after 9/11, Abu-Ras and Suarez (2009) found that 86.3 per cent of Muslim women in comparison to 54.9 per cent of men experienced hate crime and related trauma (see also S. Ahmad 2019). According to Perry (2014), the motives for Islamophobic violence against women share similarities and differences from those that underlie violence against men. Both forms of violence are underwritten and animated by persistent racialized media tropes, yet the gendered nexus of Islamophobia places Muslim women at the locus of intersectional violence that relies on Orientalist narratives.

Gendered Islamophobic violence comes coupled with a mix of racism and sexism and, as in all forms of gendered violence, an exercise of power and control. Because of Islamophobic stereotypes, Muslim women have been viewed as easy targets due to Orientalist views that they are silent and submissive and would be reluctant to speak out and report incidents of physical or verbal assault. A case in point happened at a Toronto high school during an investigation of a school shooting at C.W. Jeffries Collegiate in 2007. Allegations were made regarding an unrelated assault on a Muslim girl by six boys in a school washroom. According to a news report: "She was 'apparently chosen because (Muslims) are less likely to report it, because of their strict parents' and cultural taboos, said a source, who added: 'It's a series of sexual assaults that have happened at the school in which no action, or little action, was taken to protect the victim.'" In a separate incident, teachers reported that another Muslim female student was knocked down in the hallway and "ridden from behind like a horse" by a male student (Marlow and Rushowy 2007). These assaults play upon the vulnerability of Muslim girls who are perceived to be docile and reticent and therefore unlikely to retaliate or report these violent attacks against them. The specific ways that Muslim women's bodies are read within a context of Islamophobia then becomes not only a discursive problem but one where the consequences are a matter of personal safety. Unfortunately, despite the prevalence of these incidents, there is limited space for Muslim women and girls to address and work through the trauma of incidents of Islamophobic gendered violence (see S. Ahmad 2019).

This chapter unpacks the individual, ideological, and systemic pathways through which Islamophobia operates. The narratives offer a window into the dimensions and dynamics of Islamophobia from a gendered intersectional perspective as they affect larger systemic structures alongside the everyday life of young Canadian Muslims. The normalization of Islamophobia must be understood in both the subtle and overt ways it operates so that we can better gauge its diverse manifestations and trace the pathways through which it is reproduced and sustained.

4

Campus Culture in an Age of Islamophobia and Empire

Muslim Youth Counterpublics

In a climate of Islamophobia and racial securitization created by war on terror, Muslim student groups on university campuses are often viewed as breeding grounds of Islamist radicalism. Many of the youth connected to the 7/7 bombings in London and the Toronto 18 case in Canada were university students. Because of this connection, Muslim campus groups have become sites of interest for the security and intelligence communities (see also Hopkins 2011; Brown and Saeed 2015; Maira 2016; Guest et al. 2020). In this volatile political context, MSAS operate as corporate sites promoting Islam and Muslim identification on campuses across North America. These organizations create a space for Islamic subcultures to flourish within university campuses and provide spiritual support, affinity, and camaraderie among Muslim students. They can be alienating spaces, however, for Muslim students who do not conform to the dominant norms and standards set by these groups.

The Islamic subcultures of MSAS in Canadian universities are significant in how they negotiate the bordered spaces of race, religion, gender, politics, and identity and how the resulting tensions produce a sphere for social activism and resistance. The politics of race and empire shape the lives, experiences, and subjectivities of Muslim youth on campuses as well as in their daily lives (see also Maira 2009). This chapter examines how MSAS operate as campus-based social movements and "counterpublics" that promote religious engagement and connect Muslim youth with national and transnational struggles. In addition to exploring the ways MSAS negotiate these external political challenges, this chapter focuses on the internal dynamics of these organizations and the tensions that exist within their intra-communal Muslim subculture.

HISTORY AND SOCIO-POLITICAL CONTEXT OF MUSLIM STUDENTS' ASSOCIATIONS

Historically, the largest wave of Muslims arriving in Canada occurred after 1971, when the official policy on multiculturalism came into effect (Memon 2009). Many Muslim immigrants came to Canada for the purposes of higher education and began to develop campus-based Islamic communities to retain ties of heritage and identity. By 1963, Muslim populations were growing across university campuses in the United States, which led to the establishment of the Muslim Students Association National (MSA National). According to the organization's official history, the founding members consisted of Muslims from around the world. MSA National created a unified body to oversee the concerns of Muslim students in North America who were away from familiar ties of religiosity and studying in a land where Islam was still a foreign concept.

Most major Canadian universities have an MSA group on their campus. They are largely Sunni dominated; however, some larger universities also have Shia, Ismaili, and Ahmadiyya groups. In addition to being religiously based student groups, Canadian MSAs serve social, political, pedagogical, and discursive functions within campus cultures. In Canadian high schools, MSAs have created subcultures of resistance by challenging the Eurocentric framework of schools, fighting racism, seeking accommodation of religious practices, ensuring a positive representation of Islam, and empowering group members through various modes of support, including social, spiritual, and academic (J. Zine 2000). In Canadian universities, MSAs operate in similar ways to help students negotiate the secular framework of these institutions and create a space for an Islamic subculture to flourish.

In addition to ministering to the religious needs of Muslim students through congregational prayers and religious education, MSAs are sites of political activism. While MSAs promote religious ideologies and goals on campus, they also challenge global injustices from a faith-based perspective, allying with local and global social justice causes. In this way faith, activism, and citizenship become connected in the work of MSAs.

PUBLICS AND COUNTERPUBLICS

Jürgen Habermas's (1991) notion of the public sphere is defined as the arena where private persons come together to create public opinion. The distinctive features of this sphere posit that all individuals come together, around issues of *general interest, without* concern for social *status*, and achieve consensus by means of *critical rational discussion* (emphasis mine) (Calhoun 1992; Fraser 1992; Ambrozas 1998). The idea that the public sphere is open and accessible without consideration of social status, race, gender, socio-economic differences, and so on, is a contested one. As several authors have observed, Habermas's model of the public sphere assumes that social differences can be bracketed (Calhoun 1992). Nancy Fraser (1992) argues that for centuries the broader public sphere in Western societies has marginalized individuals based on gender, religion, class, and other forms of social difference. She argues that the exclusionary effect of these factors limits the access of marginalized groups within a dominant public sphere. Habermas's model assumes that all persons have equal access to the public sphere, have bracketed their status/difference, and that the "common good" benefits all, not only the privileged class. Religious subcultures also fall outside Habermas's notion of "rationality" and therefore cannot be accommodated within his framework. For Fraser it is imperative to recognize that subordinate groups do not have the privilege of being heard in the broader public and are therefore relegated as a "subaltern counterpublic" (Fraser 1992, 291).

In conceptualizing the university as a type of public, Ambrozas (1998) draws upon Fraser's framework. This account of the public sphere contends that it is made up of multiple intersecting publics where issues are constituted and contested and where there are no a priori determinations of what is considered "rational." Ambrozas (1998, 12) remarks, "The university today is not, strictly speaking, a single public but a number of intersecting weak and strong publics. These publics are constituted by women's studies departments, ethnic students' associations, unions, electronic mail lists for 'academic freedom,' and so on." In Canadian universities, the multiple and overlapping publics Ambrozas identifies operate within a dominant Eurocentric, secular, male-dominated, able-bodied, and heterosexist environment.

Universities are not level playing fields for members of marginalized groups whether faculty or students; therefore, the associations situated outside dominant structures of power and privilege occupy a subordinate status. Within this milieu, MSAs operate as "Muslim publics" that purvey religious discourses and practices among fellow Muslims on campus. These practices are aimed at perpetuating Islamic values and are a means to cultivate a particular type of Muslim subjecthood. They also perform an outward-facing role in presenting Islam and Muslim issues to the wider campus community among other overlapping publics.

Hirschkind's (2006) ethnographic study of the circulation of religious sermon cassette tapes in Egypt revealed that these forms of cultural production serve to expand the arena of Islamic argumentation and debate in Egypt through what he terms an "Islamic counterpublic." Starrett (2008, 1043) notes that Hirschkind draws from Michael Warner and Isaiah Berlin's notion of the public sphere as a "self-organizing space for open debate" in which popular media forms have been used either as "mechanisms allowing for open deliberation, or as disciplinary instruments meant to shape consciousness in predetermined ways." In this way, Hirschkind examines these emerging Islamic publics as sites free from state control where ideas of the common good based on religious virtues and piety provide the basis for ethical living and are not necessarily forms of religious indoctrination (see also Eickelman and Anderson 2003).

Both Fraser's and Hirschkind's notions of the counterpublic provide important ways of understanding how MSAs are constituted as subaltern Muslim counterpublics. In Canadian university settings MSAs contest the dominant secular, Eurocentric public sphere through social justice, advocacy, and the development of an Islamic subculture on campus. Hirschkind's conception of an Islamic counterpublic helps us understand how MSAs operate as purveyors of Islamic knowledge through their *halaqas* (religious study circles), *dawah*, public lectures, and events. The dissemination and circulation of this knowledge is targeted at both the Muslim public as well as the broader multiple publics that comprise the campus community. The MSAs' role of providing religious guidance and instruction is aimed at strengthening the *deen*, or faith, of Muslims on campus and building a model for pious living.

Instead of assigning the term "Islamic" to counterpublics, the term "Muslim" is more appropriate to the nature of these groups. Hirschkind's use of "Islamic counterpublics" is based on the dominant structures of religious authority in Egypt. The term "Muslim" is better suited to the context of Canadian MSA's diasporic subcultures, as their religious ideas are evolving and reflective of their age, social location, and the cultural norms they have grown up with as opposed to being authoritative interlocutors regarding Islam.

ACTIVISM AND COUNTERPUBLICS

MSAS are engaged as political actors of Islamic activism in what Wiktorowicz (2004, 2) describes as "the mobilization of contention to support Muslim causes." He identifies the broad-based activities that constitute Islamic activism as ranging from "propagation movements, terrorist groups, collective action rooted in Islamic symbols and identities, explicitly political movements that seek to establish an Islamic state, and inward looking groups that promote Islamic spirituality through collective efforts" (Wiktorowicz 2004, 2). Islamic social movements vary from grassroots protest to organized efforts seeking political change and transformation. They operate on a wide spectrum of ideals, in some cases steeped in "radical Islamism" (see chapter 6), and in others concerned with social justice issues such as anti-war activism and human rights and civil liberties. The variegated nature of MSAS as campus-based social movements and the interests they promote reflects their connection to the broader Muslim *ummah*, or global community of believers.

MSAS promote Islamic knowledge on campus, mostly rooted in conservative orientations of Islam that are disseminated through formal means such as *halaqas*, *khutbas* (sermons), and public lectures and forums, as well informal means where social interactions are guided by the normative standards for Islamic conduct. These activities align Muslim identities in accordance with the dominant religious and ideological framework of these groups. MSAS narrate the ethical boundaries for Islamic identity and practice among their members and constitute the epistemic and ontological formations for a campus-based "Muslim public."

The religious education that MSAS provide on campus make them important sites for the production and dissemination of Islamic knowledge. In some cases, this knowledge is filtered through ideological lenses that propagate conservative, patriarchal religious views. As noted in the preface, more ideologically oriented groups like the Hizb ut-Tahrir gained very limited popularity on Canadian campuses after 9/11. Hizb ut-Tahrir seeks a return to a central Islamic authority through the caliphate system (see chapter 6). As discursive communities, MSAS wield religious authority on campus and can be organized around a variety of causes (see also Abbas 2011, 2019). Wiktorowicz (2004) identifies how mosques operate as religio-spatial mobilizing structures for Islamic groups and causes. In the same way, MSAS serve as a site for organizing and operationalizing religious narratives that support various activist goals and agendas whether based more on liberal or conservative views.

Wiktorowicz (2004, 15) explains that the discursive function of social movements as a means for contention building and mobilization is accomplished through a process of "framing": "Frames are cognitive schemata that offer language and conceptual tools for making sense of experiences and events in the 'world out there.' For social movements these schemata are important in the production and dissemination of ideas and are designed to mobilize participants and support." MSAS draw upon Islamic frames of reference as cognitive tools for aligning members with religious and ideological objectives as a basis for collective identification, behaviour, and action. Conformity with these hegemonic frames secures membership in the group. Non-conformity or non-compliance with these ideological frames is addressed through religious disciplining of group members or their alienation. In some cases, this discursive disunity leads to splintering and the formation of new associations that promote alternative frames. Intra-group splintering within MSA groups can occur due to ideological or other framing differences, thereby creating multiple Muslim publics. MSAS and other marginalized student groups are also part of multiple counterpublics that challenge the Eurocentric hegemony of Western universities. MSAS have a role to play on many fronts: shaping campus life within their organizations, responding to the wider campus culture, and focusing their efforts on global concerns and causes.

CREATING AN ISLAMIC SUBCULTURE
AND MUSLIM PUBLICS

MSAS on university campuses help build a sense of community, solidarity, and affectual support among religiously observant students navigating secular, Eurocentric environments. This can be an alienating environment for students who want to maintain their religious obligations toward the five pillars of Islam.[1] The pillars that most affect their day-to-day activities at school are praying at five appointed times

daily and fasting in the month of Ramadan. The ability to carry out
these obligations has been enabled through the lobbying of MSAs for
more inclusive environments where prayer rooms, facilities for ritual
ablution (*wudu*), and halal food are made available on campus. Most
Canadian universities accommodate, and students report that these
enhance their sense of belonging and their overall experience at university (see Asmar, Proude, and Inge 2004; Peek 2005; CFS 2007).

Mahvish outlined some of the accommodations on her campus but
was skeptical of the impact that multicultural activities have in promoting meaningful understandings of Islam and Muslims:

> We brought halal food to campus. That was fabulous ... We have
> the prayer room in which we are sitting right now conducting
> this interview. Certain things had to be respected when students
> are fasting during Ramadan and there's exams or lectures.
> I've heard a lot of professors courteous enough to give a five- to
> ten-minute break to pray and eat and then resume class. When
> we have celebrations when we have Islam Awareness Week.
> But I still question the sincerity of all that. I have yet to see
> a shift in attitudes and while the displays may go up and the
> artwork is there and the speakers come in, I don't know who's
> really listening and who's not. I think that this might be formality
> we do because we are an institution of higher learning, but
> I question the true intentions behind it.

Beyond advocating for religious accommodations, in the post-9/11
context where Muslim identity and practices have come under broader
public scrutiny, MSAs provide a network that allows Muslim students
to connect with their co-religionists on campus. They offer a safe space
where members can discuss and practice their beliefs and strengthen
their religious identities (Peek 2005, 228). Awad, an international
student, described the sense of "family" and "community" he derived
from his MSA and how this had strengthened his identity and practice
as a Muslim: "I found a sense of belonging. MSA is like a family. It's
home away from home. I'm here without my family. It's where I am
five to six days a week helping my brothers and sisters, with everything
possible. From prayer to how to do MSA services. It really helps you
to become an active member and it has given me an opportunity to
reflect on my identity as a Muslim and as a person and as an individual
within society. It has really helped me redefine my goals." The MSAs
provide spaces of social and affective support that foster the familial

connections Awad describes. These social ties are also formed through identifying as "brothers" and "sisters" within Islam, as well as through the concept of the *ummah* as unifying paradigm.

Michael Warner (2008, cited in Hirschkind and Larkin 2008, 5–6) describes these types of publics as sites for religious identities to coalesce: "[A] public is a collectivity that constitutes itself by projecting a space of discursive circulation through which strangers are tied to each other and come to recognize commonalities. These modes of circulation are less about the complex cultivation of pious sensibilities – the fashioning of individual religious subjectivities – and more about the constitution of religious identity within broader public arenas." Within the subculture of MSAs, however, it is both the "fashioning of individual religious subjectivities" as well as the "constitution of religious identity within broader public arenas" that are promoted. The fortification of individual "pious sensibilities" and practices is a primary goal of the religious education and support that these groups provide and that becomes the basis for the mobilization of religious identity within broader public arenas.

As the vice-president for the new administration of an MSA, Uthman, a South Asian student from Southern Ontario, felt that the organization had to move beyond its solely religious role, which made the group far too insular and inward-looking, to instead focus on building links with other MSAs and extending the ties of Muslim solidarity: "[W]e are all Muslims and we are all within the same city and we're all in walking distance of each other so it makes sense for us to be together and helps us to develop that relationship with other [Muslims] outside [our own campus]." The recognition that "we are all Muslims" harks back to Warner's definition above of a public as "projecting a space of discursive circulation through which strangers are tied to each other and come to recognize commonalities." Cultivating these social, cultural, and religious affinities is characteristic of how Muslim campus publics are constituted. Within very diverse ethno-racial Muslim campus communities a common religious framework becomes the source of unity.

CAMPUS CULTURE IN AN AGE OF ISLAMOPHOBIA

As a response to growing Islamophobia on campuses since the 9/11 attacks and the ongoing war on terror, the Canadian Federation of Students (CFS) struck a task force to study the problem and make recommendations. The Islamophobia, anti-Semitism, and anti-racism campaign was originally motivated by an incident of hate at Toronto's Ryerson University in 2004, when a wall in the multi-faith prayer space had been defaced with graffiti that said, "Die Muslim Die." In September 2006, Arab and Muslim Students' Associations found death threats, slipped under their office doors, which stated: "Those who follow the Islam faith need to be killed in the worst possible way imaginable." Students experienced direct acts of hate, including being called a "terrorist," associated with the Taliban, accused of carrying bombs, and targeted for physical attacks. A York University student from Toronto said, "People watch us and make certain comments, like 'Taliban.' It is dehumanizing and they are demonizing minorities." Along with promoting racism and Islamophobia on campuses, such acts create the breeding grounds for radical grievances.

Muslim university students reported that they experienced less overt kinds of racism or Islamophobia when in a more educated, open, and diverse environment like a university setting as opposed to outside campus (see Peek 2003; Nasir and Al-Amin 2006; Hopkins 2011). Many students found their campuses ethnically and racially diverse, which they felt minimized the effect of potential Islamophobia. Despite experiencing incidents of racism and Islamophobia, study participants were not harshly critical of the campus culture. This ambivalence is surprising and troubling in the way everyday acts of racism and discrimination have become normalized. For example, Tahir, a South Asian student originally from the UK, described situations where he, his brother, and his friends were victims of police harassment and racially and religiously motivated physical assaults outside the campus, but they saw his Ontario university as a "serious school" where "a low-level xenophobia exists to a small extent but not really." Measured against other physical attacks and harassment, "low-level xenophobia" on campus may seem benign; however, it is the unchecked fomenting of such attitudes that normalize Islamophobia and the epistemic if not physical violence connected to it.

Mustafa described the "paranoia" that accompanies the Muslim presence on campus and expressed concerns over addressing Islamophobic bias in the classroom: "In the university setting, even though we are quite a few years removed from 9/11, there is a pervasive paranoia sometimes about the presence of Muslim students on the campus, and the students who come to the mosque. Sometimes they [students] talk about ... the intellectual dishonesty and prejudice against Muslims and Islam that's being promoted in the classrooms.

Oftentimes, they've been penalized for challenging professors for any information that's not fair or accurate with regards to Muslims."

Echoing Mustafa's concerns, it was not uncommon for students to reveal alarm about Islamophobic content in the curriculum or biases among professors. Zeenat described hearing negative comments from university professors (including those self-identified as "secular Muslims") that went unchallenged, unlike anti-Semitic remarks:

> I think U of xxd especially has a very conservative outlook on everything. They tend to shy away from looking at things in other than a mainstream way. I had a third year university prof who described himself as a "secular/modern Muslim" who called niqabis "caged animals," which was interesting. I've heard other remarks that were made within the Poli Sci International Relations field, but the university doesn't tend to reprimand these sort[s] of things. It's brushed away if you do complain about it. On the other hand, anything that is taken as anti-Semitic isn't so easily ignored.

Zeenat was critical of the double standards and biases at play within her university when it came to the representation of Islam versus anti-Semitic rhetoric. Often Islamophobia and anti-Semitism are seen as mutually constitutive, and as we see further along in the discussion, student activism in relation to Israel and Palestine is a primary source of tension in many Canadian universities.

Speck (1997) reminds us that misrepresentations of Islam had become normalized practice in the classroom prior to 9/11. Propagating misinformation about Islam persists in some university classrooms. For example, Rania describes a troubling incident she encountered in a religious studies class:

> [W]hen we were talking about Islam, the worst examples [were] used, they're given even in the religion program. For instance, I was taking this class and we had an assignment to look at the Torah and compare it to a contemporary work and discuss it. And for Christianity, it was the Bible and Jesus, but when it came to Islam, it was about Al-Qaeda! It didn't have a Quranic scripture to compare it [the Bible] to. It was just an article about Al-Qaeda and how they are an Islamic extremist organization, and the question was what does it say about Islam?! And I was like, "It doesn't say anything about Islam!"

The entry point for understanding Islam was not through scriptural passages (as was the case with the other traditions discussed); instead the class was introduced to Islam through an article about a known terrorist organization. In such instances it often falls upon Muslim students to correct the negative portrayal of Islam in some of their classes.[2] The mis-education about Islam filters through universities into the broader public sphere where, in a context of heightened anti-Muslim sentiments, these ideas circulate with relative impunity.

ORGANIZED ISLAMOPHOBIA

Organized campaigns of Islamophobia promoted by groups such as the US-based Campus Watch are some of the most egregious examples of campus-based Islamophobia. While it is more prominent in the US than in Canada, Karima, an Algerian and French Canadian student from Montreal, cited concerns about the existence of Radical Islam Week. Saleha expressed distress over a Draw Muhammad Day campaign on her campus:

> I remember they had the Draw Muhammad Day thing. Students were in the hallway drawing stupid cartoons. I went up to them and some people were yelling at them. Other people were very upset and almost crying. Being in that environment where people were yelling all around you and then some people were like, "This is great, I'm going to draw Muhammad riding a pig!" People were making really stupid comments. It didn't feel good to be in that space. It felt really horrible. It felt like they were attacking me personally, even though they are talking about freedom of speech or whatever. I was trying to have a normal conversation with someone and I was like, "You know, you guys might not have thought about this. You guys are coming at it from the angle of freedom of speech, but you don't know what it's like to be a Muslim walking around the campus and to feel that at any time someone could attack you, someone could swear at you, someone could push you into the street! Because that happened to me and my friends. So, I understand that you think you are upholding the right to freedom of speech, but what are you doing to other people? I am not saying, you don't have freedom of speech. I am not saying anything about this issue. But you are hurting me." And they were like, "Oh, yeah, we didn't

think about it that way." And one of them was still trying to yell at me and the other one – the president of the group – ended up having this whole Facebook fight about it.

Later they wrote an apology to us. But the thing was that we weren't human to them, right? We weren't actually people who live and breathe and deal with this stuff every day, right? We were just those crazy people who make threats somewhere else. Who are infringing on their right to freedom of speech. So, to look them in the eye and to say, "You are hurting me." That was different for them. That was really hard for me to say, too. Because why should I have to go up to them and tell them all the trauma that I have been through and say, "You know this is adding to it." Because that hurts too, right?

Universities are grappling with the rise of the alt-right, White supremacist, and neo-fascist groups on campus that use free speech as a rhetorical prop for their ideological campaigns of hate (J. Zine 2018). While it is important to allow for legitimate avenues of critique and political dissent on campus, free speech must be discerned from campaigns of hate to maintain an inclusive campus culture free from bigotry. Saleha's story is a reminder that the consequences of what is said can inflict harm, which must be considered when balancing free speech with human rights.

Raising awareness of Islamophobia on campus shaped the work of the MSA that challenged stereotypes during Islamic Awareness Week campaigns, as Rania explained: "We're aware that people think that Muslim women are oppressed and that guys with beards are violent terrorists. Sometimes that is reinforced in our school. *Alhamdulillah,* we are having this event, for Islam Awareness Week. Just as we have stereotypes – we're paranoid about CSIS – people are paranoid about Muslims because that's what they're learning. It really has shaped what we're doing as an MSA." As a former MSA student myself, I recall putting on Islamic Awareness Week events in the late 1980s and 1990s. Even then we were trying to combat negative stereotypes. This serves as a reminder that although the post-9/11 period of Islamophobia was particularly heightened, the impact of anti-Muslim racism was experienced on campuses long before the Twin Towers fell.

There is a psychosocial toll involved in politically challenging forms of student activism. Riyad noticed at his Montreal university the fraught political context was a deterrent for some youth to get involved in the MSA: "There are youth who became scared of the prospect of [Islamophobic] incidents happening, so they retreated from the community. The older generations, in some cases they say, 'Don't join the MSAs or participate in the community, just do your school and prayers.'" In light of such concerns, Saleha suggested that a more proactive strategy was required to ensure the safety of students: "Instead of waiting for something horrible to happen, how do we make all students feel safe and create policies where students who are particularly vulnerable feel safe? Intellectually safe, as well as emotionally safe, as well as psychologically safe, as well as physically safe." Given that the notion of being under siege creates existential tensions and anxieties, the need for constructing the campus as a safe space free from bias and Islamophobia is imperative. Engaging in proactive dialogue about safety as a holistic concept is critical for building an anti-oppressive campus culture.

GENDER EQUITY

Research has indicated that MSAs have varying commitments to gender equity (see Mir 2007, 2014). Surprisingly, women sometimes support the patriarchal structures that dominate these organizations. While she endorsed the female leadership, Zabeda explained why she preferred "brothers" take on certain positions: "[I]n the MSA, I would say [the distribution of power between men and women] is pretty fair. I know our president is male, and it could have easily been a female. Personally, I preferred, [and] most of us preferred, for it to be a male just because the president has to go through a lot of things. People yell at him, call him late at night. And we didn't want a sister to have calls from random guys late at night. We looked at those types of things. It's just what we wanted, I wanted that too." In this context, the women preferred to defer the leadership responsibilities to men to avoid what they saw as unwanted interaction with male students at inappropriate times.

In other cases, women were critical and angry about the fact that they performed most of the duties involved in running the organization but were prevented from holding leadership positions. Aisha expressed her frustration over the patriarchal structures of many MSAs, including her own:

I've had the usual MSA deal where you're not allowed to run
for president because you're female, which is insulting because
all the work is done by female students anyway. Or the pervasive
sexism that exists where women don't take positions of authority
in a lot of Muslim communities. There's the usual stuff around
mosques being inaccessible to women. Analyses of feminism
that are explicitly grounded within the perspectives of Muslim
women are often dismissed or are critiqued in ways that I find
really counterproductive. Grappling with mainstream feminism
has also been really tough. I know they [MSA] had an event
recently as part of their Islamic Awareness Week, which was
about the role of women in Islam, and all the speakers were men!

The issue of all-male panels is not limited to Muslim communities;
women are generally under-represented on academic panels or at public
events. Muslim women are critiquing the way all-male panels are
convened even when the topic is on women in Islam! In these situations, Muslim women are reclaiming their voice and agency and
challenging patriarchal dominance.

Aisha explained that her rationale for continuing to participate in
the MSA despite the patriarchal hegemony had more to do with her
fidelity to Islam than to the organization itself:

The reason I stuck with the MSA despite the blatant misogyny
was because I am committed to Islam's reputation on campus.
And so, I would put myself in these positions and I would do
that work even though all the other sisters had been like,
"We're tired," and just quietly drop off without making a big
fuss about it. I would make a big fuss about it but stick around!
It took me a few years to be like, "This isn't worth it." Not all
MSAS are like that. I know that some are more supportive, but
I think that the turnover rates, the fact that people graduate and
leave, and the lack of institutional history means for most MSAS
these things are just recreated cycle after cycle.

In choosing to use the MSA as a vehicle for promoting a more positive
image of Islam on campus, Aisha had to work against the dominant
patriarchal bent of her MSA. Even when other women would fade out
of the process without challenging it, she opted to stay and challenge

the status quo to achieve the larger aims that were important to the MSA's role as campus agent and counterpublic actor. Aisha pointed out that MSA culture is not uniform and that there are more gender friendly chapters. She also acknowledged the lack of institutional memory as students in executive roles graduated, which led to a recycling of the same structure and dynamics. In other instances, however, the turnover provides opportunities for new students to take up leadership positions and guide the organization in more progressive directions.

While there have been instances of female leaders successfully running MSA chapters, these examples were few during the period of data collection for this study. Nonetheless, as Uthman explains, his MSA is one example that has made a commitment to equity for male and female executive members:

> Every single person sitting in that room has a say and it's not
> that, "Oh, there's only three sisters, ha ha, and there's five
> brothers, so you lose." We don't have that going on. If you're
> three sisters, you're as equal to the five brothers. If one sister
> has an opinion, we all go back and forth and it's like a collective
> thing. It's basically like a family. We're just debating how we
> can make MSA better so that people can actually show up,
> and we provide more services to Muslims, so that they'll say,
> "Look, MSAs actually doing something."

While Uthman supports the egalitarian position of his MSA, this remains a form of "benevolent patriarchy" until there is true gender parity in representation and leadership. Nonetheless, Zabeda found that on occasion if the female executives were more vocal and passionate in executive meetings, they had greater influence in the decision-making. Tahir remarked that his MSA in Montreal had the requirement of gender parity on their executive board written into its constitution:

> We have a system that there's always four brothers and four sisters
> in the executive, plus the president. The president most of the time
> has been a brother, but we had an interim president who's a sister,
> a few years back. And last year, one of the people who was running
> was a sister. And mostly likely this year, there will be a couple of
> sisters [running for election]. Women do have equal opportunity.
> We try to be very inclusive. We try and give voices. Any Muslim

organization that is run through xxy university – we've got a couple of branched organizations that run different programs – we try and include sisters. On the board their input is valuable, and we need them to provide an accurate viewpoint of what sisters want as well.

Enshrining gender equity in the constitution of the MSA is a positive move to ensure it becomes part of a uniform culture instead of an ad hoc practice that could be easily subverted if a new conservative leadership were elected. Harking back to my experience in the MSA at the University of Toronto in the 1980s and '90s, I recall there were male and female executive members serving as an "*Amir*" and an "*Amira*." Interestingly I have not seen a joint MSA leadership structure during the period of this study, despite opportunities for women to acquire leadership roles and executive membership in some MSA groups. The progress in promoting gender parity over the past forty years was inconsistent. The dominance of patriarchal hegemony in the culture and administration of Muslim institutions requires sustained counter-hegemonic pressure to initiate change, otherwise the status quo is easily reproduced.

A hallmark of most MSA social structures is the practice of gender segregation, a customary practice at many MSA social events that is in line with the organization's more conservative orientation. For some women this was not exclusionary; instead, they preferred it based on the ease and comfort of being in female-centred spaces. Farheen explained that gender segregation allowed women to discuss issues they would be uncomfortable speaking about in front of men. Yet, she also found the emphasis on female modesty and gender segregation to be performative. For example, in a study of Muslim women in US college campuses Mir (2009) describes how one female MSA executive member admitted to behaving more conservatively than she would with her male friend, who was also an MSA executive, when they were in MSA settings as opposed to outside of them. The pressure to maintain more traditional norms and conventions often stems from the social disciplining that takes place within MSA circles to preserve the more conservative gender relations.

Ateeka spoke of the difficulty for Muslim women on her east coast university campus to attend the congregational prayers on Friday. Mostly men attended and space was not allocated for women. She attempted to advocate for women's prayer space but found herself up against a challenge because Friday congregational prayers were obligatory for men but optional for women: "Most of the Muslim students are from countries like Pakistan and Bangladesh where women don't go to mosques [for congregational prayers]. When it's mostly male, they dominate making decisions. I didn't have the courage to be like, 'Okay listen, I'm gonna be praying with you guys.' Not yet, maybe we work it up soon. Because I would love to do that." Ateeka felt that these different cultural expectations among the international students accounted for the lack of effort to include a space for women. Although she wanted to assert herself into the prayer space, she was hesitant to challenge the status quo on her own.

Muslim women's deferral to the patriarchal structures of the MSA are in line with the kind of female agency that Mahmood (2005) describes in her study of the Cairene women's piety movement. Mahmood (2005, 5) argues that "women's active support for socio-religious movements that sustain principles of female subordination can be a dilemma for feminists." But her fieldwork demonstrates how women find ways to manoeuvre within traditional patriarchal spaces without necessarily re-signifying or contesting the validity of these norms. Instead they create the "capacity to realize one's own interests against the weight of custom, tradition, transcendental will or other obstacles (whether individual or collective)" (Mahmood 2005, 8). Moreover, the creation of female-centred spaces contributes to the fortifying of sisterhood and solidarity for women, who despite being active behind the scenes and in front-line MSA activism, are often shut out of the top leadership positions. MSAs therefore remain sites of gender-based struggle, negotiation, and contestation as Muslim women continue to engage and challenge the dominant structures of male privilege.

RELIGIOUS AUTHORITY

As discursive actors, MSAs provide religious education to Muslims on campus through study circles or *halaqas*, public talks, lectures, and events. These forums disseminate Islamic beliefs and practices based on the teachings of religious leaders that MSAs deem the most valid and authoritative sources for sharia-based guidance. According to Hirschkind and Larkin (2008), the circulatory forms through which religious publics constitute themselves and their members are often in relation or opposition to competing forms of identity. Within MSA subcultures, religious chauvinism, sectarianism, and the exclusion or alienation of those who do not share the same religious perspectives are common. In many cases, these epistemic boundaries are policed and regulated. The guidelines for pious behaviour are circumscribed by those who wield quasi-religious authority, usually members of their executive. These are largely unspoken guidelines that nonetheless determine the legitimacy of group membership and the boundaries of inclusion and exclusion. For example, it is unlikely that a Muslim who openly identified as gay, lesbian, or transgendered would find a comfortable home within a traditionally conservative MSA group.

Lamya was frustrated by some of the narrow religious dogmas promoted through MSA culture that were bred of isolationism and judgment:

> I've struggled with the MSA. Disconnected myself completely. People have either been isolated by their families or place[d] isolation onto themselves because of fear. Fear of the *kuffar* (non-believers), fear of talking to non-Muslims. It's frustrating because I hug my friend who's gay and people are like, "What's wrong with you?!" And they're like, "You have to go do your *wudu* (ablutions) again, you shouldn't be promoting their behaviour." And I'm like, "Since when does being someone's friend and loving someone for who they are promote behaviour that I don't agree with? And what's it my business? If someone is doing something in their bedroom, even in Islam, it's none of your business." So those are the kinds of things that I feel like I had to isolate myself from. I tried different avenues, and I just feel like I don't fit in anywhere.

Lamya was rightly upset with the homophobic sentiments she encountered in her MSA and this caused her to challenge their oppressive attitudes and eventually disengage from the group.

Few MSAs adopt a truly intersectional lens to place their own oppression in connection with others and acknowledge that promoting homophobia further exacerbates Islamophobia as well as undercuts potential solidarities and alliances with other marginalized and vulnerable groups on campus. Students with more progressive views around sexuality found the MSAs repressive and problematic when it came to accepting sexual diversity. However, shifts in the MSA culture around these concerns will likely only happen when religious ideologies in the wider Muslim community provide a more open approach to addressing homophobia.

Samir found that MSA culture at his west coast university was at times too insular and exclusive, inspiring some students to consider developing more open and inclusive alternative groups that reflected the diversity of thought and identities among those who self-identify as Muslim on campus:

> The MSA suffered the same problems as traditional Muslim communities do. They are largely made up of individuals who have chosen not to integrate into the rest of society. A lot of times they are very traditional, sectarian, exclusively Muslim. At the same time, you have a whole bunch of students who self-identify as Muslim who didn't really have a place to express their views because they were more progressive or more universal or not as exclusively Muslim. So, we saw attempts to start a new type of MSA. I think there is a place for different interpretations. But I think the success of organizations such as the MSA depend on its tolerance and diversity and its open-mindedness, especially in a university setting where there are so many differing views and concepts.

Other students raised similar concerns about conservatism and the narrow religious boundaries of some MSAs, and this inspired new associations like Muslims for Social Justice on several campuses, which were less sectarian and parochial and geared to social change and advocacy. Where some MSAs were found to be too dogmatic and insular, these alternate groups provided an outlet for Muslim students who sought to work on equity and social justice goals and not be limited to a singular "type" of Muslim identity. These alternate groups helped stretch the epistemic and ontological limits set by conservative MSAs, thereby extending the parameters of and opportunities for social engagement, belonging, and political critique on campus. This relates to Fraser's (2009) notion of the epistemic variety and discursive diversity made possible through counterpublic spaces.

Heba lamented how MSAs can become the "halal police" on campus, determining what behaviour is right and righteous and imposing these standards on other students. For example, she described how the MSA at her school had tried to block the development of a Pakistani Student Association at a neighbouring university and even protested outside one of their cultural events because there was music and free intermingling between men and women. This kind of religious disciplining inhibited attempts to develop the Pakistani Student Association because potential members were wary of being harassed by the MSA. Rania, for instance, was very critical of the actions of the MSA and shared her grievances: "I mean you shouldn't do that ... you can't just push people off the wall, even if they're on the wrong path. The only thing you can do is tell them this is the wrong path and this is the right path. Like it's their choice. This is why I don't go to MSA events 'cause I think they are too pushy."

Student leaders holding the discursive reigns set the religious and ideological tone for the group. They determine which shaykhs and imams are invited to offer "Islamically correct" religious guidance and lectures. MSAs are largely conservative in their orientation but vary in their degrees of fidelity to the *madhabs* or Islamic schools of thought. The religious or ideological nature of MSAs is never entirely static and always subject to change as members who are most influential in shaping and policing the epistemic boundaries inevitably graduate, leading to a turnover in the culture.

One MSA president acknowledged that while the previous administration at his university had a single-minded ideological frame, the new executive team was committed to promoting a broader notion of Islam. Amin, a South Asian student, explained his perspective on Islam as a diverse rather than narrow path: "[T]hat is another thing that was not accounted for before [by the old MSA exec] ... making sure that Islam is not just one-stroke of colour; Islam is diverse and that's why it's beautiful because it's amazing how there are so many different ways that people can express their Islam." This MSA group sought to create a more inclusive environment where a wide variety of Muslim opinions could be accommodated. More inclusive forms of leadership can reshape the boundaries that define belonging within the diverse Muslim public sphere on campus.

Amin described how his role as MSA president was as a student club administrator and not as *Amir ul-Mumineen* or "leader of the faithful":

There's a meme going around that my sister posted to my Facebook: "Gets elected the president of the MSA and thinks he's *Amir ul-Mumineen.*" That's literally what the problem is. My job is not to be your religious leader. God knows, don't hold me to that! I'm here as an administrative helper because we're a club to help with administrative side first, and then your

religious identity and your life because Islam influences your life.
Do you want to know where all the restaurants are? Does the
university have halal food? Where do you pray? These kinds
of things ... Fine, we'll have an organized way of making your
life experience better at U of XL.

Amin's analogy about MSA leaders not being the Amir *ul-Mumineen*
is particularly apt in identifying how religious authority is often held
and perceived within MSAS as "campus shaykhs" rather than organizational leaders representing a diverse constituency of students and
assisting in meeting their social and religious needs.

Tahir complained that many imams who support youth on campuses
were out of touch with the realities and experiences of the 9/11 generation of Muslim youth:

> I think there is a crisis of leadership, and I don't think it's limited
> to Montreal. There is a general problem with regards to Muslim
> leaders: some of them are out of touch. I know in England as
> well, a lot of Muslim leaders are out of touch with youth,
> especially some of the older generation who run the mosques.
> I know some of the speakers we bring in for *jummah* [Friday
> prayers], some of the *khateebs*, are out of touch. And they will
> give us thirty or forty minutes of tirade of *X Y Z*, that has no
> relevance to what we experience as students. They will go
> on tirades, discussing the political situation in Syria. When
> most students here are engineers, they don't care about politics
> and even if they did, it has no relevance to what they are
> experiencing here.

This "crisis of leadership" as Tahir characterized it is a missed opportunity on behalf of campus imams to engage with youth facing unique
spiritual as well as existential struggles. There are limited safe spaces
to engage in open dialogue, which makes youth-friendly religious
ministry essential on Canadian campuses where few Muslim chaplains
are present. Especially at a time where Islamophobia facilitates the
recruitment of disaffected youth into violent movements like Daesh
or Al-Qaeda, socially responsive religious counselling and youth work
are important avenues to connect with youth before they are lured
into these destructive associations (see chapter 6).

BIGOTRY AND RELIGIOUS CHAUVINISM

Most MSAs in Canadian universities are Sunni focused, leaving Shia students and other non-Sunnis (Ismaili, Ahmadiyya, etc.) feeling marginalized and alienated. The hegemony of Sunni Muslims and Sunni Islam in shaping the religious, social, and cultural context of MSAs makes these groups the dominant Muslim public. Warner (2008, cited in Hirschkind and Larkin 2008, 5–6) argues that it is "precisely the circulation of discursive forms that has decisive power on forming the conceptual infrastructure of movements and creating modes of authority and power that are manifest in the relation of dominant publics to various types of marginal counter publics." The dominant Muslim public on campus maintains a privileged position in relation to more marginalized members of the subculture, and at times bigotry and religious chauvinism come into play.

In a focus group with Shia students in British Columbia, the participants told stories of blatant discrimination that led to their alienation and marginalization from the Sunni-dominated culture on campus. Adil recounted being threatened by a Sunni MSA member who began to develop more extreme sensibilities:

> I was on my lunch break, and one of the kids from the MSA came up to me. This guy used to get along with everybody, but then gradually you started to [see] changes. The beard kind of grew longer, he started to dress differently, like very, very differently. Everything about him became really, really sort of extreme. I hate using that term, but it was really kind of extreme in a sense. Like he started to look like he stepped right out of some village back home! And you can see the ideology coming hand in hand with that. He took me aside on my lunch break and said, "There is no room for people like you here. And if you say a word about any of your beliefs, I'll end up in jail for what I'm going to do to you." So, you wonder if we can't even resolve that in a university ... It is unfortunate, but it exists. I mean, it's one thing to say that no we don't have any sort of extremism in the Muslim community. I think we do. It is definitely blown up a bit in the media. The cases with CSIS really putting their finger down on it. But it does exist; I don't think it is as big a deal as they make it. But it does exist, I think at least.

While being careful so that his remarks about "extremism" would not be misconstrued in light of the stereotypes about Muslims, Adil was nonetheless understandably troubled by this disturbing encounter with the bigotry, threats, and intimidation he was subjected to by this other student.

Sectarian prejudice and violence cannot be taken lightly, but addressing these can be problematic. A lack of trust with security agencies like CSIS that surveil Muslim youth (see chapter 5) makes it difficult to seek help. The marginalization of Shia Muslim youth in Sunni-centred MSAS leads to further alienation and a lack of institutional recourse for bigoted behaviours. These anti-Shia attitudes are promoted by certain Sunni religious leaders that youth turn to for advice. Adil described how some Sunni Muslims would tell him that they were advised by their shaykh to stay away from Shias: "It goes to the extent that maybe some of them who are closer to me say, 'We talked to our shaykh at the mosque, and he told us, avoid this person.' At times they provoke it or invoke it. That division will always exist because of what they've been taught to believe." That these problematic views come from religious authorities makes them harder to challenge and dismantle. Sectarian discrimination on campus gains its legitimacy through these authorizing narratives and reproduces ingrained prejudices instead of working to ensure that the younger generations are not corrupted by these ideological divides and historical animosities. During the focus group interview, Adil and other students laughed at the story. This seemed to be out of a sense of how ridiculous the chauvinistic attitudes were, though it is sad to see how the bigotry they encounter has become so normalized that their response is laughter as opposed to sadness, disappointment, or even rage.

Rummana explained how the MSA constitution at her university stipulated that membership was exclusive to Sunnis. Shia students fought against this and took the matter to the larger student union on campus, and eventually the constitution was changed. She and other students recounted how this was met with acts of subterfuge against them. They reported that in their prayer space they would find their *turbas* (a small stone to rest their foreheads on while prostrating for prayer) had been stolen. There were acts of exclusion such as Sunni students not returning their salaams (greetings). Rummana felt it gestured to the deeper divisions among Muslims globally: "When I first started to become more involved with the MSA, they made it very clear that Shia practices were not welcome. And it was in the constitution. When I challenged it, they kicked me out of the club. So, you lose that sense of global partnership, or the *ummah,* which is unfortunate. We can't even resolve our own issues in the Muslim world, so people on the outside think that it's a war between 'us and them.' I think internally we are kind of battling it out." Through these acts of exclusion, aversion, and bigotry Muslim publics become fractured spaces, and the corporate basis for building solidarities and alliances to combat common oppressions such as Islamophobia and racism are diminished.

MSA ACTIVISM: BUILDING AND CLAIMING
A COUNTERPUBLIC SPACE

As a way of dispelling long-standing myths and negative stereotypes about Islam and Muslims, M S A s' activities such as Islam Awareness Week, Ramadan *iftars,* and Eid dinners have renewed impetus. These events are also venues for asserting religious identities within the secular sphere of university life, and they allow for a more visible Muslim presence on campus. As Schmidt (2002) indicates, M S A s in the United States participate in global social justice causes (i.e., Israeli Apartheid Week) and other forms of activism. Similarly, in Canada M S A s are active in social justice causes locally and globally. M S A s also sponsor events that cater to the wider campus community to offer education about Islam and dispel myths, misperceptions, and Islamophobic stereotypes. This has become a necessary role for M S A s to counter the backlash that has led to racism and Islamophobia on campuses across the country.

M S A s in Canada support many charitable campaigns such as orphan sponsorship programs and fundraising for relief efforts abroad. They also are involved in the Pink Hijab Day to offer more public education about veiling practices and Purple Hijab Day to raise awareness of domestic violence. One Ontario university also sponsored a Hijab Solidarity Day where non-Muslim women wore head scarves in support of Muslim women. This effort was spearheaded by a non-Muslim professor on the campus but was also supported by the M S A. More politically focused events include the Peace, not Prejudice campaign, which developed in direct response to Islamofascism Awareness Week.[3] This event is aimed at facilitating dialogue, building solidarity with other groups on campus, and promoting a better understanding of Islam to counteract Islamofascism Week.

ISRAELI APARTHEID WEEK

One of the most politically challenging and contentious causes that students discussed was Israeli Apartheid Week. This event denounces the oppressive conditions, violence, and human rights violations imposed against Palestinians by the Israeli state. Sakina described some of the backlash she experienced due to her support of this cause: "I remember during Israel[i] Apartheid Week where a lot of Muslims and non-Muslims come out to support Palestinian rights. One of the symbols of the Palestinian struggle is the kaffiyeh, the black-and-white scarf which is worn by non-Muslims and Muslims alike. I wear it on a regular basis and especially during Israeli Apartheid Week. I remember when I had the kaffiyeh, and I wear the hijab obviously, so I become that much more visible and nobody anywhere on the bus would sit next to me."

Muslims who further politicize their identities by wearing symbols like the kaffiyeh or display the Palestinian flag become further targeted and ostracized. At my university, three female students wearing kaffiyehs as a head scarves had them pulled off their heads by male students from the Jewish Hillel organization. Tactics of harassment and intimidation by pro-Zionist campus groups are meant to shut down Palestinian activism and silence criticism of Israel. In response, some MSAs fall back on performing the "good Muslim" archetype and distancing from controversial alliances and solidarities that risk further aligning them with "radical" political identities connected to global threats. Muslim youth lay themselves open to risk, negative perceptions, and potential backlash when they engage in anti-Israeli apartheid activism where the symbols of Palestinian solidarity mark them as targets for pro-Zionist campus groups.

The involvement of MSAs and other student groups in Israeli Apartheid Week has created various controversies across Canada. Overlapping subaltern counterpublic groups on campus have joined forces in solidarity against Israeli oppression. Even though they support the Palestinian struggle, Muslim students do not agree on the efficacy of Israeli Apartheid Week. This disagreement has created divisions with some students splintering to form separate Palestinian solidarity groups outside the purview of MSAs. Tahir described how altercations between Jewish faculty and students with MSA members led to a general assembly meeting bringing together the dissenting groups at his university:

There were incidents, for one, s p h r, the Solidarity for Palestine
Human Rights, put up a display with the help of m s a in a
library, showing the atrocities happening in Gaza, and the
Jewish organization was slightly insensitive to that. One of
the Jewish professors verbally assaulted a sister, and I think
some of the Jewish students attacked ... verbally abused some
of the brothers and the sisters as well. That was a big incident
because it involved a professor. It caused a huge uproar. At the
general assembly we had about 700 students. There was a physical
divide so the room was split into two. You had insults and ...
abuses across each other, religious, racial, ethnic in nature. Palestine
doesn't exist, there is no Palestine, other religious racial insults.
After that, the situation deteriorated. There were simmering
tensions. It's not always apparent, but it's there.

Given the volatile tensions on his campus, Tahir stated that the m s a
decided to not include Israel and Palestine in their Genocide Awareness
week to avoid controversy and instead establish coalitions with other
campus groups: "We did other things that are universally accepted
to be genocide. We covered Sudan, we covered the Holocaust, and
other such things. We were trying to build a wide coalition, we tried
to stay away from issues where there's huge debate. Whether Israel
is committing genocide is a whole other debate open for discussion.
People have various takes on that. So, we didn't touch on that."

Highly incendiary issues such as the Israeli-Palestinian conflict create
tensions among students and faculty. Attempts to silence these solidarity
efforts have transpired in destructive ways. Rania tried building bridges
between Muslim and Jewish students after two years of volatile interactions on her campus. The m s a extended a dinner invitation to the
Jewish student group on campus to develop a basis for a more productive dialogue in the face of dissenting positions and disagreements.
This was an important step in creating more dialogical spaces and
working across communities of difference and competing publics.

Other students were critical of the disunity the events created even
among Muslims. Students influenced by the Islamist politics of h t were
opposed to nationalism and felt that Palestine solidarity movements
celebrated nationalist symbols such as flags, so they refused to support
these events. According to Wiktorowicz (2004), this kind of controversy represents a battle between social movements for "framing
hegemony." He explains that "[p]rognostic framing in particular tends

to produce numerous intra-movement framing disputes. While social movements share a common understanding about responsibility for a problem, there is far less cohesion over strategies and tactics" (Wiktorowicz 2004, 17). In this case there were competing ideological frames where those adhering to the ideology of HT disagreed with the tactics, strategies, and political choices of MSA students supporting the Palestine solidarity movement. In vying for framing hegemony and ideological authority, neither group succeeded in achieving the dominant narrative.

Tahir observed that others disagreed with having a singular focus on Palestine and argued that MSA should broaden its activism and solidarity work to other nations, including non-Muslim causes and conflicts: "They should not fall into the stereotypical Muslim organizations focusing just on Palestine and ignoring the genocide in Sudan or other atrocities going on in the world. Kashmir for example ... Gujarat. And not just be limited to Muslim things. As Muslims we should be aware of atrocities no matter if it's Muslim or non-Muslim. So, what's going on in Sri Lanka should concern us. What is going on in China or Tibet. We should be concerned about those as well." Many students echoed Tahir's outlook about the need to engage as global citizens in a variety of political causes.

As a Nigerian Muslim student, Awad was hurt by the lack of MSA activism toward causes in Africa: "We need to be more vocal about issues facing Muslim people: Muslim men, women, children all over the world. My experience with the MSA has been that they advocate certain issues, Palestine for example ... Chechnya, Kosovo. They neglect a lot of places. I've never seen [the] MSA advocate for Muslim rights in Africa, and it hurts a lot. And I've never seen the MSA advocate for Muslim rights in Latin America or Muslim rights in China. They need to be more global with the way they approach these issues." Black Muslims experience exclusion in the wider Muslim community when their concerns and struggles are not included in the activism of the MSA. As Tahir put it: "[P]eople are suffering, we don't have to make this distinction, so anywhere there is injustice being committed around the world we have to at least acknowledge it as moral support and show that we are not in our own bubble."

MSAs AS APOLITICAL

Abbas (2011) notes that in the UK after 9/11, Muslim student groups on university campuses were unable to deal effectively with identity and political issues. Despite the campus-based activism and social justice activities MSAs undertake, many students were dissatisfied with their response to specific political issues and incidents. Students expressed discontent about the MSAs not taking a strong enough stand when Islamophobic actions occur, and they were critical of the apolitical position of some MSAs. Sakina had an especially strong reaction to how she felt her MSA had abandoned its role as critical interlocutor at a time when Islamophobia and anti-Muslim racism were major issues:

> I hated them because politically when some issue would arise, whether racist or Islamophobic, the MSA took a very apathetic stance when I thought that was a perfect time express yourself and be vocal. So, there are moments when the MSA claim to say they're the voice of all Muslims on campus, but when Muslims need them then they don't speak up. If you're not towing the party line, then you could get kicked out of the MSA which is strange because by virtue of being Muslim you should belong to the MSA. So, I hated them. I thought they didn't speak for Muslims. I didn't think they spoke for the majority of Muslims, and when they did speak it was to push their agenda. The MSA is not a religious organization. It's a political organization that pushes its own views.

Saleha felt that Muslims in general were ill-equipped to deal with Islamophobia and the backlash that accompanied attempts to address it, which she suggested might be the cause of the political apathy that others had noticed: "I think Muslims are really scared to stand up because they think that we don't have the tools to address Islamophobia. So, if we stand up and we get all this backlash, we don't know how to deal with it. So, let's just be quiet and then we don't have to deal with the backlash [*laughs*]. But the consequence of that is that it still happens, right? And it still hurts us, and we still are facing it, but we just have [fewer] tools to face it with."

The pragmatic concerns Saleha raises are germane when we consider that Muslims were foisted into a role of defending against Islamophobic rhetoric and attacks with little preparation and limited political savvy. Many Muslim students specialize in fields like science and business as opposed to social sciences, which provide some political analysis and awareness of global geopolitics. There is some warranted fear and trepidation impeding engagement in the fraught political terrain that

Islamophobia forces Muslim students into and for which they may not be appropriately prepared to challenge, either politically or emotionally.

For Sikander, a politically engaged student who worked with numerous social justice clubs on campus, the MSA had perpetuated a culture of political illiteracy:

> MSAs are largely incompetent politically. They are mostly familiar with the day-to-day ritualistic form of our *deen* [religion], and are completely unfamiliar with the political dynamics of the people they help to mould. Young Muslims are largely politically illiterate. They don't have a history of political experimentation. They go to the *halaqas* and *jummahs* and dinners and think they've lived. My views are bleak. I have been thoroughly unimpressed by the Muslim student body. It's a pathetic attempt to organize themselves into coherent political voice. Don't get me wrong, I love my MSAers ... but it's like they play on their doctrinal monopoly.

Sikander recognized that his MSA purveys a specific Islamic frame of knowledge through religious activities, which creates a particular kind of MSA subject, one he regards as politically immature and focused exclusively on "ritualistic forms" of practice. As a critical voice, Sikander positioned himself in opposition to the dominant Muslim counter-public on his campus.

Peek (2005) argues that the emphasis on religion is a means by which Muslim students are brought together and not segregated from their co-religionists, a move Sikander saw as promoting apolitical religious identities. Some MSAs adopt this strategy of focusing on Islamic practices to build unity among their diverse members and connect their MSA chapter to broader networks of Muslims. However, when this narrow focus ignores social justice and civic engagement it can be a limiting narrative and leave members dissatisfied.

Sikander was not alone in this critique of the apolitical stance of some MSAs. At another Ontario university, Awad expressed similar disapproval when commenting on the Danish cartoon controversy:[4]

> [T]he MSA is ... very, very, very inactive politically. They are very, very scared. I don't know [why]. I wasn't an executive. I couldn't understand why we're not able to put out a very strong statement against certain cartoons that were printed in Canada, and we were

always trying to give [a] statement in line with the official statement of the University [of XXD] and that was a problem for me.
[We] should be very careful because it shapes us as individuals ...
it shapes us as a community, and it shapes how we want
to see ourselves.

Awad felt the reticence of some MSAs may stem from fear of exclusion
or reprisal from the broader university public, or because law enforcement
regards the politicization of Muslim student groups with suspicion.

The sense of fear and the desire to fit in may have been impacted
by the Islamophobic acts on campuses. For example, the 2007 CFS
report mentions that Muslim candidates running for election in two
separate campaigns repeatedly had their posters torn down. These
candidates were either involved in the MSA or were visibly Muslim
(one of the candidates wore the hijab). It is possible that such incidents
compel some MSAs to remain apolitical to avoid negative attention
and harassment. However, as some students remarked, their silence
reinforces their subaltern position.

Yusra found the MSA's lack of responsiveness to certain political
issues resulted in apologetics: "Interestingly MSA has been very neutral
politically. It's apologetic. I'm not satisfied with that. I think we've
done enough of that. We need to come to an understanding that we
didn't do anything wrong. I don't understand why we have to fall
into this victim role or this oppressor role or whatever role that we're
placed into. We didn't do anything wrong, and I think Muslims should
stand up to that." Yusra's frustration stems from the way Muslims
are viewed as bearing collective guilt for the violent actions of extremist
groups. She found this translated into apathy and apologetics instead
of igniting a stronger stance against the labelling and backlash.

MSAs are more than just a student club. They form potentially
subversive Muslim counterpublics and assist students in aligning their
faith and activism in ways that create Islamic subcultures on campus.
MSAs promote education about Islam and challenge Islamophobia
and oppression affecting Muslims at home and abroad. They engage
in outreach activities and have a vibrant presence on many campuses.
Despite the shortcomings of apolitical trends in some groups, internal
sectarian divisions, and gender inequity, MSAs create communities of
faith, activism, and action. The challenge remains for them to become
truly inclusive bodies that reflect the diversity of student identities,
realities, and experiences on campus.

Islamophobia and the Security Industrial Complex

As the preceding chapters underscore, the radical, the terrorist, the extremist, and the jihadist are the new ontologies ascribed to Muslim youth that constitute them as violent, degenerate fanatics hell-bent on the destruction of the West. While a very small minority of Muslim youth engage in ideologically driven violence, these constructs neverthe-less inform the dominant paradigm through which they are viewed. The prevalence of these archetypes leaves little room for Muslims to locate themselves outside these constrictive typologies. These derogatory categories underscoring the global jihadi threat are purveyed without reference to the histories and complex geopolitical struggles that shape these terms, and without acknowledging the rôle of US foreign policies and the war on terror in creating the conditions for reactionary ideolo-gies to give rise to violent movements abroad (Abbas 2011, 2019; Kumar 2012). These new taxonomies of difference tell us who is to be watched, punished, and exiled for fear they may disrupt "our freedom," "our values," and "our nation." The boundaries of belonging and citizenship and those separating the desirable from undesirable immigrants are anchored in these distinctions. Nationhood, citizenship, civil and human rights hang in the delicate balance between the fear and moral panic generated among "good citizens" toward the Muslim "anti-citizen" (J. Zine 2012a).

Closing the degrees of separation between citizen and outsider is more than just a social or discursive shift, it is a political, legal, and ontological move. Giorgio Agamben (2005) refers to the suspension of the rule of law in times of emergency as a "state of exception." He argues that these conditions introduced under limited and extraordinary circumstances have now become normalized and serve as the dominant paradigm of government in contemporary politics. Hallmarks of the state of exception include the practices of extraordinary rendition (in both Canada and the US) and the use of security certificates as part of the Canadian Immigration and Refugee Protection Act that has effectively led to the dismantling of the rights of non-citizens through indefinite detention along with the practice of secret trials and evidence (see Diab 2008; Flatt 2012).

These techniques of governance perform a discursive function, transforming a peaceful citizen into an outlaw (see also Fadil, de Koning, and Ragazzi 2019). Political and ideological categories such as the so-called radical and the jihadist are coded into an index of suspicion that informs the practices of racial and religious profiling. These deviant identities are interpellated into the discourses of a "security industrial complex" as the apparatus through which post-9/11 governmentality and exceptionalism operate. Hayes (2006, n.p.) identifies the security industrial complex as a process by which "the boundaries between internal and external security, policing and military operations, have been eroded," and new forms of surveillance of "public and private places, of communications and of groups of individuals" have been accelerated by the "war on terror." These technologies include local and global surveillance systems; biometric identification systems; electronic tagging and satellite monitoring; paramilitary equipment for public order and crisis management; and the militarization of border controls (Hayes 2009). In the post-9/11 state of exception, military[1] and security communities along with academics and the media function as part of a security industrial complex where Muslims are profiled, studied, policed, disciplined, and indefinitely detained.

The technological and physical surveillance occurs through military and law enforcement agencies that have expanded powers through the Anti-terrorism Act in Canada or the USA Patriot Act, which were both instituted after 9/11. Relying on academic studies, these intelligence communities construct taxonomies that outline ill-defined categories such as Islamist radicals and create de-historicized and de-contextualized archetypes of religiously and racially degenerate Muslims that must be policed and regulated through controlled immigration and security policies. These typologies serve as an attempt to weed out good Muslims from bad Muslims and employ colonial archetypes of cultural and civilizational differences that now rely upon a racialized security industrial complex to identify, manage, and contain the "savage" from the "civilized."

I refer to "racial securitization" as sets of regulatory ideological and political policies, strategies, and techniques employed by the state (as well as some non-state actors) that are constituted and enacted through conflating racial and religious identities with the assessment of risk and public safety. Racial securitization links race and the racialization of religion (Joshi 2006) to the security industrial complex as the basis on which threats to public safety are determined and safeguarded against. Increasingly, non-state institutions, organizations, and actors are conscripted into fulfilling the mission of securing public safety and exercising control over all areas of social life. Public servants and private citizens are asked to profile and identify deviant individuals and groups that may pose risks to public safety and civility. For example, security agencies have called upon mosques and religious organizations to be partners in public safety and help weed out extremists in their midst. Civil society participates in the supervisory networks conducting profiling and surveillance. Schools, universities, and community organizations are recruited to perform surveilling practices in ways that further extend the disciplinary function of the state (see also Fadil, de Koning, and Ragazzi 2019). For example, programs developed for the purposes of CVE, such as the Prevent Policy in the UK, have enlisted preschool teachers to help identify "potential radicals" among the toddlers they care for.[2]

In the US, the American Civil Liberties Association documented how the American government is recruiting businesses and individuals in the construction of a surveillance society (Stanley 2004). A security program dubbed "Eagle Eyes" was billed as "an anti-terrorism initiative that enlists the eyes and ears of Air Force members and citizens in the war on terror."[3] The program offers training in how to detect terrorist activity and a telephone tip line. According to their web page, "Anyone can recognize elements of potential terror planning when they see it." This messaging secures the role of the public as part of a security apparatus to identify suspicious activity such as, "People who don't seem to belong in the workplace, neighbourhood, business establishment or anywhere else … If a person just doesn't seem like he or she belongs, there's probably a reason for that" (Stanley 2004, 4). These programs widen the reach of the security industry by asking the public's assistance to profile their neighbours, report who they deem to be "out of place," and identify potential threats. Racial biases are deeply embedded in the judgments and assumptions underlying the practices that distinguish between good (safe) and bad (dangerous) citizens. Those distinctions are a driving force shaping public policy and security practices.

BAN-OPTICON

The security industrial complex is formed through a nexus of biopolitics and necropolitics where power over life, death, and banishment are determined. In the broader transnational sphere, the disciplinary architecture of the security industrial complex regulates surveillance practices through what Bigo (2008) refers to as a "ban-opticon *dispositif*."[4] The ban-opticon encompasses a diffuse configuration of power from above and below. Muslims experience this through state-regulated controls at borders, through immigration practices, and public safety and social policies that target them (consider Trump's "Muslim travel ban" and bans on head scarves and face veils in Quebec, France, and elsewhere) alongside individual forms of exclusion, rejection, and discrimination. These dimensions relate to the systemic as well as individual forms of Islamophobia discussed in previous chapters.

Bigo (2008, 35) refers to a "collection of heterogeneous bodies of discourses on threats, immigration, enemy within, immigrant fifth column, radical Muslims versus good Muslims, exclusion versus integration, etc." These ideas reinforce a belief that a profile can be generated to ascertain people who pose potential risks: "A skin colour, an accent, an attitude and one is slotted, extracted from the unmarked masses and, if necessary, evacuated" (Bigo 2008, 44). The processes of sorting and creating typologies of abject differences are part of the new racial and cultural eugenic practices that govern national borders. Following these logics, concerns over the need to pre-emptively regulate threats has given rise to the technologies of "pre-crime" policing and surveillance and the commodification of security. Zedner (2007, 262) argues that a pre-crime focus "shifts the temporal perspective to anticipate and forestall that which has not yet occurred and may never do so." For example, Canada's Anti-terrorism Act of 2015 (Bill C-51) included a provision of the Criminal Code that made it easier for Canadian police to arrest people they fear "may" commit a terrorism offence.

Bigo (2008, 35) extends the Foucauldian perception of a panoptic society and its modalities of surveillance to offer a wider lens for "how control and surveillance of certain minority groups take place at a distance." The diverse network of surveillance technologies that include information and virtual reality are deployed in what he describes as the "'governmentality of unease' in a field of 'global (in)security'" (Bigo, 2008, 6). He argues that "security professionals have all become managers of unease," and through interconnected bureaucracies they integrate diverse institutional agents such as "customs, police, intelligence services bankers engaged in risk assessment and suppliers of new technologies of surveillance" engaged in the "management of fear." (Bigo 2002, 75). These security actors create and manage risk by "specifying specific threats or risks that can be managed together: immigration to regulate, an environment to protect, terrorism to fight and in the end a population worried by the encircling barbarians and the idea of the decline of civilization" (Bigo 2002, 75). In other words, security agencies ideologically construct the risks they seek to police and contain.

FOLK DEVILS

These ideologies and conceptions of social deviance manifest in what Cohen ([1972] 2014) dubs "folk devils." Introducing the folk devil concept in 1972, Cohen used the example of violent clashes between the 1960s music British subcultural group the "Mods" and "Rockers" as a template from which ideas about the construction of socially deviant folk devil archetypes could be extrapolated to understand how other groups are similarly cast in ways that generate societal angst and moral panics. "Folk devils" operate as scapegoats and are blamed for a variety of social problems. Cohen ([1972] 2014, 35) argues that "society labels rule breakers as belonging to certain deviant groups" and that "once the person is thus typecast, his acts are interpreted in terms of the status quo to which he has been assigned."

According to Cohen, there are three primary ways that folk devil archetypes are manifested. The first process is the "symbolization" of the folk devil who is portrayed through a singular narrative that becomes a popular indicator for deviance. The negative essentialism of deviant Muslim archetypes is a quintessential illustration for this case in point (Al-Natour 2010, Nilan 2017; Opratko 2019). Second, the controversies surrounding the folk devils become exaggerated, distorted, or fabricated and are used to fuel a moral and "symbolic crusade" (Cohen [1972] 2014, 3). The Islamophobia industry for example has been fuelled by campaigns of misinformation, deceit, and salacious lies about Muslims as the fifth column or an Islamist Trojan Horse that seeks to overthrow Western civilization (Khan 2014; Lean 2017). These discourses are purveyed and popularized through mainstream media as well as far right social media in ways that normalize and heighten Islamophobia and result in hate crimes and backlash. The third part of the folk devil dynamic involves predicting future degenerate and deviant actions based on the stereotypes generated about vilified subcultural groups. This factor relates to the securitization measures underwritten by notions of risk and what Bigo warned as the "unease" and states of "(in)security" that abject groups are responsible for creating. The Muslim folk devil, therefore, plays a key archetypal role in post-9/11 security discourses, policies, and practices as an emblem of deviance and risk.

SECURITIZED HABITUS

Understanding the social, cultural, and psychological dynamics of racial securitization, I contend that the mechanisms of the security industrial complex result in a "securitized habitus" that impacts the behaviour and dispositions of targeted groups. Bourdieu's theory of habitus refers to the socialization into specific norms and tendencies that guide thought and behaviour within specific groups and subcultures. Bourdieu (1977) argues that "structures constitutive of a particular kind of environment (e.g., the material conditions of existence characteristic of a class condition) produce *habitus* or 'systems of durable transposable dispositions'" (72) and an "endless capacity to engender products – thoughts, perceptions, expressions, actions" (95). These dispositions are products of a specific environment into which people are socialized through unconscious cultural conditioning. For example, Maira (2009) argues that there is particular subjectivity and an "imperial feeling" to the post-9/11 era that transcends the global war on terror and is connected to material and political structures of power that are evident in everyday life, pop culture, migration, labour, and the formations of national belonging. Similarly, referring to the affective conditions engendered by the war on terror, Abdel-Fattah (2021, 60) describes the "maps of meaning, ideas, feelings, and social images that are constructed to situate young Muslims as a category of youth 'at risk.'"

Habitus is enacted in the way that "social order is progressively inscribed in people's minds" through "cultural products" that include educational practices, language, values, classification systems, and so forth (Bourdieu 1984, 471). It is the way that individuals perceive and react to the social worlds they inhabit. I contend that the post-9/11 condition in the West created a specific "securitized habitus." Muslims and society at large have become conditioned to this fraught environment and the ideologies and practices produced by it. According to Foucault (2000, 107), "[C]onstraints, controls, mechanisms or surveillance that play themselves out in disciplinary techniques" are "charged with investing themselves in the behaviour of individuals." These dynamics are internalized and in turn produce specific behaviours, affective responses, and shared experiences of alienation.

For Muslims, the manifestation of the securitized habitus results in the ontological condition of feeling under siege and constantly aware of how you are perceived by others. This vigilance results in making conscious or unconscious decisions to modify one's clothing, bodily comportment, and behaviour (smiling more to not be seen as threatening) or checking what you may be carrying with you when travelling that could be deemed suspicious. We are all socialized into navigating airport security and automatically taking off our shoes, packing our personal care products into tiny bottles in transparent plastic bags, co-operating with security guards, or being wary of the person speaking Arabic sitting next to us on the plane. However, not everyone is socialized into being regarded as a potential threat the way that racialized Muslims (and those perceived to be Muslims) understand themselves to be suspect by others. Maira (2016) refers to "surveillance effects" that the 9/11 generation experiences through the normalization of these practices as part of daily life. The narratives that follow delve into the impact of this conditioning on Muslim youth and highlights their responses and strategies for navigating these fraught conditions.

NARRATIVES OF SECURITIZATION AND SURVEILLANCE: RACIAL AND RELIGIOUS RROFILING

"Whatever you do by virtue of being a Muslim in Canada you're just inviting a lot of state surveillance, policing, and all the rest of that."

Aisha, law student, BC

In the preceding quote, Aisha speaks to the experience of Canadian Muslims who are subject to state policies and practices that render them as suspect citizens within regimes of hyper-securitization based their religious and racial identities (Bahdi 2003; Caidi and MacDonald 2008;

Hennebry and Momani 2013; Jamil 2014; Nagra 2017). One of the main drivers of the post-9/11 surveillance of Muslim youth involved the arrests of seventeen young Muslims and one adult in June 2006 for involvement in domestic terrorist activities. These arrests evoked responses of shock, fear, and vulnerability among Canadians. This group, coined the Toronto 18, were Canadian-born university and high school students from middle-class backgrounds, a profile that was inconsistent with popular assumptions about disaffected or at risk youth. The case involved an RCMP mole or spy who was embedded with them (a member of the local Muslim community) and who led the youth to a paintball camp in Northern Ontario that was later branded as a "jihadi training camp." Along with the intrigue surrounding this case, the arrests shattered the complacency some argue has made Canada blind to the "homegrown" threats from within. No longer just "dangerous foreigners" invading our shores – Muslims were cast as the "fifth column" or "enemies within." Following the arrests, an Ipsos-Reid survey found that 49 per cent believed it was justifiable for Canadian authorities to focus their anti-terrorist activities more strongly on the Muslim community (Walia 2006).

The public suspicion and Islamophobic fears surrounding this case meant that Canadian Muslim youth were subjects of national scrutiny and constructed as security concerns. In a declassified report by CSIS, "Western jihadist youth counterculture" was described as the next phase in the evolution of global terrorism. This movement was identified as a "very rapid process" that was transforming some youth from angry activists into jihadist terrorists, intent on killing for their religion. The CSIS report identified "Generation Jihad" as "a significant threat to national security" and "a clear and present danger to Canada and its allies" (S. Bell 2006). Heightened fear and moral panics regarding homegrown terrorism placed Muslim youth at the centre of public safety concerns as potential threats to the nation.

According to Walia (2006), "One of the most disturbing realities of the aftermath of the Toronto arrests is the passive acceptance and normalization of a state of fear, and consequentially, further fortification of the security state." Expanding on the political context of racial and religious securitization, Roble, a youth worker, had experience with Somali Muslim youth that led him to the following realizations about how religious fidelity affects the perceptions of the 9/11 generation of Canadian Muslim youth: "If you are a religious youth who attend[s] the mosque regularly and who wants to have a religious-centred life, the assumption will be that you are an extremist." He went

on to qualify that while being religious and being extremist should
not be equated, Muslim youth are nonetheless burdened with these
labels, often without support from the larger community. While religious
fidelity is by no means a requirement for being subject to the consequences of Islamophobia – anyone perceived to be Muslim can be
affected – the attacks on mosques in Quebec, Canada, and Christchurch,
New Zealand, make mosque-going Muslims feel especially targeted
and vulnerable. According to Roble, the repercussions that youth
must face from the suspicion and labelling that they routinely encounter
follows them into classrooms and the workplace.

Mahvish highlighted how the popular Islamophobic stereotypes
and the backlash that Muslims experience felt surreal, like something
out of a movie or dystopic fiction. But at the same time, she felt these
experiences allowed her to better understand the persecution of Jewish
people who have also been scapegoated as "folk devils" to incite moral
panic and bigotry, a position that Muslims now occupy: "I have for
the first time understood what Jewish people ... started to feel. You
are that social scapegoat when every problem in the society is blamed
on you. That's what I'm starting to feel right now when I hear people
saying, 'those Muslims on welfare' or those 'sand niggers' you start
to feel like, 'Oh shit ... I saw this in a movie one time ... I've seen this
in books ... this is not headed in a good direction unless we can do
something about it really quickly.'"

As a teacher working with Muslim youth in Ontario, Safeeya reflected
on the palpable fear, paranoia, and public scrutiny that Muslim women
face: "People get a little more paranoid of Muslims. For instance, if
you are wearing the hijab and you go to places, people's eyes are
focused on you. If you drive your car and wear the hijab, people look
at you differently. It's just being singled out in a crowd all the time.
But of course, you don't know what they are thinking but you know
their eyes are looking at you." The public paranoia and the sense of
constantly being under scrutiny is palpable and viscerally felt by
Muslim women, as Safeeya described in her examples. This gendered
surveillance contributes to the kind of social conditioning experienced
as part of the securitized habitus of the post-9/11 world.

Safa, a Guyanese youth from British Columbia, tried to account
for the existential fear that she as a Muslim represented to others.
Secular paranoia and the fear of cultural change, White decline, and
fear of terrorism are at the core of White nationalist angst. "I don't
know if it's threat, we're a secular country, I think they just want to

protect that secularism, maybe we're a growing population, maybe we're going to change their laws. It might not be that they think we're crazy and we're going to bomb their country or something like that." Mahvish, too, felt the regulatory gaze of public and national scrutiny following her and shaping her encounters and interactions in various facets of her life, even though she felt she could otherwise pass and not be recognized as "typically Muslim":

> I'm afraid that racial profiling will get out of control. I've had such problems [and] I don't "look Muslim." I don't wear the right clothes, it's like "I don't look it." People are surprised when I tell them I'm from the Middle East!! I don't have [a] beard, thank God! But when people will find out at the border, at the airports, at shopping malls when I go to use my credit cards, when I make collect calls to my house, my mail, everything has to be double-checked, triple-checked because of who I am and because of my last name.

Having a Muslim-sounding name is enough to trigger greater scrutiny and oversight while carrying out everyday tasks. The shadow of surveillance is a constant looming factor in the everyday encounters and activities Muslims undertake. By jokingly stating that she was lucky to "not have a beard," Mahvish gestures to the way the Muslim men's beards are often read as a marker of "radicalization" and invite suspicion.

Talia, an Albanian community college student from Ontario, was a recent immigrant to Canada. She observed that Muslim youth were subject to undue attention and treated as being "up to no good." She commented on the negative essentialism that confines the identities of young Muslims who share a similar demographic profile with the small number of those who engage in domestic and foreign acts of terror. The notion of "guilt by association" feeds into the security industry that relies upon rash judgments to legitimate the securitization of Muslim youth as well as to justify imperial wars and aggression abroad. Keeping these ideas alive in the public imaginary serves broader political goals and interests, which allows negative tropes to maintain their currency.

Sikander put forward the same point far more bluntly: "I guess the single biggest negative impact was that the mainstream majority now probably suspects every other young Muslim male with a basketball jersey or engineering degree to be a potential truck-bomber." Being defined as a "problem" based on shared markers of identity renders Muslim youth as suspect in a manner that does not require proof or evidence to support such claims. This is a quintessential problem facing the 9/11 generation.

CAMPUS SURVEILLANCE

In addition to the discussion in chapter 4 on the politics of campus culture in an age of empire and how MSAS operate as subaltern counterpublics, this section extends the focus on university campuses as sites of surveillance and securitization (see also Guest et al. 2020). These investigations extend the reach of the security industrial complex into post-secondary institutions and bring the global war on terror into domestic campuses in attempts to weed out homegrown extremists who may become the next foreign fighters. Despite the fact the MSAS have operated within North America for over fifty years and they have strong and positive reputations on university campuses, they are nonetheless regarded by security agencies as sites of potential radicalization.

There have been limited instances where Muslim youth attending Canadian universities have been arrested for involvement with terrorism. For example, there is the Toronto 18 case and Kevin Omar Mohamed, who was arrested after having travelled to Syria and posting on social media about support of Al-Qaeda and attacks in the West (S. Bell 2020). Yet surveillance activities have targeted university campuses in ways disproportionate to demonstrated threats from these sites. National security is of utmost importance to all concerned citizens; however, racial and religious profiling as a strategy of CVE programs is counterproductive and has been shown to fuel the nexus between Islamophobia and violent forms of Islamism and radicalization (Abbas 2019).

The Associated Press released a secret report describing the activities of the New York City Police Department (NYPD) in monitoring Muslim communities in Newark, New Jersey, for several months in 2007. According to this report, the NYPD sent "mosque crawlers" and "rakers" as undercover operatives to compile pictures and descriptions of members of the Muslim community. This document reveals that the NYPD monitored fifteen MSAS on sixteen college campuses across the Northeast United States. The NYPD found no suspicious threats of terrorism, and the report contained no allegations of criminal behaviour. The Associated Press reported in the *New York Daily News* (2012):

> Police trawled daily through student websites run by Muslim student groups at Yale, the University of Pennsylvania, Rutgers and 13 other colleges in the Northeast. They talked with local authorities about professors in Buffalo and even sent an undercover agent on a white-water rafting trip, where he recorded students' names and noted in police intelligence files how many times they prayed. Asked about the monitoring, police spokesman Paul Browne provided a list of 12 people arrested or convicted on terrorism charges in the United States and abroad who had once been members of Muslim Students' Associations, which the NYPD referred to as MSAS.

An examination into the activities of the NYPD revealed that their monitoring of MSAS included religious surveillance, such as collecting data about the number of times individuals were praying. Operating on the premise that fidelity to one's faith implicates Muslims as potential terror threats has been an embedded assumption within the lines of inquiry of similar high-profile cases (Bechrouri 2018). In Canada for example, the 2003 case called Project Thread by the RCMP involved twenty-six male Pakistani nationals in their early twenties who were arrested in pre-dawn raids during militarized sting operations executed by the Public Security and Anti-Terrorism Unit, a multilateral police unit for immigration-related charges. The men arrested were in Canada on international student visas. They were detained five months based on the following "evidence": (a) they lived in scantily furnished surroundings (not surprising as students); (b) they lived in clusters among other Muslims and South Asians in Toronto (assumptions criminalizing their racial and ethnic background); (c) they had photos of the CN tower (a postcard); (d) photos of firearms (picture of a hunting trip in India); (e) photo of aeronautics (Lufthansa Airlines poster); (f) they lived close by the Pickering nuclear plant and were observed walking nearby; (g) they all hailed from the Punjab province (an alleged hotbed of Sunni Muslim extremism).

The circumstantial and otherwise inconsequential set of facts was used as evidence against these Pakistani students to demonstrate potential extremism. They were held on civil immigration charges, but their attorneys argued that their religious beliefs and practices were central to the investigation. They were asked the following questions: How often do you pray? Where do you pray? Have you been for hajj? What do think about jihad? What do you think of Osama bin Laden? This line of questioning pathologized and criminalized their religious beliefs and behaviours. Despite the lack of evidence to prosecute them, the Pakistani students were eventually deported. This case represents the fraught and dangerous intersection of race, immigration, and national security that has led to the erosion and dismantling of civil rights for non-citizens (see also Odartey-Wellington 2009).

Fahim, a South Asian engineering student from Toronto, was worried that what was said at the *khutbas* during Friday congregational prayers on campus or in *halaqas* was susceptible to outside scrutiny and bias. Fahim acknowledged concerns over religious policing: "I think everyone is still careful when they give *khutbas* or talk in *halaqas*. There is a feeling like something they say will be taken the wrong way," and he hastened to add that he did not believe the sermons had problematic political messages. The fear of religious messages being misconstrued as dangerous or a threat to Canadian values is taken seriously in Muslim communities. The term "sharia" can lead to national paranoia and moral panic because of its use in conservative and far right fearmongering campaigns. Sharia means "a path leading to water" and refers to Islamic laws derived from the Quran and Hadith but has become code for signifying an Islamist takeover of the West. Notions of creeping sharia have been popularized through conspiracy theories fomented by the Islamophobia industry (Bowen 2012; Lean 2017). The Quran lexicon has been weaponized and used as a means for promoting a theological fiction to exacerbate Islamophobic fears and public anxieties.

Muslim students on Canadian university campuses are under surveillance. Students from the MSA at my university informed me that they were receiving phone calls form a local regional police officer who was part of a counter-terrorism unit. The officer told the MSA president Sufyan and vice-president Rania that he wanted to talk about "why terrorism was bad." He was persistent in requesting a voluntary meeting to discuss matters of "national safety." The students did not want to appear evasive or unco-operative for fear they would be perceived as having something to hide. They were defaulting on the "good Muslim" approach to be compliant to avoid being relegated as "bad Muslims" and face the consequences which would lead to more surveillance. I suggested that the MSA executive arrange a meeting with the officer, and I would attend to support them. The students requested to meet on campus.

A male officer arrived in plainclothes bearing coffee and donuts. I recall thinking that this gesture was a way of making the meeting appear informal and winning the "hearts and minds" of Muslim youth. The officer was not pleased that I was sitting in on the meeting. It was clear he wanted to speak to the students alone but knowing that innocent actions can be relegated as "suspicious" if you are Muslim, I did not want to leave students in a vulnerable position. From the start of the meeting, it was clear the officer knew little about the MSA or their social activities (bowling nights), spiritual role (organizing prayers and lectures), and charitable work (sponsoring orphans in war-torn countries), and local civic engagement. Instead he was fixated on discussing "radicalization." When I asked him to give us an explanation of what he meant by "radicalization," he could not offer one, leaving the term open for conjecture. I asked, if Rania started wearing a niqab (face veil) and Sufyan grew a long beard, would these be signs they were becoming "radicalized"? The students asked how they could be expected to identify a "radical" in their midst if the markers were arbitrary. Nevertheless, the group confirmed that if they had valid concerns about any student who might be a risk to themselves or others, they would be the first to approach law enforcement authorities.

We all noticed the way the officer approached the MSA was based on profiling instead of evidence that would warrant such scrutiny. The officer expressed offence that he was being accused of racism. Meanwhile, there was no consideration for how the students were made to feel unduly targeted by his line of inquiry and the underlying assumptions. As noted in the preface, several years earlier some members of the MSA had been supporters of the HT; however, the current MSA did not espouse any specific political or theological leanings. Kevin Omar Mohamed, a student at a nearby campus, had recently been arrested on terrorism charges, which may have drawn attention to other local universities. Omar Mohamed was caught up in dangerous political ideologies, but he was not a member of the MSA, and students from his campus reported that he kept to himself and did not interact with other Muslim students (see also Nasser 2019b). Nonetheless, Muslim youth are subject to "guilt by association." MSAs would likely be one

of the least hospitable places for these ideologies to germinate and
gain traction in Canada. And yet, MSAS continue to be rattled by
encounters with security agencies that have targeted these groups as
potential sites for radicalization.

The University of Toronto's MSA reported that their executives had
been receiving unannounced visits from both CSIS and the RCMP
from 2016 onward. These visits occurred on campus as well as at their
homes (Kao 2018). At Ryerson University in Toronto, Muslim students
found recording devices behind the curtains of their prayer room
(Nagra 2017). The Canadian Council on American-Islamic Relations
(CAIR-CAN 2004) survey examined the interactions between security
officials and Canadian Muslims and found security officials conducted
visits in Muslim homes (45 per cent) and workplaces (23 per cent).
Nineteen per cent reported that security officials contacted them multiple times. Men were the primary targets of surveillance (56 per cent),
especially Arabs (54 per cent), those between the ages of eighteen and
thirty-five (62 per cent), and students (38 per cent).

MSA executives expressed concern that racial and religious profiling
and surveillance not only created an unsafe environment on campus
but also posed a deterrent to attracting and retaining members. Amin,
an MSA president in Ontario, was worried that the pervasive climate
of suspicion surrounding Muslim youth affected the perception of
MSAS. In one instance, a Muslim convert asked Amin to assure his
parents about the nature of the MSAs before they would allow him to
be involved in any of their activities: "He asked if I could give him
a signed letter on MSA letterhead so that he could show his parents
and his family that MSA is not affiliated with any political group. I said
that MSA is a U of XL student club. We are governed by the school's
constitution for clubs. You don't have to worry about it." Unlike other
student clubs, MSAS are placed in the position of proving they are
not potential sleeper cells and risks to public safety.

Raees, an executive member of his MSA, resisted these pressures
and said they should not be afraid of the authorities since they were
not doing anything illegal:

> If I was doing something wrong, then I should feel scared.
> I'm not doing anything wrong. We're just there to promote
> our religion and at the same time promote unity amongst the
> people. That's our main goal ... I don't feel like there is any
> reason to be afraid of the police coming after you or CSIS,

or the NYPD. For what? We're organizing a ski trip? A couple of guys want to go play paintball? What's wrong with that?! It's just guys having fun, guys bonding with each other. We're not going out of our way to foster hate and say, "Be against Canada" or "Be against the American government."

Although Raees's sentiments speak to how MSAs should not have to fear the authorities, this optimism is tempered by the reality of racial and religious profiling. For example, Bushra, explained how the pervasive climate of suspicion and surveillance has led to Muslim youth looking over their shoulders: "We were at the mall, and this guy got off the bus after us and we walked in together. And we're like, "Oh, my God, CSIS is here!!" We started walking fast to get away from him! And then someone else came and we're like, "Oh, my God!" ... We were laughing about it but, on the inside, we were all scared! It's not a joke. It's a real issue!" The Orwellian dystopia created through the workings of the security industrial complex creates paranoia for Muslims who feel the regulatory gaze of surveillance in everyday interactions. This sense of paranoia is another manifestation of living under siege and the affective responses it manifests.

The surveillance of Muslim students hit home for me when my son Yusuf was elected president of the MSA at my university. Early the next morning after the election my son received a phone call on his cell phone from a CSIS agent requesting to meet with him. This was odd, since not even the membership knew at that point who had been elected. Somehow intelligence was being passed along, though there was no evidence of spies having infiltrated the MSA. My son and I agreed to meet with the agent in a local coffee shop. Instead of having to convince another law enforcement agency that the MSA consisted of peace-loving students not potential radicals and terrorists, we turned the tables and asked how the government would protect Muslims who were increasingly being targeted by hate crimes. In 2015, three Muslim students in Chapel Hill, North Carolina, had been shot and killed. We used this tragedy to stress that Muslims need to be protected. The CSIS agent agreed that national security concerns should involve the protection of all citizens, but we did not receive any assurance that the escalation of anti-Muslim hate crimes was important to national security. The 2017 Quebec mosque massacre and the mosque attacks in Christchurch, New Zealand, demonstrate the clear and present danger of neo-fascism, White nationalism, and the alt-right (Perry and Scrivens 2015), yet Muslim youth continue to be a primary focus for security agencies.

Canadian security intelligence agencies have been attempting to recruit Muslim youth to their ranks. Rummana attended an RCMP conference where she felt they were trying to recruit insiders as spies, to "rat out" others in the community. She challenged their outreach tactics as a publicity stunt to garner legitimacy in the community. In her view, their agenda was to sow discord and division between Shia and Sunni communities:

> I told them, "You can't have these sessions and go into mosques and have a recruiting booth and do your own spiel and expect everyone to be okay with it!" That doesn't work! I said the same thing to officers from the Vancouver Police Department and each one of them turned to me and said, "The problem isn't in your community. It's not the Shia community we are worried about. So, don't even worry about it." I see that as driving a wedge among Muslims just to get a platform. The agenda[s] behind issues like this are concerning to me. So, I quickly stepped out. But the average youth doesn't get that, right?

Rummana was apprehensive for the youth who might be attracted to these recruiting efforts without recognizing the divide-and-conquer politics at play.

The normalization of the security state allows for the legitimation of racial and religious profiling and the focus directed on Muslim youth. Yusuf explained how instances of homegrown terror in Canada and the US provided a rationale for this heightened scrutiny, "I think because the Boston bombers were very young, that sort of attention now is shifting to MSAs because they think that's the breeding ground for these terrorists. So, there's definitely going to be a heightened surveillance on MSAs and Muslim youth more so than before. Because they think, 'Get to them while they're young.'" Muslim youth are perpetual suspects placed within narrow typologies that undermine their agency, safety, security, and mobility.

"FLYING WHILE MUSLIM"

The narratives of risk ascribed to and associated with Muslim youth impacted their travel across borders and heightened their perceptions of personal and political risk. The shared experience of "flying while Muslim" involves being flagged for scrutiny and additional checks at border security. Tariq recalls how showing up at an airport wearing Islamic attire was enough to cause security to question him: "I was at an airport and was going to Friday prayers after, so I was wearing an Arab dress, *thob* (long robe). I was just dropping my dad off in the lobby and two security agents came up to me and started questioning me. I wasn't even going on a flight! I've gotten to be a lot better with it now 'cause I know my rights and I haven't done anything wrong. I also have a little bit of cockiness to me as well [*laughs*]!"

Ziad also referred to when he and his father visited the United States, they were often subjected to lengthy interrogations. He acknowledged that this experience had "changed us in a way." An ontological shift occurs when being interpellated into discourses of risk and public safety and transforms racialized citizens into potential outlaws. This shift is deeply felt in many cases when the narratives of threat and fear are internalized. Discussing the process of this kind of interpellation in chapter 2, I use the illustration of Fanon's (1967) experience of being hailed into a discourse of abject Blackness as an example of how specific subjectivities are constituted through the relations of power enacted by dominant ideologies. Althusser's (1971) original example illustrates the process as occurring when a police officer calls out, "Hey you!" – an encounter that constructs and transforms the individual into surveilled subject or suspect. This example illustrates how Muslims are interpellated into the discourses of racial securitization. Encounters with law enforcement and security agents create a context where Muslim subjectivities are remade into transgressive archetypes that must be policed, regulated, and where possible, exiled.

Racialized religious identities attract specific kinds of scrutiny and suspicion. In a culture of Islamophobia, Islamic religiosity (e.g., praying, attending mosques or Islamic schools, wearing religious attire, adhering to sharia law) is often read as adherence to violent forms of political Islamism. These signifiers are construed as the rejection of Western liberal values and a desire for the violent overthrow of Western democracies to install an Islamic state (see chapter 6). These ideas are common tropes of alt-right and White nationalist groups that rely on the Islamist bogeyman to legitimate their Islamophobic fearmongering (Khan 2014).

Ziad reflected on how the racial and religious securitization of borders created not only social and political barriers but also moral concerns. Muslims are screened and vetted in ways that equate their religiosity with nefarious intentions. Making the decision to lie to authorities or risk being denied entry is a moral quandary, as Mahmood explained: "'Are you the kind we want or are you the kind we don't want?' They are trying to corner people. If an immigration officer is asking me, 'Do you pray five times a day?' And if you say yes or no, this might change your whole application. I have to make a choice whether to get into this country based on a lie. Where my religion just preaches the exact opposite." Mahmood lamented the fact that he must engage in a moral calculus when deciding how to respond to the questions of immigration officers or risk being denied entry.

The encounters that take place when flying while Muslim are rooted in subjective determinations, Orientalist stereotypes, and racial fears and anxieties that require Muslims to be wary and at times hyperconscious of how they are going to be perceived in these securitized contexts. Similarly, Finn, Hennebry, and Momani (2018) found that Canadian Arab youth are often forced, or feel they are forced, to perform their Canadian-ness to substantiate their innocence when crossing borders and travel transit sites.

The process for Muslims of crossing borders in a post-9/11 context is not only a situation where national identities are monitored and regulated but also where their religious identities are policed. Practices of racial and religious profiling occur where culture, bodies, and the state collide in a tension that renders Muslims as suspect citizens. These distinctions are based on the pathologizing of their faith and the politics of the colour line. Policing the borders of the nation and surveilling racialized subaltern identities takes place through a form of what I call "border eugenics" whereby culturally "desirable" versus "undesirable" immigrants are determined and those deemed as suspect are either detained or exiled. The taxonomies of difference created through these processes of racial and religious differentiation are constituted and regulated to sanitize and inoculate the nation from infiltration from illiberal and dangerous foreigners whose cultures are deemed incompatible with democracy and the rule of law. In the culturally eugenicist terms that these practices sanction, the regulation of borders and national boundaries becomes an exercise of sorting the "savage from the civilized" within racial forms of governmentality.

Zabeda remarked on how her male family members would routinely shave their beards when crossing borders, especially when entering the US, to avoid suspicion, possible detention, and unwanted delays.

Mahdi, a Shia Muslim from British Columbia, found that his name and the fact that he travels on an Iranian passport would elicit further questioning when crossing borders through the US: "I go through American borders a lot. Usually when they see my name and they see that I am born in the Middle East, and my passport has an Iranian visa ... most of the time they don't stop me, but they do ask, 'What are you studying. What are you doing?' I am kind of afraid to answer, to say that I am a chemist, because they might think that I might, you know ... make a bomb or something."

Because of the suspicion of Muslims as potential bomb-makers, the act of crossing a border breeds anxiety and uncertainty. For this reason, Muslim travellers have to decide in a split second whether disclosing the truth about their vocation can be misread and place unwarranted limitations on their mobility. Zabeda and Faiza reflected on how they navigate such a climate of suspicion:

> **Zabeda:** There is always a tight feeling in your stomach when you're going through airport security. Whenever we are at the airport I would never say, "*Allahu Akbar*" (God is great) when there are people around! I would be too scared to say that!! You know, being judged and scaring other people. Like Mahdi said, he's scared to say that he is a chemist and if somebody else is a pilot, they'd be scared to mention it. Even if you are not under surveillance, you feel that you have to hide these things because people are going to judge you.

> **Faiza:** I find that it's the way you carry yourself also has a lot of impact on how people treat you and whether you get profiled or not. If you are very nervous and look suspicious, then yeah, people will get suspicions. If you are just acting normal and are showing confidence, then I think the likelihood of being watched or judged becomes much less.

Both Zabeda and Faiza understood the implications of using the Islamic lexicon (e.g., saying *Allahu Akbar*) or simply being identified as a Muslim chemist or pilot when Orientalist and Islamophobic tropes govern many of the encounters in security zones.

Media reports validate their unease and the need to err on the side of caution. For example, in 2016 an Iraqi professor from UC Berkeley was removed from his Southwest Airlines flight for speaking Arabic.

When a passenger sitting next to the professor overheard his phone conversation and misheard *inshallah* (God willing) as *shahid* (martyr), the passenger reported him to the authorities (Milman 2016). In this way average citizens have taken on the role of profiling other citizens who they deem suspicious, which broadens the expanse of the security industrial complex in the public sphere. These circumstances exacerbate anxiety and stress for Muslims, but as Zabeda acknowledged, they also play into the racial fears and anxieties of others. Faiza found exerting confidence and not appearing suspicious when going through airport security helped mitigate negative stereotypes that might otherwise single her out for scrutiny and questioning. Yet the fact that she has to self-monitor when travelling is an example of how deeply the securitized habitus of flying while Muslim has been internalized (see also Nagra 2011).

Youth peer workers located in a low-income area of Toronto where the population was over 80 per cent Muslim described the sentiments of the young people in the community they served regarding the Passenger Protect Program, also known as the No-Fly List, which has disproportionately targeted Muslims (Jamil 2017; Nagra and Maurutto 2020):

> **Zafar:** The fact that there's security officials that are going in and harassing and questioning youth is a concern we already have. Police are discriminating against the racialized communities in the area. The tactics used by security officials is nothing more than a religious and racial profiling!

> **Idriss:** This is Canada and they can put me on a No-Fly List and don't have to tell me and I can't do anything about it ... what's next?!

> **Amna:** With no checks and balances! I'm fine with the No-Fly List if you find out something on someone, but it's almost like governmental anarchy where they can do it without evidence or proof.

Zafar's, Idriss's, and Amna's concerns for the vulnerable community they serve included over-policing and the presence of security officials. They regarded this as harassment against Muslim youth in the neigh-bourhood who are deemed suspect prior to evidence being produced to support such claims. Where law enforcement strategies rely on stereotypes versus evidence an antagonistic relationship with marginalized communities develops, breeding distrust and alienation. Having to challenge and deflect stereotypes that position Muslims as outsiders and outlaws by virtue of their faith, race, and identity takes an emotional and spiritual toll on those who must always prove their allegiance to the nation or risk being exiled from it.

Amira, who was visibly marked as Muslim by her hijab, found the gendered practices of surveillance targeted Muslim men more directly: "As a woman I have a privilege that I am not suspected as much as Muslim men. For example, I went to Palestine in the occupied territories through the Tel Aviv airport. I've seen that I was treated with a lot more respect and maybe more negligence than men. I was ignored more than Muslim men who had to go through security. They were treated really rudely because they were seen as a threat."

In many contexts, Muslim women are subject to both a hyper-vigilant gaze with respect to their sartorial choices being viewed as a threat to secular democracy (Quebec is an example) and being deemed a threat to public safety as potential "isis brides" who may be travelling to join armed conflict by violent Islamist movements abroad (see for example Saeed 2016). In other instances, as Amira noted, Muslim women may be viewed as less threatening than Muslim men for whom the terrorist moniker is a more salient trope regardless of their age, class, ethnicity, nationality, or background.

While Muslims are subjects of scrutiny and surveillance, the impact of these practices is rarely addressed. For example, fear was expressed by youth who felt that the current political climate made them more vulnerable to everything from judgment and surveillance to physical attack. Mahvish spoke of how this fear affected her and made her more self-conscious: "I have to be afraid for the first time in my life! Never until 2001 was I actually afraid for my security and for people's opinion ... because I think as women, we can all agree that we're constantly self-aware of every single action. We are conscious of what's around us and how people are viewing us and what the person next to me might think." The internalization of fear, vulnerability, and oppression can lead to trauma as a by-product of Islamophobia (Abu-Ras and Suarez 2009; Berzengi et al. 2017; Mahr and Nadeem 2019). As Mahvish pointed out, this is a heightened issue for Muslim women. While all women are conditioned to be vigilant regarding their personal safety against various forms of violence (domestic, sexual, etc.) being subjected to possible gendered Islamophobic violence requires an additional layer of caution and wariness.

Anxieties about cross-border travel also extend to Muslim children. Zabeda described a scenario where she and her relatives were panicked when they brought a children's book to the airport for fear that it would be read from the perspective of Orientalist fears and moral panic surrounding Muslims flying planes: "We were going to the US with my baby cousin and he had a book written for children about how to fly an airplane, and we were all so scared!! We were like, 'Why did we pack this?!!' Everyone was so scared because you feel that you are always on the lookout. Are we going to get judged? I should probably sit more nicely, smile more, people shouldn't be scared of me." The presumption of innocence cannot be assumed for Muslims in a climate of Islamophobic surveillance. The worry that something as innocent as a children's storybook can be used to validate the worst post-9/11 fears and suspicions about Muslims bombing planes is part of the internalized fear that Muslims face. This causes them to self-monitor and be aware of anything potentially incriminating that might be perceived by others as dangerous. Children's books are not immune from this self-policing when the content plays into contemporary moral panics. We need only recall the 2015 case of "Ahmed the clock boy" to consider how innocent actions become contrived as terrorist threats when Muslim children and youth are involved.

Ahmed Mohamed was a fourteen-year-old Muslim student living in Texas when he brought a homemade clock science project to school only to have the teacher call the police for fear that he had built a bomb. The photo of Ahmed handcuffed at school has become an iconic symbol of the surveillance attached to Muslim childhood where innocence can be easily lost. In a *Maclean's* article by the Associated Press (2015), Ahmad explains to the media, "I built the clock to impress my teacher, but when I showed it to her, she thought it was a threat to her. So, it was really sad she took the wrong impression of it." The story caught the attention of Barack Obama, who tweeted, "Cool clock Ahmed. Want to bring it to the White House? We should inspire more kids like you to like science. It's what makes America great." Ahmed's family subsequently launched an unsuccessful civil suit for damages against the school district and right-wing media, citing death threats stemming from Ahmed's labelling as a potential terrorist.

A federal judge dismissed the case with prejudice, denying the actions of the school district and police were the result of religious discrimination. Ahmed and his family have since relocated to Qatar (Limon 2018). For Muslim children and youth, the story remains a cautionary tale that speaks to how innocence cannot be unconditionally presumed when Islamophobia is normalized.

Patel (2012, 298) argues that "the rhetoric of 'national security' has always been about maintaining Canada as a predominantly white nation with a Judeo-Christian ethos, as national security is not only about keeping the physical borders of the nation safe but also about keeping its ideological borders as 'morally clean' as possible." Lamya contested the psychological and discursive borders that nationalism creates when "travelling while Muslim":

> I think the problem with nationalism is that the borders it creates mentally. Those borders might be physical and invisible lines, but they are also very entrenched in people's brains. So, you would have me as a Palestinian travelling around the Middle East, yeah, I have a Canadian passport but as soon as they find out I'm Palestinian, my Canadian passport means nothing. I'm treated like complete crap! I'm not allowed into malls. I get searched. I'm not allowed in certain parts of Jordan. It's just really messed up! Or even when I was in Dubai, it was like a double whammy because my husband is Pakistani and I'm Palestinian. We are both kind of hated.

For Lamya the borders she encounters as a Canadian Palestinian Muslim are at once physical, ontological, and discursive and are attached to how her body, faith, nationality, and identity are read within various geopolitical spaces.

Homi Bhabha (1994, 7) argues that the "social articulation of difference, from the minority perspective, is a complex, ongoing negotiation that seeks to authorize cultural hybridities that emerge in moments of historical transformation." He goes on to stipulate that these conditions position marginalized groups within contradictory and contingent relations of power. Lamya's example demonstrates how her travel experiences were dependent configurations of state, social, and political power vis-à-vis the construction and resonance of "Muslimness" and "Arabness" in a post-9/11 context.

SECURITY POLICIES, SURVEILLANCE, AND CIVIL RIGHTS

Aside from being subject to surveillance at universities and border crossings, Saleha discussed how the security industrial complex has affected Muslims in the workplace: "I have heard stuff in Toronto about people who have been constantly harassed by CSIS. CSIS coming to your workplace and interviewing you even though they don't have anything. But that whole effect of them coming to your workplace! Obviously, you're going to get fired or your coworkers are not going to have the same relationship with you afterwards, right?" The optics of being questioned by CSIS or other law enforcement agents at one's workplace would, as Saleha notes, create a potentially tainted work environment where trust among coworkers and management would be jeopardized.

As a chaplain working with American Muslim youth, Mustafa raised similar issues about how the emphasis on "radicalization" was overshadowing the way Muslim youth face the reality of spies, surveillance, and potential entrapment:

> Concerns about the radicalization of Muslim youth is at the forefront of people's minds. But my greater concern in the United States is that disenchanted young people are being entrapped by various law enforcement agencies. The FBI has been very active in sending agent provocateurs into the *masjids* (mosques) and into the circles of Muslim youth and targeting and inciting them to carry out acts they would not have arrived at themselves. We have some cases where young people who obviously have mental health issues are on trial for serious charges and crimes, but their mental faculties are somewhat diminished. So, my greater concern is not so much the process of radicalization of Muslim youth as much as I'm concerned about their being prompted and almost misdirected into certain areas.

In Muslim communities, the concerns range from how some vulnerable youth might be lured into violent militant groups to how they may also be lured and manipulated by law enforcement agents into incriminating circumstances. This dual concern underscores the various ways that Muslim youth are targeted by opposing forces and remain caught in the crosshairs of religious extremism and Islamophobic securitization.

Mahvish articulated a sense of confidence that she could handle the scrutiny from state surveillance, so long as the circumstances did not escalate to even greater Orwellian proportions:

> I'm not afraid ... I speak both languages in Canada fluently ... I can defend myself. I don't feel like there's a threat of terrorism against me as long as there aren't video cameras being set up on my corner or my phone lines are not being tapped or at least not to my knowledge. I feel relatively secure, not too afraid here ... I'm more afraid of what's happening in parts of the world where immigrant communities or individuals are unable to express themselves or to articulate their fears or are too afraid to do so and don't have the channels to do so.

Mahvish felt safer to exercise her agency and political voice in Canada as opposed to countries with more overt state repression. Having the cultural capital, political literacy, and institutional channels to express her concerns and self-advocate allowed Mahvish to feel she was well equipped should she be singled out for attention by Canadian security agents.

Other Muslims feel more reticent to report situations they face when crossing borders (Nagra 2017). The RCMP, Public Safety Canada, and CSIS have been reaching out to Muslim communities to be "partners in public safety" and engage in community roundtables as well as actively recruiting Muslims into their ranks. These initiatives speak to a desire to win the "hearts and minds" of young Muslims to make sure they do not end up on a path of radicalization, and yet these community forums are led by the very agencies policing and surveilling Muslims, which undermines the trust they hope to gain. For example, Saleha was involved in the RCMP Advisory Council in her local community but quickly became disenchanted with the process. She described doing training for RCMP officers and being asked questions about how she felt about the war in Afghanistan. Despite her efforts to present a different narrative about Islam and Muslims, there was a consistent default on stereotypical perceptions of Muslims as closet Taliban supporters: "When I am trying to tell them that Muslim youth are struggling a lot. There are a lot of difficult things that we're going through, and this is not helping. And then they throw something back, like, 'Well what do you think of Afghanistan?' I'm like, 'Well, Afghanistan is nothing to do with me!!' You are making the connection between

Afghanistan and me, right? So, you are kind of politicizing our identities in a way that we are not trying to do."

Saleha was also critical of how the security agencies were out of touch with the local Muslim community, which eventually made her decide to stop working with the RCMP Advisory Council: "If there are national security concerns in the local Muslim community, I have no idea where they are or how to address them because I have never met anybody who's planning anything violent. I have seen people who are angry. I have seen people who are frustrated. But I haven't heard anybody close to saying, 'Let's blow up the Parliament building,' or anything like that!!" Saleha recognized that legitimate community angst and anger could be misread as a potential threat to public safety and therefore felt that taking part in a security advisory group was counterproductive and not responsive to actual community issues.

Tariq had also participated in national security consultations as a youth community representative and concluded that the tension between security and human rights cannot be reconciled without addressing the underlying systemic racism at the heart of many security policies and initiatives:

> I think things like security certificates, racial profiling, Passenger Protect lists are absolutely forms of racism. From a civil rights point of view, they are basically infringements on human rights. The idea that you can't fly restricts your right to mobility. The fact that you could be detained for a couple days without any charge and then deported to your country, is obviously [a] huge human rights problem. I am very concerned about it. The thing about national security and racial profiling in the current age is most evident for Muslim communities, but it is an issue that can be associated with all minorities. In the same light, different stakeholders can come together against these ideals.

Tariq's awareness of the erosion of civil liberties in times of heightened securitization co-existed with the hope for solidarity among other racialized groups that experience similar circumstances.

This hope is important to foster the political alignment of marginalized communities who face similar challenges. The global context of surveillance and militarization affects policing and racial violence at home, a fact that has galvanized social movements such as Black Lives Matter. Connecting these issues on a wider geopolitical scale allows for a more integrated and intersectional analysis of racism, securitization, and militarism within the global politics of empire and imperialism. Tariq's observations gesture to possible spaces of collaborative solidarity and resistance in addressing these interrelated concerns.

THE SECURITIZED HABITUS AND PANOPTICON OF SELF-SURVEILLANCE

Youth participants were asked about how 9/11 impacted them since they all experienced this event and the Islamophobic backlash that ensued during their formative years. To my surprise many stated that "9/11 didn't affect them." However, when I would then ask them questions about the kind of activities their youth groups were doing, I would hear examples explaining how their MSA decided not to go up north to play paintball because they did not want to be seen as if they were running a jihadi training camp. But "9/11 didn't affect them." Or some said that they stopped playing violent video games on their laptops when sitting in public spaces so that people would not fear they were engaging in a rehearsal for a violent attack. But "9/11 didn't affect them." It became clear that for the 9/11 generation, self-surveillance was a normative practice. These youth were not aware of a world where securitization didn't impact their lives, and they were socialized into accommodating these conditions.

Maira (2016, 201) observes that the "surveillance stories" the 9/11 generation of Muslim youth tell "help to do the regulatory work of surveillance in deepening anxieties and producing self-regulation among those who are objects of surveillance by virtue of their race, religion, nationality, citizenship status or political activities." The surveillance Muslims have endured since 9/11 has resulted in a panopticon effect where people become self-surveilling subjects avoiding suspicion by second-guessing and curtailing otherwise innocent actions for fear they might be misread as subversive. Foucault (1995) describes this effect within a "panoptic society" where individuals are objectified as subjects under constant surveillance and in turn, they begin to regulate their own behaviour and actions in accordance with dominant norms. He outlines how the regulatory gaze is inverted and interiorized so that the subjects themselves perform the work of the governmental surveillance: "There is no need for arms, physical violence, material constraints. Just a gaze. An inspecting gaze, a gaze which each individual under its weight will end by interiorizing to the point that he is his own overseer, each individual thus exercising this surveillance over and against himself" (Foucault 1995, 155).

I refer to the way Muslim youth navigate the realities of the post-9/11 context as the "panopticon of self-surveillance" where they internalize the regulatory gaze they are subject to and hence become self-policing. Zabeda expressed how these existential fears reinforced the internalized panoptic experience: "I think even when there isn't surveillance, we feel there is and we are scared. We are on edge. So even if people aren't watching us, we feel that we do need to be on the lookout and we have to be on our best behaviour."

Safia and Ateeka echoed similar feelings of being watched and interiorizing the gaze:

> **Safia:** I think they've just been trying to be more careful, so the cops don't come after you. Make sure you have everything ready at the airport so you know you're not held back … make sure you're good … make sure you don't do this, make sure you don't do anything that could target you! It's a big fear and that shouldn't be.

> **Ateeka:** I'm Brown and I'm Muslim. So, I have two issues to worry about!! I'm always making sure that I don't look suspicious. Why do I have to do that?! I don't find anyone else doing that! Like on my passport I'm always making sure I have all the papers … my bag is not like … I'm not looking suspicious. That's always something I'm worried about no matter what it is.

Speaking as a Muslim and mother of two young adult sons the concerns about the surveillance of youth are not purely academic. When my son was president of the MSA at his university, he told me they were planning a retreat in a wooded area so they could have a bonfire and "chill." I was immediately concerned about how the optics of [a] large group of Muslim youth lighting fires and praying outdoors might be perceived by others. We discussed this with other MSA members in a focus group, and Yusuf shared why they had to consider how their innocent actions would be read because they are Muslim:

> It's not just how other people are going to see us but how we see ourselves. Like how we internalize it. Even when we were planning the MSA retreat we wanted to do something in a forest

like go build a bonfire. But then we had to start thinking about that. And it's even kind of funny. We were joking that if somebody did see all us visibly Muslim folks there all kinds of suspicion[s] that would arise. So, there's that type of thing that we internalize that fear. We have to monitor what we do so it doesn't come off as suspicious even if it's not.

For many Muslims already feeling under siege, the securitized habitus and hyper-surveillance of the post-9/11 world impacts daily activities and choices (see also Maira 2016). The internalization of the regulatory gaze causes Muslim youth to be wary of how they may come to be associated with perceptions of terrorism and radicalization (see chapter 6). Similarly, a study of the effects of surveillance and security measures on Canadian Muslim men reported a "chilling effect" that created fear, paranoia, and anxiety along with pressure to monitor their behaviour to avoid undue suspicion (Akseer 2018).

Idil described how Somali Muslim youth self-censored themselves because of the fears of their community and family: "You have the right to say things, but the youth or community members might tell each other not to say those same things out loud. I think the youth are censoring themselves because of the fear. It is reality. Laws don't apply because there is no equality. If you are a Muslim woman or man, you will be profiled differently from the next person who may be in exactly the same circumstances and have the same beliefs. That is the reality."

Where civil liberties can be arbitrarily suspended in a "state of exception," Muslims are fearful that the law will not protect them and is instead being used to target them. Muslim youth can feel inhibited to speak freely for fear they will be misunderstood and vilified or subject to arrest or detention. In a study of Islamophobia on UK campuses, Guest et al. (2020) found that the Prevent policy discouraged free speech on campuses among staff and students when it came to talking about the subject of Islam, especially when the topics involved terrorism, fundamentalism, or military conflict. Zahir spoke of the perils of misunderstood speech and alienation: "There is definitely a concern post-9/11 that's in the air. There is a certain vibe. You always have to watch out not to have your words misinterpreted. You don't want to leave open-ended sentences that someone can take away a wrong message from. Inside the community, there is a feeling of being *the other* and a feeling of victimization. Whether or not that's true, that's the feeling out there."

Similarly, Sohail, a South Asian international student, described how he resorted to self-censorship to avoid having innocent speech misinterpreted and jeopardizing his academic career and future: "Being a Muslim automatically makes you want to censor a few things. Because I am an international student, I am a little more careful. I don't want to compromise my education, an investment from my family. I can't risk it, so I have to follow a strict line." The stakes are high for international students who are fearful that if they do not toe the line they will be seen as trouble-makers, which could forfeit their education. Cases like Project Thread, discussed earlier in the chapter, which targeted as potential terrorists Pakistani nationals studying in Canada, make other international students fearful should they end up under the scrutiny of authorities. These fears are compounded by the fact that precedent has shown innocence is not a guarantee for fair treatment under Canadian immigration and security laws.

Reasons why youth felt on guard and compelled to self-monitor their behaviour and actions were tied to other political issues. For example, Saleha was impacted by the Maher Arar case where a Syrian Canadian dual citizen was detained at JFK airport when returning home from a family holiday in Tunis. Arar, an engineer, was suspected of having ties to Al-Qaeda and was held in solitary confinement for two weeks in the US without charge and later deported to Syria where he was tortured. He was eventually cleared of all charges by the Syrian and Canadian governments. The information that placed him under suspicion was provided to US authorities by the RCMP who later issued an apology to Arar.

The differential treatment of Muslims under federal immigration and security policies creates feelings of insecurity, frustration, and resentment, as Saleha lamented: "You see things like that [Maher Arar] and you know, that wouldn't have happened to somebody who was not Muslim. I think the pervasiveness of anti-terrorism legislation is not really fully known or seen by the ordinary person, right, until something like that happens. Or until you see someone who is targeted destroyed." Arar's case is a cautionary tale for Muslims who feel they may be subject to similar treatment through state policies that target their faith, ethnicity, race, and identity. Muslims are increasingly alienated when their citizenship and belonging are questioned rather than affirmed.

Study participants expressed concerns that spies might be secretly surveilling them. Suheir recalled reports about spies at an Islamic school: "I was just talking to one of my friends and she was saying how there was an article written somewhere about secret police at an Islamic school. They went skiing, and they put someone who is spying, a secret worker, and he was working at the ski place, but he was spying on these kids! These are kids. They wanted to have fun, why is this still happening?" It is unclear whether this was a verified report or panoptic paranoia. Yet they considered that since the NYPD was spying on Islamic schools, restaurants, community centres, and mosques (Pilkington 2018), rumours might well be facts. The truth can be difficult to discern in a climate of fear and paranoia. Ali (2016, 79) notes that in the US "young people need not be watched, for they watch themselves and their peers through disciplining particular forms of engagement out of public space."

Sareena, Innaya, and Ziad feared they were under surveillance in their homes and in public spaces:

Sareena: I don't think I'm being paranoid but I feel like my lines are being bugged and everything ...

JZ: What makes you think that?

Sareena: Just really weird things happening on the phone these days ... I know I'm not doing anything weird, but they check everyone these days. I feel like I can't even speak my own opinion. If it was a Canadian person saying the same things I say, it would be seen differently. It would not be used against me. I can't even talk to my own friends normally sometimes. Even though I am not saying anything bad, but you feel like you have to watch everything you do these days.

Innaya: I know one friend of mine is very careful when he texts and chats that he doesn't say, "That was so bomb!"

JZ: Yeah, avoid any terms that involve explosives!

Sareena: Even when I just said the word "bomb" earlier, I was like, "Oh, no!"

Ziad: You have to rephrase and substitute words in the sentence of a joke. I've been told be careful of the jokes that you say nowadays, so I'm not really as funny as I used to be!!

In other interviews, participants were careful not to make "terrorist jokes" in public for fear that they would be taken seriously. Sareena's comment about how speech is read differently when uttered by a "Canadian person" versus the policing of Muslim speech underscores how a Canadian/Muslim dichotomy is internalized by some youth as mutually exclusive categories.

Ateeka described how her family's experiences living under a repressive regime in Libya influenced their adaptation to life in Canada. Gaddafi's dictatorship was a shadow from the past that created existential fears and political paranoia for her family. In Canada they felt they were still under the regulatory gaze of the state. Ateeka described how these fears and insecurities infiltrated the sanctity of their home:

> Someone's hearing this. Someone is gonna arrest you. My dad is so scared! Even if we say, "Oh Bush did all this, he's hiding Osama Bin Laden" just around the dinner table, he'd be like, "Ssshhh ... don't say this!! No political discussion in my house!" He's scared. If I'm on the phone with my dad and I'll be like, "Remember the India bombing thing?" He'd say, "Don't say stuff like that on the phone!! We could be arrested!! Someone could be listening to our phone calls right now!!" So that's fear for me. Youth might come off strong, but we're scared.

Panoptic fears may be imported as Ateeka's example shows, but they are compounded by the realities of surveillance in Canada. Many Muslims emigrate from countries characterized by repressive political regimes and state violence. Arriving in the West, these experiences converge with diasporic anxieties creating ongoing political paranoia and angst. A securitized habitus is created where looking over your shoulder, self-censoring, modifying your behaviour, speech, comportment, and clothing are strategies to avoid undue scrutiny in a post-9/11 context. The panoptic gaze reinforces feelings of alterity and fuels the trauma that Muslim youth experience growing up under the spectre of suspicion. The security industrial complex and its archipelago of interconnected disciplinary networks shape the experiences of the 9/11 generation of Muslim youth and govern their actions and choices in a post-9/11 state of exceptionalism.

6

Being Cast as the Bogeyman

Muslim Youth on "Radicalization"

To be a "radical" once held a broad resonance and represented involvement in a variety of justice-oriented ideals and movements (see for example Bramadat 2014). When applied to Muslims the term has been reduced to a label that conjures images of wild-eyed marauding Muslim terrorists wearing suicide belts and seeking to overthrow Western civilization and replace it with an Islamic state. Hollywood's stock Muslim terrorist character has a deep legacy within Orientalist fears and fantasies and is reproduced as the Islamist bogeyman in Islamophobic conspiracy theories as well as in security discourses. The 9/11 generation of Muslim youth faces the discursive ambush of this term and must contend with the consequences of being associated with this category. Yet, how they grapple with this labelling and its repercussions and why they think some youth among them might fall prey to violent ideological pathways have not been considered. This chapter highlights the voices of the 9/11 generation as they talk about radicalization and provide important insights into understanding the problem.

CSIS has focused its attention on Muslim youth and homegrown terrorism as well as on how they evolved from radicals to violent terrorists through a "jihadization" process. Reporting on a declassified CSIS report, MacLeod (2008) notes that Canada's intelligence service says a "very rapid process is transforming some youths from angry activists into jihadist terrorists, intent on killing for their religion." The same CSIS report also warns that "Western jihadist youth counterculture" is the next phase in the evolution of global terrorism, and that "generation jihad" poses "a significant threat to national security" and "a clear and present danger to Canada and its allies" (S. Bell 2006, n.p.).

These reports confirm that religious radicalization has been identified as a prominent threat by Canada's main security agency and Muslim youth are viewed as subjects of concern when it comes to safeguarding national security.

According to the Centre for the Prevention of Radicalization Leading to Violence (CPRLV), radicalization can be understood and defined as "a process whereby people adopt extremist belief systems – including the willingness to use, encourage or facilitate violence – with the aim of promoting an ideology, political project or cause as a means of social transformation." An Angus Reid public opinion poll on "Radicalization and Homegrown Terrorism" found that four in ten Canadians believe "radicalized individuals" live in their communities,[1] and "radical Islamic attitudes" were cited by a majority of Canadians (54 per cent) as a cause for "a great deal of concern." The survey concluded that "homegrown terrorism is a 'serious threat' to this country rather than something that has been 'overblown' by politicians and the media."[2] When asked to assess what they saw as the causes of homegrown radicalization, nearly half (47 per cent) said that religious or cultural factors are to blame, and roughly one in three blamed feelings of marginalization and mental illness (Angus Reid 2018, 6).[3] Public concern was focused on "the possibility of attacks motivated by radical Islamic beliefs" and not on the prospect of White supremacist or White nationalist homegrown terrorism, though both concerns were acknowledged. The same survey found that 54 per cent believed that radical Islam is cause for "a great deal of concern," while 44 per cent said the same of White supremacy. These findings demonstrate that "terror" is synonymous with Muslim bodies, markers, and identities.

Supporting this negative association, Sian (2015) notes that while far right extremists are often portrayed as victims or angry, vulnerable, misguided youth, the focus on Muslim radicals emphasizes faith, culture, and religion. While most Canadians saw the Muslim community as a partner in the fight against radicalization and domestic terrorism, rather than the problem, they did not feel that community leaders were vocal enough in condemning these acts (Angus Reid 2018). Therefore, while Muslims were viewed as "good" so long as they were partners in identifying radicals in their midst and condemning their actions, they still could be deemed "bad" if those condemnations were not loudly proclaimed. As Muslims scramble to fall on the right side of the "good Muslim/bad Muslim" archetype, public perceptions, suspicions, and accusations keep re-inscribing this divide.

It is not my intent to try to ascertain the pathways of radicalization based on my study participants' insights, rather the aims in this chapter are to (a) better understand how Muslim youth make sense of these actions; (b) examine how the collective negative labelling affects them; and (c) examine the dialectical relationship between Islamophobia and radicalization. In our discussions, participants sought to make sense of Muslim youth radicalization not to justify the actions of misguided youth who engage in acts of violence but rather to provide a context for how some might become lured into various kinds of reactionary ideological movements. Rather than be held captive by how others perceived and labelled them, these youth expressed illuminating views that allowed for a better understanding of how the narrative of radicalization has affected their sense of identity (individually and collectively) and how they engaged in ways to resist and shift these narrow and limiting ideologies. It is important to examine the impact of how the "radical" label affects Muslims and how this false narrative has real consequences in their lives.

It is also instructive to gauge participants' responses to the phenomenon of the small number of Muslim youth who have taken the path of extreme ideologies that at times have led to violence. Being subject to many of the same social pressures and pull factors, the perspectives of the vast majority of Muslim youth who do not seek these pathways helps ground an understanding of what lures some youth into destructive ideologies while others articulate their dissent and resistance in more productive ways. Before turning to the narratives of Muslim youth, I first outline the contested drivers of radicalization. It is useful to set the stage with an overview of what radicalization research has to say about the factors that might lure young Muslims into such dangerous liaisons.

MOTIVATORS FOR JIHADIST RADICALIZATION

There is a variegated set of conditions, dispositions, and practices that in different permutations may or may not lead some youth down a pathway toward militant views and potential violence. This uncertain chain of causation is the unresolved paradox in radicalization research; the factors that may be a catalyst toward extreme ideas and violent behaviours for some do not incite violent ideologies or actions in others. Given that there is a very small minority of Muslim youth in Western nations who gravitate toward these pathways, it is difficult to discern what the complex triggers are let alone make any decisive or generalizable claims. The practice of racial and religious profiling lacks clear, consistent markers that would indicate someone might be inclined toward violent extremism.[4] Empirical evidence does not support a specific "profile" of a Muslim "radical." Therefore, racial and religiously targeted surveillance and profiling are part of a pernicious and vicious cycle that exacerbate rather than ameliorate the problem (Sageman 2008; Abbas 2019). Moreover, as Kundnani (2015, 123) observes, "[R]adicalization discourse claims predictive powers but lacks explanatory powers." As a result, the often spurious and unsubstantiated claims feed into the faulty premises underlying the CVE industry.

There are various social, political, economic, and ideological factors that underlie the root causes of radicalization; however, as Rabasa and Bernard (2015, 2) point out, "[W]hile the presence or absence of these variables helps shape the conditions under which radicalization is more or less likely, structural variables rarely bear out as proximate causes of terrorism." Kundnani (2015, 140) furthers the point by arguing that what is sought lies beyond predictability and ready-made criteria: "[W]hile policing agencies search for scholarship that can give them a magical formula to predict who will be a future terrorist, the microlevel question of what causes one person rather than another in the same political context to engage in violence is probably beyond analysis and best seen as unpredictable."

For example, psychological approaches have limitations and cannot point to specific drivers for radicalization and the adoption of extremist views, yet these approaches are being employed in service of "deradicalization" programs (Trip et al. 2019). What motivates and potentially "causes" something called radicalization is disputed epistemic and sociological terrain and engaging in it runs the risk of authorizing perspectives that have been destructive to Muslim communities. Kundnani (2012, 5) responds to the question, "[W]hy do some individual Muslims support an extremist interpretation of Islam that leads to violence?" by qualifying the fact that "[t]his question, of course, takes terrorist violence to be a product of how Islam is interpreted and, therefore, renders irrelevant any consideration of terrorism not carried out by Muslims." Echoing this stance, I undertake this inquiry to dislodge the settled notions that underwrite the false equation between Islam and terrorism.

Religion has been the primary culprit associated with jihadist radicalization. Islam is often cast as inherently violent and anti-Western with predatory aims for global domination. This has been a prevalent narrative within Islamophobia circles, the news outlets that purvey anti-Muslim ideologies, and in Orientalist academic works. Samuel Huntington's (1996) influential "clash of civilizations" thesis and Bernard Lewis's (1990) "roots of Muslim rage" set the stage for academic writing that supported the idea of Islam as the West's post–Cold War nemesis and a nefarious threat that would lead to the downfall of Western civilization.[5] Yet notable studies have challenged the assertion that the Islamic faith is a causal factor in the radicalization process (Roy 1994, 2017; Pape 2006; Sageman 2008; Khosrokhavar 2009; Atran 2010; Pape and Feldman 2010; Abbas 2011, 2019; Kundnani 2012, 2015). Research has instead pointed to how religion is instrumentalized in service of violent movements that allow for emotions like frustration, anger, moral outrage, and humiliation to be translated into an Islamic register (Khosrokhavar 2009).

Sageman (2008) explains that while the aims of global jihadist movements are couched in a religious vocabulary, they are overtly political in nature. Abbas (2019) also finds that religion is used as camouflage and political cover rather than a central driver in the process of radicalization. Roy (2017) notes that religious scripture is secondary within the jihadi imaginary and that their internet posts are more action-oriented and geared to restoring the honour of the *ummah* against foreign aggression. Sageman's (2008), Khosrokhavar's (2009), and Roy's (2017) research in the European context confirms that jihadis are not well versed in religion,[6] and the "keyboard jihadis" who self-radicalize on the internet are not familiar with Arabic.[7] As a further case in point, Hasan (2014) notes that some British wannabe jihadists ordered copies of *Islam for Dummies* and *The Koran for Dummies* from Amazon before heading to Syria.[8]

The phenomenon of Islamism as a political and social movement is largely viewed as a response to and retreat from secular modernity. Many studies that attempt to make sense of violent Islamist movements cite the failure of secular modernization projects in the Middle East and North Africa (MENA) region (Wiktorowicz 2004, 2005; Sageman 2008; Khosrokhavar 2009). The notion that Islam is incompatible with modernity and the values of secular liberalism places Muslims in an antagonistic relationship with the West. Mazarr (2007, ix), for example, refers to "radical Islam" as a manifestation of "unmodern men in a modern world" who are waging a "war on modernity." The Manichean cultural and civilizational divides that this rhetoric re-inscribes animates Islamophobic fears of atavistic and uncivilized religious zealotry as popularized within Orientalist literature. These notions continue to underwrite the ideological formations and military agendas within the war on terror.

Abbas (2011, 139) outlines Barber's (1996) views on how the "jihadi world" meets the soft imperialism of "McWorld culture," where the vices of unbridled Western capital consumerism and homogenization of global markets create a "dialectic response to modernity." The interdependence of these culturally irreconcilable social and political systems results in a dialectic exchange that is mutually constitutive. As Roy (1994, 1) argues, "[M]odernity itself produces its own forms of protest," citing how political Islam has arisen from that encounter as a "third world movement" with anti-imperialist roots.[9] These movements are understood as failing to adapt to Western political modernity. Such views emphasize Western exceptionalism and Eurocentric hegemony and override the existence of multiple and overlapping modernities. So long as Islam is viewed as incompatible with Western modernity it will continue to be relegated as a pre-modern and illiberal threat.

Fundamentalism is another attribute attached to Islam as an anti-modern force. This term is used in association with Islamic revival movements connected to the Saudi-inspired Wahhabi and Salafi ideologies that follow narrow and literal doctrinal interpretations and practices. According to Sayyid (2003, 4), "Islamic fundamentalism is considered to be the vehicle by which many of the victims of the western enterprise seek revenge and redress" (see also Wiktorowicz 2004; Sageman 2008). The rhetorical value of the term is employed as a coded language that invokes fear and securitized panic where the repertoire of "veiled (Muslim) women and bearded (Muslim) men, book burners and suicide bombers have emerged as fundamentalist icons enjoying recurrent Hollywood canonization" (Sayyid 2003, 7–8). Sayyid prefers to move away from the language of fundamentalism, which fuels Western anxieties and is otherwise limiting,[10] and instead focus on "Islamism" or political Islam. He defines Islamism as a political discourse and a political project that asserts Muslim subjectivity (Sayyid 2003, 16). While often characterized as a "full[-]blooded attempt to reconstruct society on Islamic principles," (translated into Islamophobic idioms, Muslims in the West are a Trojan Horse ready to unleash a violent overthrow of democracy), Islamism is based on a wide spectrum and can also manifest as "diffuse strategies of 'intellectual moral reform' of civil society" (Sayyid 2003, 17). Essentializing all Islamist groups as violent, pre-modern, and irrational reduces a broad political spectrum to the most extreme manifestations.

As noted in the preface, the MSAs at my university were politically oriented toward the Islamist group HT in 2005, when I started my position. Followers of HT seek the return of a central religious authority or caliphate to the Muslim world. They see this reform as offering the best means to inculcate Islamic principles and live by them. Their focus is on aligning Muslims to their political and ideological goals and the narrow theological purview that goes along with them. They do not endorse or promote violent means to achieve their aims (unlike the militant offshoot Muhajiroon) and instead operate on a philosophy of gradual ideological, political, and cultural change within Muslim communities. Among the HT-inspired MSAs I interacted with, I found they showed little interest in combatting Islamophobia (despite using it as an alibi to call others to the cause) nor did they promote any political concerns that were not connected to the goal of a return to a Muslim caliphate.

According to Sayyid (2014, 118), "The growing prominence of the idea of the Caliphate among Muslims can be seen as a dawning recognition that the institution of the Caliphate may provide an escape route for Muslims from a world of constant subjugation and marginalization." In this way we can see that colonial modernity has bred the dialectical development of political Islamist movements that are finding renewed impetus in the post-9/11 imperial era. As Abbas (2011, 39) notes, HT has galvanized around what it regards as the "imperialistic, non-Islamic control of Muslim lands seized by the kuffar (non-believers)." The occupation of Palestine through Zionist settler colonialism is a cautionary tale among HT circles. The failure of the Arab and Muslim communities to resist this domination gives renewed impetus to their cause to unite Muslims under a centralized banner of religious and political solidarity. The restoration of the idea of a transnational, pan-Islamic caliphate has been connected to groups like Al-Qaeda and used by the US and its allies to safeguard against what they see as a form of "Islamist revanchism" (Sayyid 2014). Islamist revival movements spark fear in Western nations where they are viewed as the source of potential radicalization and extremist violence, although most of these groups do not support or condone such actions. Nonetheless, in Western political and cultural terms,

Islamism in any form has become synonymous with a source of potential radical and cultural upheaval, if not the violent overthrow of Western civilization itself.[11]

In Western nations, HT groups reject political participation in democratic processes (such as voting in elections) or the promotion of nationalism, which they regard as conflicting with their goals for a supranational system of Islamic governance. In a study of Islamic radicalism in the UK, Abbas (2011) identifies HT recruitment operating largely through campus-based student networks that secretly distribute their propaganda, which caused them to be banned by student unions and college authorities in Britain in the 1990s. The HT student group at my university disbanded a few years after I started my position, once the key leaders graduated. They were eventually replaced by far more open-minded students, who shifted the culture to a more inclusive space in contrast to the limiting ideological and political goals of their predecessors.

Political drivers are especially salient in animating extremist causes and violent actions. For example, Pape and Feldman (2010) identify the conditions of occupation as a cause for suicide bombing. Based on sociological data from 315 terrorist attacks and 462 suicide attackers, Pape (2006, 21) found that religion is rarely the root cause of suicide attacks; instead, the primary catalyst is "coercing a foreign state that has military forces in what the terrorists see as their homeland to take those forces out." Collective victimization and humiliation have been cited as central to understanding how imperialist violence and militarism impact ideologies of retribution. According to Khosrokhavar (2009, 191), "Victimization brings Muslims together within an imaginary community where suffering is the paramount feature: Bosnia, Iraq, Afghanistan, Palestine, Chechnya, etc. Disaffected youth extend their own mental agony to other parts of the world, their task being facilitated by TV and the internet, which broadcast vividly Muslims' unequal fight." Currently India, Kashmir, Myanmar, and China are added to the list of countries along with Palestine, where Muslim populations are subject to extensive Islamophobic nationalism, militaristic and state violence and surveillance, denial of citizenship, and even genocide (as is the case with the Rohingya in Myanmar and the Uyghurs in China). Religious extremism and political and economic imperialism backed by a military and security industrial complex are mutually reinforcing links in a vicious cycle (Abbas 2019). Focusing on only one part of the equation (i.e., religious extremism versus political and economic imperialism) allows the other to gather strength and momentum.

Khosrokhavar (2009) argues that the sense of victimization experienced by the *ummah* as a result of global conflicts and rampant Islamophobia in Western nations is one of the drivers behind jihadization. He argues that this dynamic fuels "humiliation by proxy" and a "subculture of internalized indignity," leading to a sense of helplessness and withdrawal into an "imaginary world of estrangement." The hypermasculinized response to these conditions is a means to recuperate power and subordination (Khosrokhavar 2009; Abbas 2019).[12] Death features in these subcultures to demonstrate the fearless valour of the Muslim who is transformed through martyrdom from "slave to master" (Khosrokhavar 2009, 198). These dynamics translate into a cult-like fascination with emulating emblematic jihadi heroes and engaging in a vernacular known as "jihadi cool" which makes it "cool" and thrilling to be part of a clandestine movement as "warriors in pursuit of fame and glory" (Sageman 2008; Atran 2010; Joosse, Bucerius, and Thompson 2015). Among the small number of Muslims engaged in these activities, economically marginalized youth are more likely to become active in these subcultures in Europe than in North America; however, there is no consensus that economic conditions are predictive of involvement in radicalization or extremist behaviour. Failed integration policies in Western nations leading to a lack of social cohesion are cited as mitigating factors. This logic is often used to promote ethnonationalist values and cultural rehabilitation for Muslim immigrants lacking the predisposition for multicultural modernity. These deficit paradigms play into the problematic racial logics of CVE programs.

In other psychosocial theories, Wiktorowicz (2004) describes the rationale for participation in radical movements as based on factors such as gaining a sense of belonging and purpose amid social anomie, despair, and cultural anxiety. Atran (2010, xii–xiii) breaks down the complexities of this phenomenon to a central overriding factor: "Terrorists generally do not commit terrorism because they are extraordinarily vengeful or uncaring, poor, or uneducated, humiliated or lacking in self-esteem, schooled as children in radical religion or brainwashed, criminally minded or suicidal or sex starved for virgins in heaven. Terrorists for the most part are not nihilists, but extreme moralists-altruists fastened to a hope gone awry."

Similarly, Abbas (2019, 74) maintains that young people drawn to these subcultures are searching for "hope and opportunity to replace fear and discord." He argues that jihadist groups and the rhetoric and ideologies they promote, operate in a symbiotic relationship with far right extremism, with Islamophobia fuelling these dialectical movements. Islamophobia further fuels extremist logics on both sides (be it religious extremism or far right political ideologies) and should be viewed as a threat to civil liberties and democratic values. The nexus between Islamophobia and radicalism (whether jihadist or far right) cannot be ignored and must be acknowledged in underscoring the need to combat anti-Muslim oppression. The narratives that follow explore the perspectives of Muslim youth who are impacted by the jihadist bogeyman trope, despite never engaging in radicalized behaviours or actions.

NARRATIVE ANALYSIS: POLITICAL UNDERPINNINGS AND RELIGIOUS ALIBIS

Many participants felt that Islam had been hijacked on 9/11, and the faith they revered had been perverted by both media and fanatics. They saw Islam as peace-loving and just and were frustrated by public perceptions that cast Islam and Muslims as radicals out to destroy the West. Their concerns were not unfounded. Jiwani's (2017) study of 400 articles in the *Globe and Mail*, a Canadian national newspaper, described a predominate pattern of portraying Muslim youth as "barbarians" seeking to destroy Canadian society. More than half the stories that refer to Muslim youth in her sample focused on radicalization and terrorism, criminal activity, violating deportation orders, and their inability to assimilate into Canadian society. These depictions reflect narrow stereotypes of Muslim youth as dangerous foreigners, even if they are Canadian born.

Other predominant representations depict religious leaders promoting cultural chauvinism and narrow interpretations of religious texts that stoke extremist sentiments. The voices from the *minba*r (pulpit) may purvey problematic readings of religious texts based on authoritarian views. Not all fundamentalist views, however, promote violence or aggression. The majority of Muslims denounce the violence derived from authoritarianism and religious zealotry. By centring religion and extremist ideologies as the sole culprit of this phenomenon, we lose sight of how the structural relations of power and domination under-score global unrest and create the conditions for violent extremism to flourish.

Study participants were quick to redirect the source of the extremism as being political rather than religious, which echoes the research findings noted above. There was a commonly expressed understanding among the youth that geopolitical struggles that imposed Western imperialism and militarism in Muslim majority countries led to reaction-ary movements. They unequivocally asserted that drastic and violent measures like suicide bombing have no basis in Islam and are con-demned. Miguel offered a counter-theology of 'radicalization': "Islam is a religion of moderation and balance. It's not a religion of extrem-ism. The words of the Prophet are very clear: 'Don't be extreme in what you do.' Those Hadiths are very authentic and very clear. It's a huge problem because it [radicalization] doesn't follow the Sunna of the Prophet and it just keep[s] giving more room to people using those examples as means to bash Islam." He argued that the term "radical" needed to be removed from its connection to political violence and redirected to being "radically spiritual," referring to the peaceful tenants of the faith. He rejected using Islam as a tool for political ends.

In a focus group discussion, Mohammed provided his thoughts on what might be motivating some youth to engage in violent and fun-damentally un-Islamic acts: "I guess when you push someone enough, they will push you back. Some people are calling it: 'enough is enough.' It's time for us to take a stand. Sometimes these stands are taken in different forms. Some individuals will try to get a group to go back to our scriptures and see what our religion tells us to do. If someone guides them the right way, there wouldn't be a problem."

Tariq pointed out that in some cases, family socialization might not offer appropriate guidance based on Islamic principles. If extreme ideological views are espoused within families, this would affect vulnerable and impressionable youth. Innaya felt heightened discrimina-tion and the lack of a strong social network could lead vulnerable alienatèd youth to become frustrated and follow more destructive options to seek redress for political grievances: "You and your family and people around you are discriminated against, then that is all you see, and not the other side of things. And if you do not have a strong social network to say that those are just specific crazies or it is not always like that, then you will be inclined to think it's time to take a stance."

Many participants warned that the war on terror can lead to "self-fulling prophecies" among marginalized youth. For example, Bilal referred to the situation in Pakistan, where his family originated from, and how the proliferation of US drone strikes under the Obama administration and high numbers of civilian deaths created the conditions for reactionary extremism and self-fulfilling prophecies to take root. He recounted the "word on the street" as a local perspective on the war on terror: "There was this one quote that really struck me, from a villager, 'You killed my whole family, none of them were terrorists. But you're turning me into one. If this is what you want from me, if you are labelling my whole family into terrorists, then I am now what you want me to be.'" The cycle of violence depicted here reminds us that many innocent people pay the price for the dialectics of war.

Ateeka explained how the negative perceptions of Muslim youth limit the narratives through which others come to know of them, which can, in turn, affect how they see themselves. As an international student, Ateeka experienced anti-Muslim discrimination and harassment when she moved to New Brunswick from Dubai. She felt the alienation first-hand and talked about how this might be processed differently by youth who feel more allegiance to their countries "back home" as opposed to Canada if they are not accepted and feel like they do not belong. Ateeka described how the self-fulfilling prophecy could play out in this context: "It's like blaming a kid for something he didn't do and he'll do it. So, it's having that negative effect on youth and making them angry." When Muslim youth become estranged from a society that sees them as suspect, dangerous, and undesirable, this can create the breeding ground for recruitment into reactionary movements abroad (Wiktorowicz 2005; Sageman 2008; Abbas 2011, 2019). Problems arise when alienation from society becomes a rationale for targeting these youth with undue surveillance rather than addressing the conditions that create this estrangement.

Anisa suggested that the stronger indicators of violent behaviour were not always political: "I imagine that the people who are attracted to super violent acts have their own personal reasons, just like mental health issues or like coming from really violent homes. The same reasons that anyone commits a violent act. They don't always have to necessarily be political or religious." The notion that violence committed by Muslims must always be religiously or politically motivated places these crimes in a different category based on the Islamophobic fears and racial inscriptions that govern these distinctions. The social determinants that create pathways leading to individual criminal activity (social exclusion, poverty, etc.) are ignored in Islamophobic formulations in lieu of fearmongering that places Muslims in a category of inherent political and cultural deviance dictated by Islam. The perceived epistemological and ontological difference this narrative generates becomes essentialized and justifies and reinforces public safety measures that target Muslims for surveillance, profiling, and intensified scrutiny.

Zahir contested and rejected the label "radicalization," arguing that the civilizational divides and racial and religious dichotomies generated through dystopic radicalization narratives result in irreconcilable differences between "Us" and "Them":

> I hate the term "radicalization," but it's common these days. There's a concern about the creating of the *Other* and *Us versus Them* mentality. Muslims are feeling under the microscope and on the hot seat. There is a tendency for some to react and say that the rest of the society does not understand who we are and are out to get us. That's not a healthy way of living in a multicultural society like Canada. Radicalization is a by-product of the *Us versus Them* mentality and it's something that we need to work against.

Zahir points out how the *Us versus Them* dichotomy positions Muslim youth as outsiders to the nation and potential outlaws. Being coded as socially deviant "folk devils" galvanizes the rationale for moral panics as a justifiable threat rather than a product of racial anxiety and cultural angst (Cohen [1972] 2014; Jiwani and Al-Rawi 2019). The actual threat of violent jihadi Muslim youth in Canada is based on Islamophobic social anxieties instead of evidence-based concerns. For example, Beyer (2014) asserts that there is little evidence to support concerns over potential radical behaviour among Canadian Muslim youth. In a study of thirty-five Muslim males, Beyer found the modelling factors associated with radicalization were not significantly present in his sample. Nonetheless, being a potential radical and jihadist are prevalent stereotypes that frame public perceptions of Muslim men.

I asked Safeeya, a teacher in Toronto, if she was worried about Muslim youth radicalization. She recognized that it was possible for youth to become disaffected and "pushed to the fringes," making them potentially vulnerable, but did not feel this was a major concern:

Well, I mean, not [concerns] in the "CNN headline" news
sense! I think any group of youth has the potential to become
radicalized if they are continually pushed to the fringes.
Do I see this as the case with our youth? Yes, in many ways,
Muslim youth deal with a whole set of assumptions by society
just because they're Muslim. I think that needs to change
systematically. We can ensure we don't have radicalization
in our community by dealing with the challenges that are
specific to our youth. Most of them are just good kids that
need an outlet for their frustration.

Many youth echoed the sense of frustration that Safeeya described.
In a focus group of university students in Southern Ontario, we discussed
the 2013 Boston bombings. Rania tried to make sense of the senseless
violence and what factors may have been at play. We discussed their
frustration about the war on terror and the dystopic global conditions
of militarism, violence, imperialism, poverty, and occupation that
Muslims face. The inability to respond to these tensions in productive
ways often left only destructive possibilities. Rania warned that the
pent-up frustration could be become directed in negative ways in
the absence of meaningful outlets for this political anger and dissent:
"I think, the problem is that these susceptible youth that get involved
with these like, fringe organizations or whatever they are, have that
same frustration but they don't have that outlet to deal with it."

The discussion raised concerns that mosques and community leaders
were out of touch with the lived experiences and frustration of Muslim
youth. Rania felt they were too focused on playing on the right side
of the good Muslim/bad Muslim divide and were not paying enough
attention to the needs of young people at risk: "The Muslim community [was] almost sweeping it under the rug. Like, 'We're the good
Muslims, we're not the bad ones,' so we don't need to discuss these
issues that are actually happening outside of the mosque doors." She
cautioned that in the absence of sound guidance, the discontentment
of some youth could find expression in more extreme outlets: "So
there's like that one angry person and the kid that feels the same anger
and feels like that's the leader that they want to follow, because
that's the person that's actually addressing the issues." While the community is not the source of the problems that create pathways to
radicalization, it can nonetheless have a positive or negative impact
on that trajectory.

As a social worker and youth coordinator working with immigrant communities in Toronto, Shahnaz offered her insights into the motivations of youth who may become lured into more radicalized actions or associations. She felt that while the issue was "overblown" and not as widespread as it was made out to be, there could be risks for some impressionable youth to be led astray:

> I think that the majority of the people that are involved in any sort of radical activities tend to be in their teens and very highly impressionable. So, if there is someone who they see as an authority figure that will feed them this kind of rhetoric, I think they are very quick to jump on it because they are at that age where they will cling to really strong opinions and ideals that they want to embody. Especially if there is a backlash against Muslims. It's kind of a cool thing to do. You kind of stick to your identity. This pushes them further away from the mainstream. So, I think radicalization is partly a response to Islamophobia.

Shahnaz highlights the symbiotic relationship between radicalization and Islamophobia that in some instances creates a dialectical response that gravitates toward this destructive register (see Abbas 2019).

Ijaz, a Pakistani student in Montreal, used the metaphor of the *ummah,* or global community, of Muslims to put the sensibilities of the geopolitical imperial context in an Islamic perspective:

> There are Hadiths that say that if part of the *ummah* is hurt, then the entire body suffers. As an *ummah*, we are concerned about Palestine, Chechnya, Darfur, and so many places that it's a topic of discussion among our friends and family. So, when someone else talks about these things, you relate to it very easily and say, "Oh yes, this person knows what I'm talking about," or "My family were there," or "I know a family friend who was there." It's like a snowballing effect. If you're able to use that [to the wrong end] you can do a lot of damage.

Ijaz was quick to point out how this common concern for the suffering of fellow Muslims could be taken out of context and misconstrued by extremists: "The Prophet Muhammad (s a w),[13] didn't say anything without any meaning and whatever he said was said in the best of words. But people, I think, are able to misuse that very easily."

Ijaz's concern over the malleability and misinterpretation of religious messages was valid in the way many groups like Al-Qaeda and Daesh pervert religious meanings to recruit believers to their cause. Wiktorowicz (2005) describes how the persuasive strategies used by these extremist activist groups create a "cognitive opening" achieved by challenging the previously held beliefs and world views of prospective recruits to indoctrinate an alternative ideology. White nationalists use similar ideological and rhetorical strategies to recruit members to their fold. Both challenge the existing world views and beliefs of prospective recruits as a means of indoctrination. A tactic used to foster this cognitive opening is what Wiktorowicz (2005, 21) calls "moral shock," which refers to "rhetorical appeals to the moral sensibilities of predisposed audiences already primed for outrage when prompted by particular events or situations." Ijaz characterized these social movements as a "kind of activism" (echoing Wiktorowicz 2005) and noted while being Islamically misguided and dangerous, not all the critiques they raise about the plight of Muslims with the post-9/11 war on terror are without merit, even if the means for addressing those concerns are destructive and create a vicious cycle of violence.

ON VIOLENCE AND ROOT CAUSES: WAR, TRAUMA, AND DISCRIMINATION

Radically violent social movements use Islam as a rallying cry for their political and ideological agendas. Many youth I spoke to pointed to the conditions that led to these reactionary movements. They did not condone or justify violent reprisal but tried instead to make sense of the breeding ground for these actions. Using Palestine as an example, Idriss and Zafar graphically described the asymmetrical relations of power and brutally oppressive conditions that give rise to reactionary violence:

> **Idriss:** I'm not gonna spew which side is right or wrong but what I am saying is one side has military and are able to build a fence and go in with tanks while on the other side of the fence people are throwing rocks, seeing their children die, their grandparents and their parents die. They're being left with their homes being demolished. At what point do you say, "Enough is enough"? I think that Islamophobia and propaganda

[are] contributing to us avoiding looking at the contributing factors. What happens when living means you have to strap
on a suicide vest? No reasonable happy soul would do that.

Zafar: People ask me, "So what about suicide bombing?" I go,
"Bro, you know if you are living in Palestine right now and an
army came into your house raped your mother, raped your sister,
killed your brother, killed your dad, and took your mom and
sister away and you're alone, what do you have to live for?"
So, these guys go and blow themselves up … I don't agree with
it, but I sort of understand where they're coming from …
stories you hear out there, it's really scary you know.

Others also contributed to unpacking the rationale for radicalization
and the ways in which global conflict, militarism, imperialism, and
Western hegemony impact this process. As Muslim youth bear witness
to violence and the desperate conditions in their homelands they are
triggered by the injustice. Mohsin used Afghanistan as an example to
historicize the conditions that led to groups like the Taliban gaining
traction and power as a by-product of US militarism and intervention
in the region. He criticized the US government for leaving a social and
political void in Afghanistan which gave rise to violent insurgency
and the spillover of the conflict into Pakistan, where his family was
from: "When the job was done the Americans didn't establish anything.
No schools, no government. What they gave Afghanis was how to shoot
and how to kill and how to survive based on that. So, they became
a threat. They didn't know how to get themselves a decent job or
train for a profession. There was no established government, no laws,
no police, no army … there's no system."

Mohsin's views on the political backdrop of war and conflict in
Afghanistan are informed by his connection to the region. As with
many transnational Muslim youth growing up in Western diasporas,
he was impacted by the political conditions that affect his homeland
as well as the domestic conditions that shape his experience as a Muslim
immigrant. Straddling both contexts uniquely impacts the lives of
diasporic Muslim youth who must navigate the nexus between these
colliding worlds. Dealing with these turbulent circumstances may
enhance the sway of reactionary ideologues who offer ways to recuperate Muslim pride and safeguard the *ummah* through violence.

Jessa, a White convert, did not have connections to conflicts abroad, but came to similar conclusions about how the fraught geopolitical context inspires radically violent reactions. She commented on the precarity of identity and the need for stability in a chaotic world: "How a lot of young Muslim youth find stability in their life when nothing else is, is through their Muslim identity. Perhaps, in my opinion, if that comes under attack, when they are attacked viciously, or when they see their kin … for example the war in Afghanistan, the war in Iraq, etc., they think, 'This could be me,' and they want to support their kin." In acknowledging the frustrations that aggrieved Muslim youth are facing, Jessa tried to make sense of the existential tensions some youth are grappling with and how these emotions may be negatively channelled: "I think they have an angst within them, which is multi-layered, coming from ethnic issues, family issues, social issues, economic issues, religious issues. All of these different issues. Some people channel it a different way. Some people have a very different approach to it while others … use whatever outlet is there. It's unfortunate."

The "multi-layered" angst, grievances, and frustration that marginalized Muslim youth face in both the Global North and South create a social, political, and psychological vortex where their identities and emotions converge and must be negotiated. Where there are positive supports these tensions can be resolved productively. However, where the pull factors toward more militant actions are compelling, and alternate spheres of socialization do not exist, some youth may find themselves surrendering to a more destructive path.

War casts a shadow on the experiences of diasporic Muslim youth in Canada who may have fled countries where they were subjected to political conflict and strife. Simone discussed the experiences of youth she worked with who had endured the trauma of violence:

The specific reality of Muslim youth is that they might be coming from a country that's being bombed, they might have been bombed themselves. They still are dealing with that. They are stil dealing with trauma. They think they are gonna die. That does affect how they perceive certain political situations. There are often not a lot of spaces for them to talk about their specific experience, even in the Muslim community. If they are angry at America for something there's often not a lot of space to talk about that. Not even angry, just scared and traumatized. They feel like they are gonna die and they talk about death all the time. For those sorts of specific experiences, there needs to be space for healing.

Youth who were socialized into conditions of existential fear and anxiety can internalize the trauma of war and civil strife. As they adapt to new conditions in Canada, the residual angst and fear can remain imprinted on their psyche. Without appropriate spaces to voice their frustration and work through the internal tensions and anxieties, their ability to heal from trauma is compromised. Youth with unresolved frustrations and alienation are more likely to be preyed upon and recruited into gangs, ideological violence, or other negative kinds of associations. While these circumstances may account for potential problems, there is no evidence to indicate that Canadian Muslim youth are necessarily more at risk. Simone clarified that she has not encountered any youth with terrorist tendencies: "Again, these groups I met are not going to be terrorists, they're not going to blow things up. But there's a negative impact in their lives. In terms of Muslim youth, there can't be this obsession around radicalization because very few Muslims are involved in that and it's more of a state-level interest."

Islamophobic narratives that cast "dangerous Muslim men" as potential jihadis result in undue forms of targeting and racial and religious profiling (Razack 2008). These practices exacerbate the problems they aim to prevent. According to McKenzie (2018, 11), current security approaches to dealing with radicalization involve surveilling youth until they cross the line and then arresting them. He asserts that with such tactics "[it] is not inconceivable that an alienating CVE agenda could in fact create the very problem it sets out to solve."

Youth workers were concerned that the securitized narratives about radical Muslim youth alienation and marginalization were based more on clichéd stereotypes than evidence. Roble found that overblown concerns about the danger of youth radicalization in Canada drew attention away from the more pressing concerns facing Muslim youth: "I don't see a lot of youth who are Muslim going in groups to become extremists. That's not the major issue. I would rather focus on the issues that are facing some Muslim youth: unemployment, identity issues, intergenerational gaps: things that I know are going to cause them difficulty as they try to go on with their lives. I focus on those and how we can support them through that. But I don't think this [extremism] is an area that I am really concerned about."

Marwan, a student in Montreal, highlighted problems of unemployment and discrimination among Maghribi youth that contribute to conditions of alienation and isolation from society:

> We have really huge discrimination here in Quebec in terms of jobs. Many Arabs, mainly those who come from Al-Maghrib, speak French at least as the common language here and they don't find jobs as others find. So, they get fed up and don't identify and they can't go back home so they just they get stuck here. They go to the mosque to fill the void they have inside them or maybe to feel more like home. They just go and stay in the mosque and go back home and that's their whole life.

Multiple systemic barriers lead to social exclusion and inhibit integration as Marwan points out. In Quebec, policies have favoured secularism or *laïcité* over free and open religious expression. The suppression of religious identity can lead to forms of social and cultural distancing among minoritized groups who do not find belonging and acceptance.

HOMEGROWN TERROR

Incidents of homegrown terror in Canada were important flashpoints in shaping the experience of the 9/11 generation. Cases involving youth who were being recruited to fight abroad or arrested for plotting domestic terror attacks were few but had profound impact on the lives of Muslim youth. While they do not condone these acts or the ideologies driving them, they are nonetheless impacted by public perceptions, surveillance, and CVE initiatives, as we have seen.

Foreign fighters returning to Canada who have travelled overseas to Syria, Iraq, Turkey, Afghanistan, Pakistan, or North and East Africa, have been the source of domestic concern over potential extremists wandering Canadian streets (Dickson 2019). In 2017, a Nanos poll found that 62 per cent of respondents supported the prosecution and laying of criminal charges against Canadians suspected of involvement in jihadist groups abroad, while 28 per cent stated the government should prioritize rehabilitation and "deradicalization" (Zilio 2017). Living under the spectre of the jihadist bogeyman, Muslim youth are interpellated into these discourses and fears in ways that collapse their identities into destructive and limiting stereotypes. As previous narratives described, social rejection leads to alienation and dissonance.

In a report titled *Radicalization Leading to Violence in Quebec Schools* the CPRLV (2016) states that Quebec's Muslim youth are feeling rejected and victimized due to global and domestic concerns. The US-led war on terror, Israeli-Palestinian conflict, Abu Ghraib, and Guantanamo Bay, and civilian casualties of Western military interventions in the Middle East are highlighted as key concerns. The report focuses on the case of six young Muslim Quebecers, five of them students at Collège de Maisonneuve, who were suspected of joining jihadist groups in Syria. The catalyst for this case study was that "[f] or the first time, Quebec was witnessing the phenomenon of clusters of departures for Syria; a small group of interconnected individuals seemed to have become progressively radicalized to the point of wanting to leave the province to join the Syrian conflict and armed groups on the ground" (CPRLV 2016, 9). After talking to Muslim students at Collège de Maisonneuve, the report concludes that the policies and debates that have targeted Muslim religious practices and identities in Quebec have contributed to the feelings of alienation and that these sentiments were preyed upon by "shady charismatic figures who feed identity malaise and feelings of victimization" (CPRLV 2016, 23).

The CPRLV director Herman Okamba-Deparice argued that the discrimination that Muslim youth face in Quebec was "exaggerated." He contended that issues like the Charter debates were used by radicalization agents to make vulnerable youth feel their identity was under attack, when in fact Islamophobia was not a greater concern in Quebec than elsewhere in Canada (Solyom 2016). The nexus between Islamophobia and radicalization has been well documented (Abbas 2019). Not acknowledging the role Quebec's policies play in institutionalizing Islamophobia under the guise of upholding secularism ignores the systems of oppression that operate within law, civil society, and Québécois culture. The report findings indicate that aggrieved youth who feel isolated from society become susceptible to the propaganda of "radicalization agents." This trajectory leads to self-segregation and insularity from mainstream society. Radicalization agents leverage Islamophobia in the West to their rhetorical advantage: "By positioning itself as a radical critique of the West, this type of discourse therefore encourages the rejection of a pluralist society and the adoption of a Manichean interpretation of the world" (CPRLV 2016, 24). A shift to more religious behaviour was a salient factor, according to friends of the youth described as "undergoing radicalization," or in some cases, having left for Syria. However, the report overdetermines religiosity as an indicator of radicalization. All observant Muslim youth could therefore be deemed suspect by some unknown measure where their adherence to Islam would be flagged as "deviant."

The difficulty lies in assessing and addressing credible threats among the small number of youth who may be vulnerable to recruitment by violent reactionary groups versus wholesale vilification and undue suspicion of all Muslim youth. The latter scenario is one that leads to a vicious cycle and reproduces the very conditions it seeks to contain. The affective registers activated by discrimination such as frustration, alienation, identity malaise, etc. cannot be taken as rationale for or a given trajectory toward radicalization. The realities are far more complex. Yet it is instructive to have a clear sense of the dynamics of oppression that youth face and the myriad of responses this generates. Some youth may seek destructive paths that resonate with their frustration, fear, and social and political disengagement.

The 2013 case of four former high school friends in London, Ontario, who were lured into becoming foreign fighters came up in an MSA focus group. According to media accounts, Ali Medlej, Xristos Xatsiroubas, Aaron Yoon, and Mujahid Enderi (aka "Ryan") attended London South Collegiate Institute in Southern Ontario where they were "average teenage boys," high school jocks sporting hoodies and headphones and flirting with girls. Aaron and Xristos were reported to have converted to Islam while in high school, though little information has been made public about this. A few years after graduation, Ali and Xristos died along with thirty-seven hostages and twenty-seven militants in Algeria while taking part in the seizure of a natural gas plant with Al-Qaeda. Aaron Yoon was arrested and detained in Mauritania allegedly at a training camp for a North African branch of Al-Qaeda, while Enderi's whereabouts remain unknown (Canadian Press 2013).

Trying to make sense out of a senseless tragedy raised some speculations among youth who saw this as an unfathomable situation. Some wondered whether having an MSA in the high school would have made a difference. Others remarked at how new converts can be more easily lured into extremist groups since they do not have a strong foundation in Islam. There was a consensus that the Muslim community should be more welcoming of new Muslims so that they could find spaces free of judgment. They acknowledged that new converts needed to be guided by "proper Islamic principles" rather than find misinformation on the internet or connect with groups that brainwash them into extreme ideologies and movements.

"DISAPPEARING" SOMALI YOUTH

Another case with transnational ties is called "disappearing Somali youth." This refers to the recruitment of Somali youth as foreign fighters for the extremist network Al-Shabab, or "the youth," an insurgent group that gained traction in Somalia after Ethiopia, a majority Christian country, invaded in 2006. According to Wise (2011, 4), the Ethiopian occupation of Somalia was responsible for "transforming the group from a small, relatively unimportant part of a more moderate Islamic movement into the most powerful and radical armed faction in the country." Al-Shabab pledged allegiance to Al-Qaeda in 2012 and promotes opposition to Western-backed governments. In areas where they have gained control, they have implemented harsh interpretations of sharia law and seek the establishment of an Islamic state in Somalia. Somali youth in Canada, the US, Europe, and Australia are reported to have "disappeared" from their communities and re-emerged in Somalia to fight with Al-Shabab (Shephard 2010). One Canadian religious leader reported that these youth were being misled and shamed by accusations that their faith was questionable (Hamid Slimi, cited in Shephard 2010).

Toronto has a large Somali population clustered in the west end of the city in an area known as Dixon, a community renown even in Somalia. I went there to speak to a group of Somali high school students and youth workers. The students were unfamiliar with the fear over recruitment of foreign fighters from their community, even though this was the focus of international security. Idil, a youth worker, felt that many Somalis were disconnected from the political and human cost of the conflict, although she noted that community organizations and young professionals were trying to raise awareness.

Simone, a youth worker in Ottawa – another city with a sizable Somali population – found the conversation about Al-Shabab was a focus of community concern. In her view, the reasons some youth wanted to be foreign fighters were the same reasons they get involved in gangs. She argued for the necessity of creating alternatives for marginalized youth to avoid these trajectories and for youth workers to counteract the messaging that might draw youth into these dangerous alliances. Simone stressed the saliency of an intersectional analysis when examining the conditions Muslim youth experienced, especially when trying to determine what factors might lead some youth toward extreme ideologies and paths: poverty and low-income coupled with anti-Black racism and Islamophobic discrimination are key factors leading to the vulnerability of Somali youth. Fuad, a youth worker in Dixon, echoed these arguments and spoke of how the "double jeopardy" of being Black and Muslim subjected youth to multiple derogatory labels, such as "gang banger" and "terrorist." He also saw the hostilities with police and border security exacerbating the alienation of youth who were "not being treated with dignity."

Jiwani and Al-Rawi (2019, 3) examined Canadian media representations of Somali youth and found the dominant signifiers included the stigma of criminality and terrorism as well as depictions of being "lost," inassimilable, and "unruly others." In a data set of 1,067 news articles about Somali Canadians from seventy-six Canadian news outlets, the four predominant themes of the news coverage were: Somali Canadian youth, violence in the community, trouble with police, and Islamist terrorism (Jiwani and Al-Rawi 2019, 21). These findings demonstrate how Somali youth are associated with criminality, deviance, and terror in the media, which then shapes the hegemonic views adopted more widely in society. As the repetition of these tropes becomes normalized, Somali Muslim youth are more easily viewed as culturally prone to imported violence and conflict.

Yunus, from Toronto, argued that the conflict in Somali could not be construed as jihad since the battle was waged against other Muslims. He characterized it as a "tribal feud" and felt it possible that some vulnerable youth who experience a violent unrest in their homeland may be lured into militant campaigns. Yunus and Jaleel discussed how jihad could be mobilized for various political motives:

> **Yunus:** They're coming back with a war mentality already. So now you're telling them there's something that they can die for righteously – Oh, ho ho! Cutting up by the dozens! But for them, they feel it is like finishing up an unfinished sentence, from a historical Islamic perspective. Somebody called for jihad, they just heard the jihad call. They don't know where it came from. There wasn't actually a voice, it was just some idiot online, who said, "www.fatwa.com," and that guy is off!

> **Jaleel:** For all you know, the FBI is launching fatwas against other Muslims!

Yunus provides an interesting insight about how the clarion call for jihad is often instrumentalized for reasons outside the parameters of what legitimately constitutes jihad as a defensive war. This call to action can be politically leveraged to finish up an "unfinished sentence" from a historical perspective, as he put it. Old grievances are deployed by extremist groups to redress an unfinished history. For example, rhetoric involving the Crusades is leveraged both by jihadist groups against the "Crusader infidels" as well as by far right White nationalist groups to animate and valorize their battle against the Muslim "menace." Jaleel interjects the suspicion that the FBI were behind the erroneous "fatwas" to bait Muslims into violent reactionary campaigns. Being suspicious of the agents of securitization is a product of the scrutiny that Muslims face from these sectors (see chapter 5). These tensions and anxieties are reproduced in ways that invert the prism of suspicion back onto the agencies that target them.

Fuad noted that Somali parents were being vigilant and discouraging their children from following misguided ideologues who might lead them astray. Joosse, Bucerius, and Thompson (2015, 814) found that Somali community strategies were effectively creating powerful counter-narratives: "[T]he Somali-Canadian community are involved in a narrative dialectic with the activities of al-Qaeda affiliate al-Shabaab, and as such it has already developed narrative tools that render it largely resistant to the radicalization process." While grass-roots counter-narratives are important strategies of resistance, social workers noted that the Somali communities were under-resourced and overburdened.

Soraya, a youth worker from Dixon, complained that too much emphasis is placed on Somali youth changing their behaviour, instead of society changing to address the racism and interlocking forms of oppression that produce marginality. The onus falls upon marginalized communities to find solutions to problems they face or else have solutions imposed by the state that result in over-policing and securitization. These dialectics become a vicious cycle whereby Islamophobia underwrites the allure of extremism (see Abbas 2019).

THE TORONTO 18

The Toronto 18 case sparked conversations about what factors might lead some Muslim youth astray as well as how the backlash from this case affected them. As a teacher, Safeeya discussed the impact the Toronto 18 arrests had on Muslim youth, including the fear and angst it created among them: "Muslim youth who may have felt marginalized on the fringes before the arrests, certainly did after. Toronto was home to many of the youth that were arrested so it was only natural to feel the repercussions. Some of the boys were skeptical that the eighteen did anything illegal. The case is shrouded in some oddities, and I think the youth pick up on that. It scares them and creates a climate [of] fear in which they're left to live." This case raised complex emotions and responses from youth, as Safeeya noted. Everything from suspicion and disbelief about the facts surrounding the case to a realization that they were back in the spotlight as potential terror threats and being apprehensive about how this would affect them.

This was a high-profile case that garnered widespread national media attention. I recall seeing a front-page headline that read, "The Face of a Terrorist?" above a photo of one of the accused, a young South Asian male. I wondered how this headline and photo would impact Brown male youth (Muslim or not) who had to cope with the repercussions of this salacious representation and the racial backlash it invoked. For example, Samir noted that while the impact of this case was not as strongly felt where he lived in British Columbia, he was worried about sensationalism surrounding the case and the way it was handled by law enforcement: "The sensationalism of the story itself, the way that the police went about arresting them, even what led up to the arrests, made us realize that we are not living in the same environment we were living in before 9/11. And that things are different when it comes to how the state deals with the Muslim community." For Samir and others of the 9/11 generation, this case wakened them to the fact that the world before 9/11 had changed and would continue to impact them. Samir also noted it brought home the reality that there was extremism in the community and that some youth were being lured into dangerous activities and associations.

A transcript of a phone conversation between two of the accused youth referring to "beheading" the prime minister created media panic and public alarm. Idil feared this conversation was overheard without full knowledge of the context and facts and that this undermined the presumption of innocence for these youth. Others expressed concerns about "entrapment" and how some vulnerable youth were susceptible to manipulative tactics by law enforcement. Anisa described her misgivings about the RCMP's use of a mole or spy who befriended the youth. The mole facilitated actions that included procuring ingredients known for bomb-making: "Maybe they weren't actually going to do it. But the thing is, they said it. And then on the other hand you have someone going after them, pressuring and putting them in a situation where they will say it. When the people entrapping you tell you that that is what Islam says you should be doing ... you end up doing it. Entrapment plays into that notion that you are assumed to always be going down that path, so you might as well." Luring these young Muslim men from dangerous ideologies to dangerous actions involved measures that relied upon and reinforced stereotypes that would ultimately become self-fulfilling prophecies.

Tariq related to the age group, ethno-religious background, and university-oriented life of the Toronto 18, but he could not relate to their actions. He wondered out loud: "What went wrong in their philosophies versus my philosophy?" While he was unable to fathom their choices, he was aware of the impact this had on other Muslim youth: "I've had friends who are a little bit more visibly religious, or a bit more conservative in their views, but by no means to the point of what these eighteen people were planning. But they have come under scrutiny as well."

Simone pondered the motivations that would drive youth to these extremes. She felt that the existential struggle to find belonging, identity, and meaning in life played a role: "I think it's this issue around belonging and identity and trying to figure out your purpose in life. It's true for many radical groups. It's not just about my struggle with the government. It's also about what I think my life is about. What is its meaning? It's essentially the thing that is driving a lot of radicalization in the West." She added that at risk youth living in poverty were more susceptible to being lured into gangs or transnational organizations like Al-Qaeda or Daesh/ISIS. The fact that the Toronto 18 were from middle-class South Asian backgrounds made it hard for her to fathom their actions. Simone's confusion signals the problem of seeking a specific profile for someone who may become radicalized. The factors that play into such trajectories are not predictable and defy typical assumptions and judgments (Sageman 2008; Khosrokhavar 2009; Roy 2017).

Dawson (2014) was also confused about why these well-integrated South Asian and Arab Muslim youth with "good" families and solid educational paths would feel alienated. His study sought to make sense of homegrown radicalization by examining the Toronto 18 case as documented in media and court transcripts. His analysis did not examine racism or Islamophobia as sources of alienation and instead relied on other indicators, thereby underestimating the impact of the socio-political context on the 9/11 generation. Dawson (2014, 79) argues that members of the Toronto 18 did not experience the marginalization and hardship that Somali youth experience. He cites newspaper reports describing the youth as "ordinary and seemingly well integrated" and "honours high school students who loved to play soccer" with "parents who were hardworking homeowners." He questions how these youth could experience alienation if they are well integrated into the same norms and values as other hard-working Canadians. It is important to recognize that racialized Muslim youth may be able to do well in school, play sports, and have hard-working, middle-class families but may still be affected by racism and Islamophobia in profound ways.

Research among British South Asian youth, for example, indicates that they feel alienated and politically excluded from British society (Abbas 2011; Hoque 2019) as well as feeling victimized through derogatory media representation, anti-terror legislation, and collective victimization as enacted by institutions upon Muslims as a group (Mythen, Walklate, and Khan 2009). In interviews with British Pakistani Muslim youth, Mythen, Walklate, and Khan (2009, 746) found "the anger of personal victimization was firmly indexed to the suffering of Muslims in the country generally, and, subsequently – often through reference to the Ummah – the suffering of Muslims worldwide." Muslim youth alienation is therefore also produced by the vicarious trauma of the global conditions faced by Muslims.

The determination of who may or may not be a radical played out through sectarian divides, underscoring the good Muslim/bad Muslim dichotomy. Samir explained that because the Toronto 18 were Sunni Muslims, the response in his Shia community in British Columbia was one of distancing:

> In the Shia community, we have this notion that the extremist issue is beyond our doors. The Toronto 18 arrests were not even spoken about in our mosques, not even in our Friday *khutbas*. So, we have been sort of aloof to what happened. It's not an issue that we have to deal with. It's an issue that other communities, especially the Sunni community and maybe the Wahhabi and Salafi communities, have to deal with. And I don't know how accurate that is. I think there is still potential for extremism within the Shia community, but I think for the most part our community doesn't view it as so much of an issue.

He clarified that the impact of 9/11 and its aftermath, which precipitated concerns about radicalization and domestic terrorism, was felt by all Muslims and should not be viewed through a sectarian lens: "9/11 definitely impacted all of us because most of society doesn't really differentiate between Sunni and Shia. And probably they shouldn't in terms of this type of thing." Therefore, the intra-sectarian politics of the Muslim community reproduce the good Muslim/ bad Muslim trope as a Sunni/Shia divide. Yet the label of "potential jihadi" transcends sectarian as well as ethnic boundaries and is often deployed in ways that fall prey to divide-and-conquer strategies.

CONVERTS

Security agencies often associate the identity of the Muslim "convert" with potential radicalization (Sageman 2008; Khosrokhavar 2009). Sageman (2008) argues that the over-representation of converts involved in global terrorism is based in part on the inability of new Muslims to evaluate the religious claims of charismatic leaders who offer false narratives. Those new to Islam are often unfamiliar with reliable sources of information and can easily be led astray. Sageman (2008, 80) argues that "[i]n their eagerness to demonstrate commitment to their new religion, they (converts) are all too willing to accept the words of any Arabic speaker who claims special expertise as a representative and legitimate voice for Islam." New seekers who come across questionable religious and ideological influences that masquerade as authentic versions of Islam may not be able to discern these indoctrinating forms of propaganda.

As new Muslims try to make sense of their life in new ways, they are in search of meaning, purpose, and a place of belonging and community. Daood, a White male Muslim convert in his early forties, ran a community-based program for Muslim youth in Ontario and provided spiritual outreach to new converts. He began working as a "deradicalization counsellor" based on his own past affiliation with extremist groups abroad. In recounting his story, Daood recalled coming across people who claimed to be "true Muslims" attempting to recruit impressionable converts who they could indoctrinate into their extreme world views. They kept a distance from the mainstream Muslim community that they felt were not "true believers" and were hypocrites. They fomented distrust of the mainstream Muslim community and isolated people they were trying to recruit. Daood was angered by the war on terror and American imperialism that was taking the lives of innocent Muslims in the Middle East and Afghanistan and felt solidarity with these politically reactionary groups. He headed to Iraq in 2003 during the US-led Shock and Awe campaign. In describing the kind of people he encountered in these movements, he remarked: "There are people with delusions of grandeur ... they really think they're somebody special ... Gonna change the world!" But he later found that the people who recruited him had no regard for average Muslims who they did not accept as "real believers." Daood became disenchanted with their ideology, despite being sympathetic to the cause of combatting imperialist military aggression.

These groups created paranoia through promoting conspiracy theories about the Illuminati and Freemasons and provided their own fake news videos to support their claims. Daood described how they viewed the 9/11 attacks: "These were the Towers of Babylon where Western civilization was from and they're going to be taken down. The people were 'collateral damage.' And they should not have been there anyways because they are all adulterous, and alcoholics ... Whatever, [they said this] to desensitize you from the actual idea of someone dying." These groups brainwashed and indoctrinated people who were vulnerable to messages about redressing the aggrieved circumstances of Muslims globally. In a context of Islamophobia, fed by the war on terror, the purveyors of extremist ideologies can exploit feelings of victimization, and in some cases instrumentally guide those susceptible toward violence.

THE PERFECT STORM

Returning to Canada from his sojourn in Iraq, Daood worked as a deradicalization counsellor and ran a centre that provided youth outreach services. It was in this capacity that he was introduced to some of the youth involved in the Toronto 18 case before and after their arrests. I asked him what he thought were the factors that resulted in the perfect storm that led some youth astray while the vast majority could hold similar political grievances and not resort to making the same destructive choices. He replied, "I feel like there are so many factors that go into the perfect storm. The biggest factor is that they are very self-righteous and delusional. They have mental health issues in that they see themselves as the solution to all of the *ummah*'s problems. That they are going to save the world. They are judging others and putting themselves on this pedestal." Daood's observations add "delusions of grandeur" to the other psychosocial pull factors, such as seeking a sense of purpose, adventure, being righteous warriors, and so forth, as discussed earlier. He was concerned about the mental health issues some of these youth were experiencing, which did not make it into media reports (unlike when terror suspects are White). None of these factors should be read as sole predictors of radicalization, however when they come together with other pull factors, they may create the perfect storm within an individual's life. This remains an idiosyncratic process, however, and thus impossible to predict.

Khalid, an African Canadian convert, outlined the "ingredients" he felt created a mindset that might lead to destructive actions. His views are recorded here at length as they synthesize issues raised by others in this chapter:

What it really comes down to is, "I'm not well integrated into society, I want to hurt society, because society wants to hurt me, and people like me." You know, they can't identify with their neighbours. They see their society as being the enemy and they see Islam as being the vehicle through which they can achieve retribution against their enemies.

When you see young Muslim men, the ingredient for this is the same ingredients as to why people join gangs, do drugs, drop out of school. It's when people get to a point where they are desperate, when they see that people around me, society around me, can't empathize with them. They see them opposed to them. They see them as enemies to them. They can't see any hope to achieve something through the system. So, they see the system as being oppressive, keeping them down. So, anything that hurts that system is fair game and is righteous. That's the thing, it's righteous.

What I think it really comes down to is kinda like doing drugs. Somebody doesn't just wake up and say: "Hey I am gonna try crack this morning!" That's not how it starts. It starts with despair, it starts with a lack of something, and it moves on to something else. So, the first person that comes along that "sells some dope," next person says, "Drop out of school," another person says, "Blow up this metro station." That is a righteous act.

So, they fall into that. It's a whole story of revenge. The little
gang life, the little criminal activity isn't going to affect society,
but when you put on a beard and a *kufi* and blow something up,
you put fear inside of everybody, you get everybody. If you
blow up the metro, you have just touched everybody in that
city. You've taken power away from everybody in that city.
If somebody can come to you and tell you, "If you do this,
you die you would go to heaven." It gives them a purpose:
"I don't like this place anyway, I'm gonna die, and I'll get
a better place."

Khalid tells the story of how racism, poverty, systemic barriers, imperial wars, and oppression, and alienation and frustration can find
destructive means of expression. Most Muslim youth process and
manage these concerns without violence and find other outlets for
political dissent. Khalid admitted that he thought about these issues
a great deal and had discussed them with his parents. His mother was
worried not that he might join these groups, but that he may know
others who would.

Feeling alienated, isolated, and frustrated is a common malaise of
being young and marginalized, but this is not to be mistaken as a sign
of potential radicalization. The pressures felt by the 9/11 generation
need to be understood in their uniqueness without defaulting to
Islamophobic fears and moral panics. The following chapter examines
how Muslim youth are finding spaces of resistance against Islamophobia
and anti-Muslim racism by engaging in the arts.

7

Muslim Counterpublics

The Arts and Anti-colonial Public Pedagogy

Previous chapters outline how Muslim youth are targeted as potential radicals or terrorists at a time when anti-Muslim racism and Islamophobia are part of a global phenomenon. This chapter examines how Canadian Muslim youth artists and cultural producers are creating spaces for subaltern voices and experiences to be heard and from which to speak their own truth. Drawing on the notion of "anti-colonial pedagogy" outlined by Dei and Asgharzadeh (2001) and Dei and Kempf (2006), I situate these artistic interventions as politically subversive acts. An anti-colonial framework challenges Eurocentrism and reclaims subaltern knowledges through praxis and resistance. For example, Dei and Kempf (2006, 2) note that "[t]he power of the anti-colonial prism lies in its offering of new philosophical insights to challenge Eurocentric discourses, in order to pave the way for Southern/Indigenous intellectual and political emancipation." Drawing on the work of scholars such as Fanon, Said, Bhabha, wa Thiong'o, Trask, and others, Dei and Asgharzadeh (2001, 300) further articulate the emancipatory imperatives that ground the anti-colonial framework: "As a theoretical perspective, anti-colonialism interrogates the power configurations embedded in ideas, cultures, and histories of knowledge production, validation and use. It also examines our understanding of Indigeneity, pursuit of agency, resistance, and subjective politics." Animating political praxis through education and public pedagogy opens creative possibilities for liberatory struggles. Muslim cultural production in Canada is part of a subaltern counterpublic space that operates within the hegemony of White Canadian secular nationalism.

According to Fraser (1992, 82), there is a dual nature to subaltern counterpublics that allows for their emancipatory possibilities: "In stratified societies, subaltern counter publics have a dual character. On the one hand, they function as spaces of withdrawal and regroupment; on the other hand, they also function as bases and training grounds for agitational activities directed toward wider publics. It is precisely in the dialectic between these two functions that their emancipatory potential resides." As a resistant form of intervention, the subaltern Muslim counterpublic challenges clichéd stereotypes within diasporic and minority contexts. Community spaces are incubators of cultural production for youth (such as arts-based programs and collectives). These forums provide the opportunity for the "withdrawal and regroupment" that Fraser notes is necessary for critical reflection and action. It is through this dialectic and praxis that counter-stories can be nurtured and developed. While not all forms of cultural production created by Muslim youth are necessarily political (neither do they need to be) the focus here is on artists whose work contributes to a political critique.

COUNTER-STORIES

Youth artists who engage in "counter-storytelling" according to Lee Anne Bell (2009, 113) are involved in a political practice that creates "new stories that challenge the status quo ... give an alternative version of reality and can resonate with people who have been excluded from mainstream stories." In this way, counter-stories become part of an anti-colonial public pedagogy where Muslim youth can engage the politics and poetics of resistance. Within the framework of critical race counter-stories, promoting empowerment is a primary goal (Rappaport 2000), along with galvanizing critical consciousness and socio-political action, personal and collective memory and memorial, and healing (Smith 1999; Solórzano and Yosso 2002; S. Dion and M. Dion 2004; L. A. Bell 2009). Counter-stories provide a means of contesting epistemic privilege and centring subaltern voices and experiences. They represent strategies of survival and resistance among marginalized groups in an effort to speak truth to power.

According to Solórzano and Yosso (2002, 36), counter-stories provide the following functions:

(a) They can build community among those at the margins of society by putting a human and familiar face to educational theory and practice, (b) they can challenge the perceived wisdom of those at society's center by providing a context to understand and transform established belief systems, (c) they can open new windows into the reality of those at the margins of society by showing possibilities beyond the ones they live and demonstrating that they are not alone in their position, and (d) they can teach others that by combining elements from both the story and the current reality, one can construct another world that is richer than either the story or the reality alone.

These goals of counter-storytelling situate marginalized voices as critical interlocutors of the imperial present as well as being architects of alternative futures. According to L.A. Bell (2009, 113), counter-storytelling is a political practice that creates "new stories that challenge the status quo ... give an alternative version of reality and can resonate with people who have been excluded from mainstream stories."

Through counter-storytelling Muslim youth are changing the dominant cultural currency through which their lives are represented. Youth artists are employing cultural production as a corrective to the limiting narratives that have been used to contain their experiences. For Muslim youth, like other racialized and marginalized youth, telling their stories through the arts is also a means of countering Eurocentric epistemic privilege and gaining discursive control over their identities and experiences. This chapter begins with Muslim youths' responses to dominant Orientalist narratives that hijack their experiences and then explores how artists and cultural producers are responding to these challenges by reclaiming centre stage.

CONTEMPORARY ORIENTALISM AS CULTURAL PRACTICE

In the documentary *Reel Bad Arabs*, based on Jack Shaheen's (2006) book of the same name, he notes that of the 1,000 films that have Arab and Muslim characters (from the year 1896 to 2000), 12 were positive depictions, 52 were neutral portrayals of Arabs, and 936 were negative. The repetition of these images allows for Muslims to be interpellated into discourses of racial fear and religious degeneracy. Said (1979) points out that Orientalist tropes and imagery continue to be reproduced in media, film, and literature, and they shore up the positional superiority and dominance of the West. As Holmlund (1993, 4) asserts, "Orientalist discourse channels and organizes the fascination

and threat posed by the unknown for purposes of domination." In this
way, tropes of Muslim terror have maintained currency and colluded
with the imperial aims of the war on terror and global Islamophobia.
Sensationalized representations are pervasive and ideologically fixated
upon a limited taxonomy of Muslim stock characters. Guyanese youth
participants in a focus group in Surrey, British Columbia, related this
in the following exchange about these representations:

Safia: Yeah, they don't show like the normal Muslims.

All: Yeah, right.

Safia: Like the Muslims that go to school, the Muslims that,
you know, who are born in America or born in Canada,
they don't show those Muslims. They only show the –

Samiya: The ones that hijack some plane with a bomb
or something [*laughs*].

Munaza: They don't even have proof for that, right? They just
accuse Muslims.

Muslim youth are keenly aware of how their experiences are reduced to
stereotypes and used to support a particular narrative that has nothing
to do with their sense of identity or faith. These youth were very cognizant
of how Muslims fail to be normalized in dominant mediascapes.

Nabila, a Canadian Palestinian theatre actor and comedian, discussed
the challenges of working against the dominant stereotypes: "It's very
difficult for people to see Muslims as being funny when you watch
the media all you see is head scarf–wearing ladies slapping themselves,
and Arab men ... or you know Pakistan men or Indian men ... anyone
from Muslim faith ... burning an American flag! Do we ever see head
scarf–wearing women playing with [their] children? Or do we ever
see Arab men being loving to their wives and being loving to their
children? This is the majority! Why don't I see this in the media?"

Zeenat also lamented the narrow and limiting representations of
Muslims: "When was the last time you saw a positive, uplifting story
to do with Muslims? They are only in the news as perpetrators of evil ...
I think it's really far from the case. Our community does great things,
like interfaith gatherings and community clean ups, but I haven't seen

press coverage of that." Despite the integration of some visibly Muslim newscasters on Canadian television, the mainstream media landscape is entrenched with recurrent Orientalist representations, making it difficult to make Muslim lives intelligible outside these frames of reference. Alternative representations of Muslims as people who live peaceful lives with loving families and may even have a sense of humour are not part of the repertoire of stock images that mainstream media or Hollywood draw from. This representational history makes producing more nuanced counter-narratives far more difficult.

The challenge is compounded by the growing fake news industry that supports and purveys global Islamophobia. A 2018 study conducted by the UK-based Hope not Hate examined social media, fake news, and Islamophobia (see also Townsend 2017). The ubiquity of false information spreading via social media and websites of far right groups is fomenting a climate of fear, moral panic, and Islamophobic hate: "The growth among Twitter accounts and websites spreading anti-Muslim hate is alarming. In such a key area of public interest, it is an indication of increased interest in these views and, as each account or site grows, more people are exposed to deeply prejudiced anti-Muslim views." The study also found that terror attacks in the UK were exploited by these anti-Muslim activists, who acquired significant followers in the aftermath of these incidents.

The Islamophobia industry in Canada operates in similar ways, using media outlets such as Rebel Media and popular far right-wing commentators such as Ezra Levant, Faith Goldy, Lauren Southern, Barbara Kay, and Kevin Johnston. The Islamophobic rhetoric of these media ideologues is a dog whistle to White supremacist groups. The fake news industry manufactures a form of agnotology, or the "willful act to spread confusion and deceit" (Proctor and Schiebinger 2008; Kenyon 2016), which is usually done in the service of capitalist consumerism to sell products, but also occurs through the right-wing propaganda machine that relies on the propagation of ignorance as currency in their campaigns of hate.

MUSLIM YOUTH AS CULTURAL PRODUCERS

Canadian Muslim youth are engaged as storytellers, spoken word artists, political cartoonists, hip hop artists, filmmakers, actors, visual artists, musicians, digital media producers, as well as participating in other forms of literary and cultural production. Muslim storytelling,

whether through literature, cinema, poetry, theatre, or film, is a powerful form of public pedagogy featuring new and insurgent subaltern
voices. Muslim storytellers are creating their own content and producing
films and documentaries in Canada and elsewhere. In talking with
artists about what drives their vision and purpose, some traced this
back to the roots of Islamic culture. Aisha, a poet, spoke of how
contemporary Muslim artists are continuing an Islamic cultural tradition: "Islam came out of a tradition of orality and of storytelling and
narrative. And I think that's really beautiful. I want people who are
invested in scriptural history to know that and take a lot of strength
from that." Situating contemporary Muslim storytelling within this
historical legacy is a recognition of the rich and textured culture
production of Islamic traditions.

Sakina was critical of the repetitive imagery that promoted overt
and subliminal connections between Islam and terrorism and was
troubled about not having an equal platform to challenge these views:
"The thing that's really damaging about the media is that they have
a much wider avenue to sit there and claim for you what your identity is,
and you don't have the same avenue to counter it. I don't care if you
say that I'm a terrorist but give me the same mic to say that I'm not."
Many Muslim artists/cultural producers are "claiming the mic" in
order to speak truth to power as a conscious political choice after
9/11. According to Munir Jiwa (2010, 77), "For Muslim visual artists,
and Muslims in general, 9/11 has become a significant marker of time
in thinking about issues of identity, belonging and representation.
Even in the art worlds, the larger tropes of Islam/Muslims – terrorism,
violence, veiling, patriarchy, the Middle East – become the normative
frames and images within and against which Muslim artists do their
work." Muslim cultural production therefore performs critical counter-
hegemonic work in the re-shaping of post 9/11 imaginaries.

Within these knowledge economies, Muslim artists serve as critical
interlocutors creating new narratives through counterpublic discourse.
Jiwa (2010, 77) tells us that "Muslim artists are exploring new ways
of thinking about being Muslim, not necessarily as a theological or
aesthetic unity, but as a minority identification in the West/America."
In doing this cultural labour, they forge new aesthetic horizons that
allow alternative constructions of identity and faith. As Jiwa (2010, 77)
notes, "Muslim artists as cultural producers are not only contesting
art world boundaries in terms of new and emerging forms of identification, but also the various sites where they are being forged." A growing

number of Muslim artists are working to interrupt and decolonize spaces of epistemic and material power that constrain their ability to articulate their identities, realities, and struggles.

VOICE, AGENCY, IDENTITY, AND RESISTANCE

Through storytelling, contemporary voices are added to the historical repository of resistant Muslim narratives. Muslim youth are re-presenting their lives and experiences in ways that subvert colonial and imperial scripts. Sahar, a spoken word poet of South East Asian and Pakistani background from Montreal, described the challenge to claim her voice outside the perception of others: "At a certain point, I felt that the power to know who I am was placed in the hands of others and it was time for me to take it back. As I grew older, I began to realize that taking back your voice, preventing others from keeping you in a box, and standing up for who you are is a lifelong struggle. My poetry is the vehicle that helps me navigate through it all."

As Sahar notes, engaging in the arts is a way to negotiate the complexities of identity and agency for the 9/11 generation. She described how poetry allowed her to work through her contested identity:

For me, poetry is about expression, feeling, emotion, trying to make sense of the world and seeing the world through your own specific lens. In that sense, my poetry is not objective. This is where being multiracial, a visible minority and a woman come into play. Historically and even to this day, if you are part of any of these groups, you will experience racism, sexism, abuse, alienation ... some form of oppression. These are all meant and intended to marginalize, humiliate, degrade, and essentially, reduce you to nothing. The people who are committing these acts intend to place fear in you and control you; infringing upon your rights as a human being. At a certain point, you have to raise your voice and fight to take it back. It's a never-ending struggle to be who you are and to be who you want to be, but what is more difficult, is to peel away the images others have placed on your being, to reveal who you truly are.

Using the arts to negotiate the ontological struggle of post-9/11 Muslim intersectional identities was a way for Sahar to regain narrative control and reframe the meanings others attached to her identity.

Developing a Muslim counterpublic sphere for artistic and cultural expression creates an affective space to work through the challenges of marginality as a personal and political project. Engaging in artistic forms of expression allows for a catharsis beneficial in fostering the resilience that marginalized youth need to weather the multiple social, political, emotional, existential, and spiritual challenges they face.

Nabila, a Palestinian Canadian actor, described the existential angst and ontological struggles of the 9/11 generation:

> Growing up between Canada and the Middle East brought up a lot of issues for me: Who am I? What am I? Why am I here? What is my purpose? I kept repeating these questions over and over again and I thought, what defines you? Is it your culture? Is it the choices you make? Is it your past? Is it what you aspire to in the future? Who are you? Who are we? Or, who am I, really?! Very existential questions that I had no idea how to answer!! So, you go through a filtering process. You go into your weaknesses, your traumas, your pains, and some of it is of course very uncomfortable.

Exploring these emotions and self-reflective questions was part of her development as an actor and allowed Nabila to put the complex facets of her identity as a diasporic Muslim into context. She was negotiating two cultures that were both fraught with expectations and limitations rooted in histories of pain and struggle. Nabila saw this introspection as a part of the deeper emotional work she needed to do as an artist who wanted to use her craft to affect change and transformation in both herself as well as the world around her.

Sahar spoke of the specific challenges she faced as a Muslim woman in hijab performing in public venues:

> I would get verbally harassed, and there were a few instances where I was spat at. But I eventually used all the anger and hurt I was feeling to fuel my poetry. I wanted to dispel any type of ignorance that Muslims were facing, and I specifically concentrated on Muslim women since many of us are silenced and made to feel intimidated. And since I knew all too well how that felt, I felt the need to speak since many of those around me felt like their concerns, stories, and voices weren't being heard. There was so much dialogue in the media about what it meant to be a Muslim,

but I felt like our own Muslim voices were not part of that discussion. If you have no representation, how will your voice be heard? If you have no voice, do you exist?

A slam poetry collective called Speakout developed in Toronto and provided a forum for a youth-based subaltern counterpublic sphere. This initiative began within the Muslim community but was open to Muslim and non-Muslim poets. Other programs sought to develop spoken word poetry in lower-income racialized communities in the city. Muslim arts-based collectives such as Outburst! in Toronto became a platform to support and promote Muslim women spoken word and visual artists. The *(mus)interpreted* exhibit hosted by the Truth and Dare Project focused on photography and art-making workshops for Muslim women. These spaces have allowed local emerging Muslim women artists to interrogate questions of identity, spirituality, politics, and storytelling through various artistic genres and showcase their work in curated exhibits across the city.

Claiming space for intersectional Muslim identities is an important concern for many young artists. Spoken word artist Timaj Garad, has critiqued the erasure that homogenized notions of Muslim identity bring to bear upon Black Muslim women:

Black Muslimah voices are systematically suppressed by a dominant narrative that seeks to erase us. From every angle, whether it's the Muslim community, Black community, or within larger Canadian society, we are demanded to fragment ourselves in ways that diminish the complexity of our multi-layered identities. We experience the violence of anti-Black racism, Islamophobia, and misogyny in ways that are intersectional, informed by all of our identities, yet we rarely see representations that give voice to these experiences. Instead, we are asked to check our Blackness at the doors of our mosques and our Muslim-ness at every other door. For those of us that are visible hijab-wearing Muslims, our Blackness is questioned. At every turn we are asked to choose between our identities, which is no choice at all. Expecting us to make this choice is to expect us to leap out of our skin, out of our own hearts. (Muslims Actually 2017)

Artists like Garad find the arts play an important role in expressing and navigating the politics of exclusion based on anti-Blackness and gendered subordination that she and other Black Muslim women face within Muslim communities as well as outside of them. Using spoken word and other artistic outlets allows them to "speak back" to the various spaces of oppression where they are otherwise silenced and their identities are disavowed.

ART, FAITH, AND FIDELITY

Navigating secular art worlds as an observant or practising Muslim adds additional challenges to an already difficult terrain of racial politics in media and cultural production. Yusuf,[1] an actor, writer, director, and filmmaker of Moroccan and Pakistani descent from Toronto, was engaged in both comedy and documentary film work. He wrote, directed, and starred in a web series called *Fame & Fidelity* that took a comedic look at his own experience as a Muslim actor trying to break into the business but constantly being typecast as "terrorist number two." The series was featured at the Los Angeles Webfest in 2014 where one of the cast members won an award for Best Supporting Actor.

The series addressed the struggle of the lead character, a Muslim actor, who tries to maintain fidelity to his religious values in an industry geared to contrary social values. Roles that involved drinking alcohol, using drugs, or engaging in sexual activity created moral challenges for Yusuf as a practising Muslim actor:

> I pursued acting professionally for about six years, until I started to face some moral and religious quandaries. I became unhappy with some of the problematic representations I was being asked to audition for, such as the "terrorist" roles. As I got older, I faced the dilemma of having to do certain things on camera or on stage that went against my beliefs as a Muslim. Even though I'm acting and it's all make-believe, I wondered whether it was permissible and appropriate for me to do from an Islamic standpoint. I came to the realization that the only way I could be satisfied was to create my own content. I started a production company with some friends where we produce films, web series, documentaries, and plays. So now we can control the narrative that goes out into the world, and I get to play better roles than I'd have opportunities to do otherwise.

Sahar also discussed the existential challenges of being a role model and maintaining fidelity to her faith and values:

> Before I'm a poet or anything, I'm Muslim … if I'm saying one thing on stage, I need to represent it in my life, or I shouldn't say it at all. And I don't like to show an image of myself that isn't who I am. People look up to you when your words resonate with them. They feel such a strong connection with you. Personally, it's a constant reminder to always keep yourself on the right track because people are watching you and whether you like it or not, you are an example. If I see a five-year-old or a ten-year-old saying, "Oh, you're so cool" or "I wanna do what you do" or "I wanna start writing poetry," in my head I'm thinking, I don't want to mess up!

Yusuf saw faith at the core of his artistic work. The challenges he faced as a Muslim actor in a secular entertainment industry served to enhance rather than diminish his commitments: "Being able to express my ideas and thoughts through a video or on stage is also my expression of faith. It shows that I am taking the tools God gave me and putting them to good use. Internally, I think it strengthens my identity. Entertainment is not a very Muslim field, and it can be easy to want to assimilate to a Western identity. But in a weird way, when I feel uncomfortable in these settings, it deepens my identity and makes me want to assert it more."

While some artists were able to reconcile their faith and their art, Zareena felt she could not pursue her interest in music and singing, which she believed compromised her standards of modesty. Zareena's Islamic ideals were based on a more conservative Islamic orientation that regards Muslim women's voices as part of their *awrah*, or modesty, that must be guarded so as not to incite the sexual attention of men. She felt that as a veiled Muslim woman she had a responsibility to maintain strict Islamic standards of decorum: "Because the thing is that when I have this scarf on I have a responsibility to carry it properly and to be modest because we cover our hair as part of our beauty and our sexuality and we are not supposed to make men attracted to us. Even though I am doing this wrong because I am wearing makeup … [*laughs*]. You know you can't just be a covered girl and go out rocking to a song!"

Zareena was told she had a talent and she wanted to continue to develop her voice as a singer but stopped when she began wearing hijab because it was inconsistent with her religious ideals. Muslim women who wear hijab are involved in art and public performance; however, Zareena felt that acting and singing were inappropriate for her. She was also a painter and felt more comfortable with the medium of visual art as opposed to singing in public. Despite her religiously conservative ideals, Zareena wanted to make it clear that she claimed her agency through voicing her opinions rather than singing and performing: "I am still a public person, even though I wear my scarf, I am out there. People notice me because I am not just that quiet girl who hides in the corner. It's not like I like to get attention, but I am not quiet either. I like having my thoughts spoken out. But singing is a whole different thing from just showing my painting, you know? Because if I was going to sing, I would not want to have my scarf on. This is just a responsibility that I have to carry."

Zareena came to an artistic compromise and found an expression for artistic voice in ways that she felt were more in line with her interpretations of Islam and the values she wanted to represent. Conservative religious views regard music, and especially women singing in public, as contrary to the values of modesty. Such views tend to have less traction among younger Muslim women who do not find music and dance to be inconsistent with their faith and Muslim ideals.

Reconciling Islamic attitudes and beliefs in the arts has led to the development of "Halalywood" a new and growing "halal" Muslim entertainment industry of faith-based film and digital media. Aggarwal (2019) describes the impetus and goal of this genre: "Reacting to the world they see around them, a new generation of young, modern Muslims are carving out new ways to entertain themselves – yet remain loyal to their faith. This new generation is showing that Islam and entertainment can go hand in hand. Along the way, they are shattering stereotypes about what it means to be Muslim in today's world." From YouTube videos featuring comedy sketches about Muslim families, spoken word poetry and Sufi-inspired rap (Van Nieuwkerk 2011; Aidi 2014) to the latest modest fashion tutorials by hijabi vloggers, Muslim cultural producers have found a growing audience of faith-conscious youth. The growth and popularity of the halal Muslim entertainment industry is reflective of this generational change: "Many young Muslims across the world, growing up in a profoundly different time to their parents, are interpreting and exerting their religion in new ways. This perhaps explains why it's young Muslims who are spearheading most of these trends. You could even say a young Muslim revolt is taking shape" (Aggarwal 2019).

Trying to reconcile faith, fashion, and the arts in a globalized world and maintain fidelity to faith while keeping step with millennial lifestyle trends on Instagram characterize this new industry and provide the conditions for it to thrive. This genre often features overt Islamic messaging, which can come across as "preachy" or too religiously transparent with heavy-handed morals guiding the storytelling instead of allowing the stories that resonate with a wider audience. Catering to a Muslim audience and promoting a "good Muslim" narrative limits the demographic appeal of the Muslim entertainment industry. The Halalywood industry risks insularity and inaccessibility to wider publics where the by-product of 9/11 has meant a greater interest and fascination with Muslim lives. The Muslim entertainment industry operates in a precarious tension with the Orientalist foundations upon which Muslim narratives have been subsumed. Muslim cultural production is uniquely poised to do important political work through counter-storytelling as part of an anti-colonial praxis. Muslim entertainment is not limited to addressing only Islamophobia or other political concerns; however, even films that address topics like romance or comedy are read within an Islamophobic context and thus impact the way non-Muslim audiences perceive the narrative.

MuslimFest, a cultural festival showcasing Muslim arts, began in Ontario in 2004 attracting over 30,000 attendees annually. The festival features art, film, comedy, spoken word, and music albeit mostly religious songs (*nasheeds*) and limited instruments. While the MuslimFest stage has been male-dominated, in recent years women have been invited to perform spoken word poetry but not to sing. The festival has traditionally followed more conservative religious practices, but the boundaries are slowly shifting. These changes are driven by youth who view the arts as an important avenue of expression, agency, and voice that should be open to showcasing the diversity of the community in terms of gender, race, ethnicity, and sectarian identities.

Promoting, funding, and supporting Muslim youth artists is otherwise limited. Yusuf was critical of how the Muslim community in Canada has not adequately supported the arts:

As a Muslim creator trying to create meaningful (or non-meaningful) work in the entertainment industry, I try to rely

on the Muslim community for support. But very rarely is there
any real support. Art in the Sunni Muslim community is still seen
as a "waste of time." It feels like the Sunni Muslim community
doesn't appreciate or value the arts as an effective or legitimate
form of social justice, activism, or discourse. Unless you're donating
money to a charity or you're a doctor or lawyer, you're wasting
your time and not going to make a difference. It really frustrates
me. Media is one of, if not the most, effective way to spread
a message to the masses. It's the quickest way to connect
with somebody on another level. Yet we disregard it.

Yusuf made the distinction between Sunni Muslims and other Muslim
groups, noting that he found Shia and Ismaili Muslims to have a
greater appreciation of the value of arts through their films and patron-
age. He noted the discrepancies along sectarian and ethnic lines:

Iranians are demonstrating their incredible talent for filmmaking
and storytelling. Maybe that comes from the secular Iranians and
their shared experience of a violent, post-revolution Iran? Some
of the best art comes from communities that experienced shared
trauma, such as comedy from Jewish artists. Maybe the Muslim
community is just too big to unite under one shared goal of
healing through arts. Or maybe it's because we're afraid it will
tarnish Islam. It feels like we're still concerned with trying to
humanize Muslims and tell people we're not terrorists all the
time. Playing the "good Muslim." I like to think we're past that
point. Or at least we should just act like we are. We can never
progress if we don't stop trying to prove ourselves to everyone
all the time.

The nascent arena of Muslim comedy is constrained on the one hand
by religious mores, and on the other by the need to prove that Muslims
are not terrorists. These discourses converge and at times dominate
the representational politics.

More recently, the comedy series *Ramy* challenges the boundaries
of conventional Muslim representation and delves into otherwise
taboo topics, such as premarital sex, pornography, queer and trans
identities, and drug and alcohol use among Muslims. The show
grapples with the challenges of trying to maintain fidelity to Islam
while being tempted by worldly vice, a struggle for many Muslims.

The groundbreaking series has had popular success in Hollywood where the show's creator, Egyptian American actor Ramy Youssef, won a Golden Globe and the show was nominated for multiple Emmy awards. Yet, reactions from the Muslim community have been mixed. Some champion the show for its daring and refreshing take on real issues in the Muslim community, while others reject it as being "un-Islamic." These polarizing tensions continue to drive debates on the boundaries and limits within Muslim cultural production.

Yusuf reflected on how other marginalized communities have developed counter-narratives over time due to the value they placed on artistic and cultural production:

> Look at the Black community and see how much they value
> the arts as a real, legitimate factor to social change. They embrace
> music, theatre, film, dance, visual art, and more – and are thriving
> in it! Like Muslims, they have their own history of racism
> and colonialism through representations by the dominant
> White elites. In Hollywood, they had blaxploitation films
> and representations of Blacks as either slaves or thugs. While
> a lot of that still exists, there are so many Black artists, writers,
> directors, actors, rappers, and more who are doing incredible
> work to undo all of that. How can we keep complaining about
> how Muslims are portrayed in the media if we're not there to do
> anything about it?

As Muslim youth artists and cultural producers in the West are working against the odds of an industry that has vilified and stereotyped their identities, they must also contend with the lack of importance that their community places on the role of the arts and media.

Nabila described how her family reacted to her decision to pursue a career in theatre and comedy: "Oh, whoa! No! 'What are you, nuts?!' Ha ha! You know, like, you have a fabulous Muslim Arab Canadian daughter who has aspirations to do social and humanitarian work and is going to change the face of poverty and then comes home and tells you, 'I want to be a comedian!!'" Nabila's decision to pursue a career in the arts would be difficult for many first-generation immigrant parents to fathom. They want to see their children excel academically and have careers in fields like medicine, law, or engineering that provide stability and prestige. Pursuing a career in the arts is often met with resistance and considered an irresponsible choice.

Aisha, a poet and writer, described how in a climate of pervasive Islamo-phobia, parents also fear for their children's safety and well-being:

> My mother has read some of my writing that's been published recently that wasn't fiction and was initially like, "Why are you writing this?" It was stuff about Islamophobia in Canada. I didn't respond because I knew that she was just afraid. The next day she called me back and was like, "I really admire the work that you do, and I want to be proud of you but I'm afraid for you." And I think that was the perfect encapsulation of what it is like to be a Muslim parent in Canada in this day and age.

Challenging Islamophobia in the wider public sphere often opens the door to receiving hate mail and even death threats. With the rise of alt-right and White supremacist groups in Canada (Perry and Scrivens 2015), being publicly Muslim can make individuals a target of hate groups and the media trolls that support them. Muslim youth artists and activists may face racist backlash as public figures, which creates concern among their family members for their well-being and safety.

COUNTER-STORIES:
ART, RESISTANCE, AND POLITICAL ENGAGEMENT

Hisham Aidi examines in his book *Rebel Music* how Muslim youth have engaged within the cultures of hip hop, rock reggae, as well as Sufi and Andalusian music as a means of political expression since 9/11. He also outlines how the US and other Western governments tap into hip hop and Sufi music for de-radicalization programs abroad. Muslim youth cultures are being recruited into the security industrial complex in ways that reinforce the surveillance of Muslims as potential radical threats to public safety and national security (see chapter 5). Many Muslim youth artists are responding to these kinds of political aims that further marginalize and endanger them. While not all Muslim artists should be expected to do work that is expressly political or Muslim-focused, the artists interviewed for this study wanted to situate their work within this context.

For example, Sahar described how connecting personal struggles to larger political concerns became a catalyst in conveying her thoughts, feelings, and emotions: "I started writing poetry when I was very young, it was mostly about myself or the things that I was going through. As I got older, I started using poetry to deal with the issues, problems, and the struggles that I was having in my own life and that slowly evolved into the struggles of other people. I started getting into social issues, activism, and political issues that I wanted to speak about and that was what made me want to do spoken word."

For Sahar engaging in the arts from a personal standpoint led to a political awakening and a mission to further social justice through her craft. Like many other artists, Sahar saw her role within the arts as a responsibility and not simply a choice. She described how her goals were oriented within this larger vision of claiming political voice and agency: "I have a responsibility to speak out and to lend my voice to certain struggles. I also feel responsibility to live my life as I speak of in my poetry. It's a responsibility that I've had to undertake ... it's not such a simple thing."

Sahar reflected on how her poetry and public performances were received, recalling a story where after reciting a poem about how being a Muslim woman and not only "demanding but commanding respect," it was met with affirmation from women of all ages in the audience. While the poem was not overtly political, it nonetheless validated their experiences as well as their hopes and dreams for the future: "I really believed I'd say one poem and girls wouldn't be scared to go out in their hijab. Women wouldn't be scared to voice their opinions and men would feel proud that they were respecting women for those who were, and those who weren't would feel ashamed. I felt that if I had just stood in front of a crowd and said this poem, that it would change people completely. I wholeheartedly believed I could change the world by just saying something." For Sahar, the role of the arts lay in asserting power, voice, and agency. She believed artists help imagine and build alternative futures based on principles of justice and equity.

Yusuf also saw his purpose as an artist tied to political and social change and wanted to reflect this in his cultural production: "I feel like it's hard for me to avoid putting some sort of political or social message in my work. As much as I try to avoid it, it sneaks in somehow! But I feel like it deepens the work, gives it more resonance if done well." He was direct about using the arts as a form of political resistance and a catalyst for challenging oppression:

I think the fact that I'm a Brown Muslim actor, writer, and director is a site of resistance in and of itself. The stories

and the perspectives that I tell are not seen in this industry very
often. The same goes for other creators of colour. The work
I have done recently has very much been about resistance.
Particularly resistance to dominant hegemonic structures.
There are too many powerful forces telling people what Muslims
are like, and none of these forces are Muslims. That bothers me.
Why are there not any Muslims in entertainment telling our
stories? If we were authentically represented more often it would
be much easier to combat Islamophobia. So yes, I think it's all
about resistance now. It has to be. Look at where we're at in
the world right now. The way I see it, anything I put out there
that represents myself or my community is an act of resistance.

Yusuf argued that by virtue of his racial and religious identity his
cultural work becomes a de facto resistant intervention in a dominant
entertainment industry that has largely excluded Muslim narratives
or reduced them to Orientalist frames. The production of new narratives lies within the subaltern Muslim counterpublic sphere as
emergent space, albeit with its own challenges and constraints.
    Canadian artist Boonaa Mohammed, a poet, writer, actor, and
filmmaker of Oromo descent has worked to reclaim the dominant
narrative on the radicalization of Muslim youth. He has produced
films such as *Tug of War* and *Detainee X* that address this phenomenon
from a community-based perspective rather than Hollywood's rendi-
tions of maniacal jihadist terrorists. *Tug of War* depicts how the path
of radicalization manipulates some Canadian youth into joining
extremist causes and highlights the nexus between Islamophobia and
jihadist movements. Mohammed warns that Muslim youth are essentially living under siege, – a "generation on the defensive" and that
"Islamophobia feeds right into ISIS's 'you're not wanted here' narrative" (CBC Radio 2015). The terrorist is one of the most difficult
narratives to re-appropriate given the infamy of groups such as Daesh
and Al-Qaeda who are the jihadist bogeyman within the Western
imaginary. This new iteration of older Orientalist, racial fears retain
their currency due to ongoing imperial wars and the Islamophobic
alibis that underwrite the violence and demonization of Muslims.
    As a filmmaker, Yusuf was committed to challenging the status
quo of the industry but argued that storytelling needed to allow for
a variety of representations, including Muslim terrorists: "For the
record, I don't have an issue with representing Muslims as terrorists.

Sometimes it's necessary for a filmmaker to tell their story. What I do have a problem with is that there aren't any other representations to counterbalance the terrorist roles. If we had other representations of Muslim characters, it would balance things out. But there are no counter-narratives."

Said (1979) reminds us that the existence of Orientalism precludes the existence of a free space of thought or action in the Western imaginary; therefore, in the absence of more balanced and diverse representations of Muslims, the stock caricatures and tropes are difficult to dismantle. Nonetheless, there are some role models for Muslim actors breaking through the Hollywood industry such as Riz Ahmed, Mahershala Ali, Aziz Ansari, Aasif Mandvi, Hasan Minhaj, Kumail Nanjiani, and, Ramy Youssef, and though fewer in number, female Muslim actors such as Shohreh Aghdashloo, Nazanin Boniadi, and model Iman. In Canada, actors Zaib Shaikh and Aliza Vellani from *Little Mosque on the Prairie* created by Zarqa Nawaz, drew national attention in what is otherwise a very limited field for non-White talent achieving success in mainstream television. Though they are few, these actors open the door for other emerging artists to envision possibilities for wider recognition in the industry.

CONFLICT RELIEF: "TACKLING ISSUES OF CONFLICT THROUGH COMEDY"

Theatre and spoken word artists discussed how they used these genres to educate, inform, and challenge the status quo. As a theatre performer and comedian Nabila co-founded a Palestinian-Israeli comedy troupe called Conflict Relief, based in London, UK. According to their YouTube channel, the goal of Conflict Relief is "generating original comedy work that tackles social, political and cultural issues."[2] Using sketch comedy and theatre as a platform to break down stereotypes and misconceptions about various religious, social, and cultural groups, Conflict Relief provides a unique way to hold up these biases and political divides for examination and catalyze productive conversations. The cast members use their skits to inspire critical thought and action and their performances are followed by a facilitated dialogue with the audience. Involving the audience in a dialogue is similar to the ideas behind Theatre of the Oppressed developed by Augusto Boal (1994). Drawing inspiration from Paulo Freire's work *Pedagogy of the Oppressed* (1970), Boal (1994, ix) describes the revolutionary possibility of theatre as a vehicle for social change and transformation and as a weapon that can be used for liberation. The idea that theatre can help develop critical consciousness and political mobilization is a philosophy shared by Conflict Relief.

The company is comprised of artists from conflicting backgrounds (Palestinian and Israeli). They co-developed a unique mission to use this social and political conflict as a site for critical introspection and learning across communities of difference:

> We are obsessed with the concept of making mankind see we are all mirrors of one another. Our early experiences of cultural and religious wars fueled our passion for creating theatrical works that help people realize we are alone, and we must learn to work as one unit. We are made up of different people and tribes so we may get to know one another. We must celebrate our differences and realize we are stronger because of them. Now more than ever it is crucial to show cooperation between different religious, cultural, and social communities. We must learn to see that we are not separate from one another and the nature of how we have grown is through difference.[3]

The company uses physical theatre and comedy to tackle difficult social problems that arise from religious and political conflict. Ironically the idea for Conflict Relief was born out of a real-life conflict between Nabila and an Israeli-British theatre colleague. She described a catalytic moment where they were arguing about the Palestinian and Israeli conflict in a restaurant and the conversation turned into a heated argument:

> We had a very big fight. Right in the middle of the place and everyone could see it! We were in each other's faces calling each other names in Hebrew and in Arabic! You know dirty things that I shouldn't say on tape! I think the next step would have been that I punched him, or he punched me! Then I broke out laughing and told him this is ridiculous! Look at us! And then of course we had to calm the people in the place down because they're like, "Oh, my god!' They saw a Palestinian fighting with an Israeli! And we're like, "We're sorry! Guys relax, it's okay!" We were embarrassed. We left money on the table and walked out of the place, tails between our legs!

Later, she and her colleague were debriefing their outburst, and they both admitted to "feeling a fire" in that exchange, which gave them pause and made them reflect on the attitudes they had internalized. Nabila concluded, "I don't want to feel this way anymore about Israelis."

Her colleague agreed that he did not want to harbour ill feelings toward Palestinians. They underwent a process of "unlearning" to deal with the tensions from this conflict in more productive ways. They said it was like "debugging" and "reprogramming" a computer. Hitting the "restart" button involved critical introspection and a collaborative strategy on how to work against disruptive biases that transform dialogue into diatribe: "We realized that to really dig deep into the issues we needed to find a way to bring together people who are biased. But the problem with biased people is that they don't want to work with the other side. So, we had to persuade them. We went out to search for people who were very charismatic, who had strong voices and opinions. Who would say, 'It's all Israel's fault!' or 'It's all Palestine's fault' or 'It's Lebanon's fault'… And we found them and stuck them together with us in the same room!"

Conflict Relief grew out of this space of political struggle, contestation, and adversarial encounters to create a forum for critical dialogues to take place across communities of difference. According to Nabila the tensions proved to be productive yet difficult:

> It wasn't always easy. It took us a good year to write our first show. And not because we were slow. It took that long because we had to work through a lot of emotions. We really had to "deprogram." It's not easy to sit and hear the other side say things to you like, "You're wrong or your people are responsible for that." I think the greatest gift that Conflict Relief has given us, and given the world, is to take responsibility for your actions. And to take responsibility for the wrongs that you commit. I think that sometimes, that's a very big burden for certain Israelis. It's difficult to admit and it's hard to speak ill of your own country. I know this because I find it difficult to point out the bad things about Palestine.

The pedagogical strategy of using comedy to disarm hostilities and galvanize dialogue to address deeply entrenched tensions and hatred was a process that the cast members underwent and then were able to translate it into an interfaith theatrical intervention.

The challenge, as Nabila explained, was to quell the fire of acrimony while still holding onto their ideals of justice: "I'm not gonna deny that I believe in Palestine. I believe that Palestine should exist and that they have every right to exist. I believe they were robbed of their land. And I believe that we have suffered at the hands of the Israelis. But you know, my attitude before was very 'anti' … it came from a place of uh, how I do I say, like, fire! Which is fine, but the fire was not very constructive." Nabila's shift in consciousness came from having difficult conversations with Israeli colleagues and an openness to collectively move beyond the fractures and political divides despite deeply held differences.

Nabila was able to find so many similarities with her Israeli colleagues, which helped her work through the political tensions they all felt:

> We all cry the same. We all yearn the same. We all want very similar things. We're all very similar. We just choose to see the difference between us rather than consistently invest in looking for the similarities … You have to close your eyes and think about what kind of future you want to create. Because it's no longer just about us, it's about our children. What's gonna happen next?! And the reality is that what Israel is doing to the Palestinians is what Germany did to the Jews and that's really very sad.

She described how their theatre company was like a family and shared their professional and personal lives together: "We're like a family. They all love each other! We've brought our friends together so now I have Israeli friends, and Haim (pseudonym) has Palestinian or Jordanian friends. So, it's been a snowball effect, not just in our work lives, but in our personal lives. I go for Passover with my Israeli friends. I sometimes go for Shabbat dinners. They come with me to the mosque and I go with them to the synagogue. I feel that's the way it should be."

The difficult interpersonal and inter-religious work that the cast of Conflict Relief was able to do is remarkable given the strong political divides between the Palestinian and Israeli members. Their success would not necessarily be easily repeated. Without romanticizing their efforts, this is one case where the ingredients for failure were ever-present but were overcome by a shared commitment to use comedy as a catalyst for social and political dialogue and debate. Nabila was realistic in what Conflict Relief could accomplish and did not see it as a panacea for the Israel-Palestine conflict. Rather, she saw it as a strategy to build a critical mass of people willing to discuss difficult issues and commit to finding non-violent solutions to solve political problems:

> I know that I'm never gonna solve the Arab Israeli conflict,
> but maybe if I inspire enough people, those people will inspire
> enough people, until enough people say we don't want war
> anymore. Maybe I'm very utopian but I'm not going to stop
> trying! I'll die trying! I remember when the Gaza war happened,
> I had a bit of a breakdown ... I sobbed my eyes out, like, the work
> that I'm doing is pointless! Then I thought to myself – no, it's not!
> Because even if I perform to a thousand people and I change
> one person's mind, I've succeeded. If I change the thousand,
> that's great. But if I even just get through to one person,
> who knows what that one person is going to do.

Nabila recognized the power of theatre as a forum for social change and found a unique way to use comedy to disarm fears and open spaces for interrogating conflict using laughter to cross divides. Interfaith activism in the arts and comedy is a new terrain and Conflict Relief is charting a promising and pioneering path.

ETHNOGRAPHIC THEATRE

Yusuf Zine began a theatre and film project in 2015, working with fifteen Rohingya Muslim refugee youth (ages eight to twenty-one years). These youth wanted to share the stories of their families who fled genocide and persecution in Myanmar and then relocated to refugee camps in Bangladesh before coming to Canada. This project developed into an ethnographic play and a feature-length documentary entitled *I Am Rohingya: A Genocide in Four Acts* (Innerspeak Digital Media 2018). The film showcases youth storytelling and uses ethnographic theatre to address the issue of genocide, violence, displacement, and Islamophobia. Yusuf noted that the play was an act of resistance against the Burmese government that seeks to erase the Rohingya from existence through violent ethnic cleansing.

Both the play and the documentary also showcase the resiliency and strength of the youth whose stories were woven into the four-act play and are featured in the film along with their families. The documentary provides a counter-narrative to the way Muslim youth have otherwise been depicted as potential "radicals" or as passive victims, and instead allows them to be seen as agentic subjects who have overcome immeasurable hardship to tell their powerful and inspiring stories on a global stage. Y. Zine (2016, 28–29) writes: "My assumption heading into this project was that the process of ethnographic theatre would engage the Rohingya youth to construct or reassert an ethnic and religious identity that has been vilified and under siege." His project harnesses and amplifies the voices and experiences of marginalized Muslim youth from the Global South living through ethnic cleansing, violence, and displacement.

Global forms of Islamophobia have created a generation of transnational refugee youth. Having the opportunity to share their stories is not always possible when sheer survival is often the most they can hope for. For the Rohingya refugee youth and families that Y. Zine worked with, finding a safe haven in Canada opened up the possibility for sharing their struggles and the plight of their people. Taking to the stage was a testament to their survival amid the perilous odds they had faced. They were not silenced and oppressed victims, instead they claimed a space of resistance and resilience. He reflected on how theatre became a liberatory space for the renegotiation of marginalized identities and relations of power: "While the theatre space can be used to construct identity, it can also be used to challenge and subvert hegemonic ideologies and the typical 'refugee identity' of the victimized and silenced" (Y. Zine 2016, 21–2). As these youth worked toward negotiating a new and empowered identity by taking to the stage, they were also trying to adapt to a new way of life in Canada, knowing that those they left behind remained imperiled.

These youth did not want integration into Canadian society to come at the expense of losing their cultural heritage which was being annihilated in the ongoing genocide in Myanmar. Y. Zine (2016, 20) put this dilemma in perspective: "Many of the youth expressed what can be described as the struggle for the delicate balance of asserting a Canadian identity and reclaiming the Rohingya identity that is on the brink of extinction." After the first theatre performance of *I Am Rohingya*, one of the eldest refugee performers invited the audience to shout "Rohingya!" Hearing the crowd shout "Rohingya!" was a powerful and poignant act of defiance and resistance against the erasure of their people.

Ethnographic theatre and performed ethnography (Goldstein 2000) allow the stage to become a site of reclamation and resistance for refugee storytellers so that their marginalized experiences can finally be centred and heard. Y. Zine (2016, 20) writes, "It's important to be aware that by bringing those stories from the margins to the centre, we are collaboratively engaging in an act of resistance towards hegemonic structures that seek to ignore and silence the Rohingya people. Oral narratives push back and create new realities in a post-positivist world." Both the play and the documentary film took risks since the process involved children and youth re-enacting the violence their families had experienced. A social service agency offered counselling during this process, but the act of sharing testimonies through theatrical re-enactment proved to be therapeutic and healing.

Commenting on how theatre created this affirming space, Y. Zine explained, "The theatre space acted as a place where healing could occur, personalities could transform, and the realities of the plight of the Rohingya people could be confronted and re-lived." He shared a quote from Maryam, one of the youth who took part in the play, who said, "I could express myself in a theatre more than a movie. When I was on the stage, I thought that it belonged to me, it's my time to tell the story" (Y. Zine 2016, 40). Using theatre and the arts as a space for healing and empowerment is a powerful intervention for marginalized youth to work through and negotiate the complex challenges they face. The liberation of claiming and asserting their voices as a means of social uplift, political praxis, and artistic subversion was part of a shared experience. While the re-enactments in *I Am Rohingya: A Genocide in Four Acts* are often hard to watch, they are a compelling and inspiring tale of resilience against insurmountable odds.

As a form of public pedagogy, the play and the documentary became an important platform to raise awareness of the plight of the Rohingya people, and at the same time help Rohingya youth negotiate their identities and come to terms with the tragedies they experienced. Y. Zine (2016, 30) writes, "Counterstories then become a way to assert or reassert identity and make people less willing to accept oppressive valuations of themselves by transforming the person into a competent moral agent and opening up a space to exercise their agency more freely." As a testament to the political work this film performed, the youth from *I Am Rohingya* met with the Canadian prime minister and the premier of Ontario who donated $1 million of provincial aid to Rohingya refugees. They have been invited to speak at the United Nations and have toured with the film across Canada and the UK, engaging with audiences for whom it was their first exposure to hearing and witnessing the plight of their people. It is these stories of uplift and resilience in the face of tragic circumstances that distinguish this generation of Muslim youth who refuse to be victims and dare to imagine and enact alternative futures for themselves and the generations to come.

Conclusion

This book has covered a lot of necessary and previously neglected ground. It was an ambitious undertaking but one that was compelled by an urgency to unpack and address the dynamics of Islamophobia and its impact on a generation of young Muslims who knew little or nothing of a world before they became constructed as potential villains and outlaws on a global stage. As the twentieth anniversary of 9/11 approaches, the conditions created by Islamophobia and the war on terror do not ultimately define who these youth are or take away their agency, it has nonetheless shaped the world they must navigate because of it. I hope that this book will not be read as a story of victimhood. It is the resistance and resilience of these youth that should be the takeaway. Muslim youth have been uniquely faced with circumstances not of their making. These conditions have profoundly shaped their coming of age from adolescence and early adulthood in ways that their non-Muslim peers have not had to face.

There is a built-in exceptionality to the 9/11 generation because of the way they have been socially and politically constructed and positioned. This generation cannot be collectively labelled and essentialized, a framing that this book has resisted. I want to acknowledge that the experiences of Muslim youth cannot be solely reduced to what they have shared in this book. They live rich, diverse, and textured lives outside the political context engaged here. The shared experiences of growing up against the political backdrop of global war and terror give us important insights into how their lives are shaped by these conditions, but it is not the whole story. Muslims are not defined by the negative labels, conspiracy theories, and industries of hate dedicated to maligning, containing, and banishing them from Western nations.

Collectively they face these challenges as conditions to be managed, contested, and resisted. But these difficult facets of their lives cannot be avoided or overlooked in favour of more palatable stories.

The voices of these youth force us to look deeply into the shadows of our democratic societies and unearth hidden truths lying behind the façade of multicultural pluralism. Their stories take us to places that many would prefer to ignore or dismiss in favour of a view of Canadian exceptionalism. Securing Canada as a benevolent nation and saying, "If you don't believe it just look south of the border" provides a convenient alibi. Yet, what happens "south of the border" does not absolve the Great White North from its history of racism and exclusion. We cannot do justice to the testimonies in this book by reading them against a more debased standard. We must include the flaws as well as strengths of our nation as part of our collective consciousness.

There must be an unflinching examination of what lurks behind the veneer of civility and multicultural diversity. For example, Canada is a country that allows for secret trials and secret evidence to be held against non-citizens who face "indefinite detention." Five Muslim men dubbed the "secret trial five" (later adopted as the name for a Muslim punk rock band in British Columbia) have been subject to these laws for almost two decades. When I teach about the legal exceptions of Canada's Security Certificate regime in my university classes, students (non-Muslim and Muslim) are shocked to learn such conditions exist and that there is little public outcry. When these laws and practices exist in the shadows of the state and are obscured by the myths of a benevolent nation, they operate with impunity. It is only by telling these secreted stories that we shine a light into the dark corners of our political system that supports and sustains racial, xenophobic, and Islamophobic logics.

Everyone who reads this book is a witness to the lives and experiences of young Muslims caught in the crosshairs of global geopolitical struggles. Meanwhile, national multicultural fantasies of "saris, samosas, and steel bands" are the dominant imagery behind celebratory ethno-racial difference. The multicultural "Islamophilic" impulse of celebrating "exotic" Muslim cultures (through song, food, and cultural exhibits) operates in tandem with widespread Islamophobic disavowal. Circling back to Du Bois ([1903] 1995) in *The Souls of Black Folk* (discussed in the introduction), he tells us of the double-consciousness produced in response to the question, What does it feel like to be a problem? This dynamic is front and centre for Muslim youth today. Diverse groups of Muslim youth are constructed as a "problem" to be feared, managed, and rehabilitated by a racialized state security industrial complex (see also Abdel-Fattah 2021). Double-consciousness interiorizes the external gaze of others but does not entirely replace one's notion of selfhood and identity. Dealing with the consequences of being Muslim is based on how others define and infuse meaning into that category, but it does not mean self-knowledge and truth must be sacrificed to those presuppositions.

Similarly, living under siege is a predicament for Muslim youth (and all Muslims), though it does not define Muslimness or the diverse ways that category is lived. In other words, no one is captive to their experiences or circumstances. The breadth and range of issues covered in this book should make it evident that Muslim youth find creative and challenging ways to navigate the social and political complexities that accompany their identities. I have argued that there is an ontological dimension to being under siege as it shapes the habitus and dispositions surrounding these lived experiences. This does not mean, however, that this reality defines Muslim identities to the exclusion of the meanings they attach to themselves. Being under siege may be internalized and cause trauma, but it is also struggled against and resisted. It is important to understand how spaces of transcendence accompany marginality. This is not to romanticize what for some are insurmountable social, political, emotional, and psychological challenges. But it is a call to see beyond victimhood and examine the multiplicity of conditions through which oppression is countered as well as to acknowledge what it diminishes.

This book was intended as an eye-opening journey to alert us to the ways that some lives are lived against the grain of social acceptance where belonging is always contingent. The youth who have shared their stories in this book did so not to be pitied or patronized. They wanted to set the record straight about the Islamophobia they experience, and they want you to understand the political complexities within which their lives have become entangled. Tuhiwai-Smith (1999, 4) explains this best as a concluding note: "To acquiesce is to lose ourselves entirely and implicitly agree with all that has been said about us. To resist is to retrench in the margins, retrieve what we were and remake ourselves. The past, our stories, local and global, the present, our communities, cultures, languages, and social practices – all may be spaces of marginalization, but they have also become spaces of resistance and hope." The hope for an alternative decolonial future underwrites the imperative for this book and must be held as a trust for the generations to follow.

Notes

CHAPTER ONE

1 Throughout this book, I follow the definition set out in my earlier work
   (Taylor and Zine, 2014) where the terms "West" and "Western" reference
   a dynamic but persistent geopolitical configuration constructed through
   coloniality/modernity (Mignolo 2000) of former European imperial powers
   and White settler states combined with the neo-liberal economic might
   of the Global North and discursively undergirded by Eurocentrism.

2 While the term "ISIS" or "ISIL" is commonly used to denote the extremist
   group that identifies itself as "Islamic State in Iraq and the Levant," I use the
   alternate term "Daesh" to refer to them in pejorative terms that challenge
   the legitimacy of the group. According to Irshaid (2015), "Daesh is essentially
   an Arabic acronym formed from the initial letters of the group's previous
   name in Arabic – 'al-Dawla al-Islamiya fil Iraq wa al-Sham.' Although
   it does not mean anything as a word in Arabic, it sounds unpleasant
   and the group's supporters object to its use." This alternative term is being
   more widely employed, with governments such as France and the UK
   adopting it as well as many media outlets. However, when participants
   in the study use the term "ISIS" I have kept it, deferring to their usage.

3 See YouTube at https://www.youtube.com/watch?v=DjET-FjFa2Q.

4 Throughout the book where "White" is used to signify a racial identity it
   is capitalized in keeping with other racial categories like Black and Brown.
   By not capitalizing the term we risk setting the category of White/Whiteness
   apart as a normative standard and diminish its resonance as a signifier
   of unearned privilege, social dominance, and cultural power. This choice
   was made to disrupt the seemingly innocuous ways the politics of naming
   can reproduce racial power. Nguyễn and Pendleton (2020, np) add the

following rationale for this editorial choice: "We believe that it is important to call attention to White as a race as a way to understand and give voice to how Whiteness functions in our social and political institutions and our communities. Moreover, the detachment of 'White' as a proper noun allows White people to sit out of conversations about race and removes accountability from White people's and White institutions' involvement in racism."

5 The Canadian federal government has also chosen to adopt this definition of Islamophobia.

6 The aftermath of the 9/11 phase of Islamophobic history has made "Muslimness" salient for those who would otherwise not identify with the category due to lack of religiosity or more secular lifestyle preferences. For these more culturally affiliated Muslims (i.e., those who acknowledge a cultural connection to Islam but eschew religious practice), or even those who identify as atheist and distance themselves from Islam, they are nonetheless still affected by Islamophobia by virtue of racial affiliation and origins within Muslim countries or by their Muslim-sounding names.

7 People misidentified and perceived to be Muslim have also suffered the impact and violence of Islamophobia. For example, Balbir Singh Sodhi, a Sikh man mistaken for an Arab Muslim because of his turban, was killed in reprisal for the 9/11 bombings.

8 *Taqiyya* refers to a denial of Islamic belief and practice or concealing one's faith, to prevent persecution, which has been used by White nationalist and other Islamophobic groups and ideologues as a way of suggesting that Muslims are deceitful and hiding their presumed nefarious aims to overthrow Western civilization behind a friendly facade.

9 Bissonnette was originally sentenced to forty years with no parole and his sentence was subsequently reduced to twenty-five years without parole. The verdict angered the local Muslim community, which sought a harsher penalty for this heinous crime.

10 On the day of the terror attack, Trudeau tweeted, "To those fleeing persecution, terror & war, Canadians will welcome you, regardless of your faith. Diversity is our strength #WelcomeToCanada."

11 See for example the following public campaign to designate 29 January as a National Day of Remembrance and Action against Islamophobia, spearheaded by Canadians for Justice and Peace in the Middle East: www.cjpme.org/mend_4_1.

12 "An Act respecting the laicity of the State" (French: *Loi sur la laïcité de l'État*) was tabled by the ruling Coalition Avenir Québec (CAQ) on 29 March 2019. See http://legisquebec.gouv.qc.ca/en/showdoc/cs/L-0.3.

13 Angus Reid Institute executive director Shachi Kurl suggested the deadly
   mosque attack may have contributed to an increase in support of the Muslim
   religion (Global News 2017).

14 Nadeau and Helly (2016, 6) analyzed Facebook pages supporting
   Quebec's Charter of Values and isolated five predominant themes:
   (1) the fear of a return of religion in the public space; (2) the emergence
   of a Muslim enemy whose values are perceived as irreconcilable with
   those of Quebec culture; (3) the inertia of the political class and its complicity
   with media and minorities; (4) the predominance of legal over political
   powers and of individual over collective rights; and (5) multiculturalism
   as a factor of denationalization and social fragmentation.

15 See for example an 11 May 2018 press release from National Council of
   Canadian Muslims (NCCM) and the Canadian Civil Liberties Association
   (CCLA) at https://ccla.org/
   bill-62-niqab-ban-guidelines-cannot-save-unconstitutional-law/.

16 CAIR's report notes that this funding is derived from multiple sources such
   as private donations, membership fees, and investment vehicles. Data was
   collected about the overall financial capacity of the Islamophobia Network
   by analyzing its total revenue capacity through a list of each organization's
   revenue between 2014 and 2016.

17 While many participants were Canadian citizens either through being
   naturalized or being born in Canada, this ad hoc category refers to those
   who are connected to White settler histories or who were African Canadian
   and impacted by this colonial history. I also want to acknowledge how
   this limited characterization of "Canadian" may inadvertently obscure
   and erase the presence and legacy of Indigenous communities in Canada.

18 No participants identified as LGBTQ, although they were not specifically
   asked to disclose information regarding sexual orientation.

19 One of my sons, Yusuf, was a participant in this study. He was actively
   involved in the executive committee of the Muslim Students' Association
   at one of the universities where fieldwork was taking place, and he figures
   as a prominent Canadian Muslim youth cultural producer. It made sense,
   therefore, to include him although I want to ensure that his involvement
   is read transparently.

CHAPTER TWO

1 The Quran is considered by Muslims to be the word of God revealed to
   the Prophet Muhammed in the seventh century. The term "Sunna" refers

to the prophetic example as a model of righteous behaviour for Muslims to emulate, and the Hadith are the documented words and actions of the Prophet used to further elaborate the religious edits and laws derived from the Quran.

2 Hijabi is the term used for a Muslim woman who wears the hijab or head scarf.

3 The *ummah* refers to the supranational transnational community of Muslims.

4 In 2015, the Canadian government introduced the Zero Tolerance for Barbaric Cultural Practices Act. The backgrounder states that "Canada's openness and generosity does not extend to early and forced marriage, polygamy or other types of barbaric cultural practices." The naming of this act invokes the idioms of colonial racism and the typologies of the savage, barbaric, and civilized that emerged from the scientific racism of the Enlightenment. Practices like honour killing, female genital mutilation, and forced marriage are often misaligned with Islam and Muslim cultures. The scope and wording of this act embeds these problematic assumptions in Canadian legislation, normalizing Islamophobia. In 2017, the Senate passed a bill tabled by Senator Mobina Jaffer to remove mention of "barbaric cultural practices" from the name of this law introduced by the Conservative Harper government. Jaffer stated that pairing "barbaric" and "cultural" was turning individual practices into cultural pathologies that malign specific groups with whom these practices become associated (Smith 2017).

CHAPTER THREE

1 As a result of Steyn's article, human rights complaints were filed against *Maclean's* magazine by the Canadian Islamic Congress in British Columbia and Ontario as well as with the Canadian Human Rights Commission. The complaints cited twenty-two articles published by *Maclean's* that maligned Muslims. While these complaints were dismissed, the Ontario Human Rights Commission (2008) made the following statement:

> While freedom of expression must be recognized as a cornerstone of a functioning democracy, the Commission has serious concerns about the content of a number of articles concerning Muslims that have been published by *Maclean's* magazine and other media outlets. This type of media coverage has been identified as contributing to Islamophobia and promoting societal intolerance towards Muslim, Arab and South Asian Canadians. The Commission recognizes and understands the serious harm that such writings cause, both to the targeted communities and

society as a whole. And, while we all recognize and promote the inherent value of freedom of expression, it should also be possible to challenge any institution that contributes to the dissemination of destructive, xenophobic opinions.

2 The researchers controlled for factors like target type, number of fatalities, and whether or not the perpetrators were arrested before reaching their final statistics. The findings were based on all terrorist attacks in the US between 2006 and 2015 according to the Global Terrorism Database (Chalabi 2018).

3 "Sharia" refers to a corpus of Islamic religious law codified in the ninth century. Metaphorically the term also refers to "a path leading to water," signifying a quest for spiritual sustenance. Sharia has been negatively popularized in Islamophobic discourses as a source of barbaric customs that Muslims seek to impose on the West, hence the deployment of the term "creeping sharia" problematically ascribed to attempts by Muslims to assert within secular nations their religious practices, including requests for religious accommodation for Islamic dress codes, halal food, or prayer as well as building mosques and Islamic schools. Increasingly, the notion of creeping sharia is being leveraged by the alt-right to promote Islamophobic fearmongering and foment anti-Muslim racism and violence.

CHAPTER FOUR

1 The five pillars of Islam are the foundations of the faith and include (1) the *shahada* or declaration of faith in Allah and accepting the Muhammad as his messenger; (2) *salat* or prayers offered five times daily; (3) fasting in the month of Ramadan; (4) payment of *zakat* or alms, a portion of one's wealth spent annually on charity; and (5) performing hajj, the pilgrimage to Mecca.

2 This kind of curriculum bias was also acknowledged in the CFS report on the needs of Muslim students, which urged university administrators and faculty to combat Islamophobia and discrimination in the classroom (CFS 2007, 24).

3 Organized by neo-conservative critic of Islam David Horowitz and the Horowitz Freedom Center, Islamofascism Awareness Week was started in 2007. According to www.terrorismawarness.org, 114 college campuses across America participated in its inaugural year. The central aim of the campaign has been to draw a link between Islam (Muslims and MSAs) and terrorism and to clarify that "Islamofacism" poses a real threat on college

campuses and to national security. In addition, Horowitz has further claimed that faculty and students who are sympathetic to terrorism have hijacked university departments of Middle East Studies, Women's Studies, and Islamic Studies (see also Bazzano 2010).

4 In 2005, the Danish newspaper *Jyllands-Posten* published editorial cartoons that vilified the Prophet Muhammad. The cartoons were considered blasphemous since most Islamic traditions prohibit visual depictions of the prophet. The derogatory caricatures incited widespread backlash and debates about the boundaries between free speech and hate propagation.

CHAPTER FIVE

1 Military organizations dominate research and development in these areas under the banners of "security research" and "dual-use" technology, avoiding both the constraints and controversies of the arms trade.

2 The UK Counter Terrorism and Security Act (2015) places a Prevent Duty on early years settings "to have due regard to the need to prevent people from being drawn into terrorism." To demonstrate conformity the act outlines the following: staff are able to identify children who may be vulnerable to radicalization, and know what to do when they are identified; they assess the risk of children being drawn into terrorism, and work in partnership with local partners such as the police, Prevent Coordinators, Channel Police Practitioners and their LSCB, to take account of local risks and respond appropriately (see also Sian 2015).

3 See also "Joint Base San Antonio: Eagle Eyes program urges people to say something if they see something" at www.jbsa.mil/News/News/Article/2035476/eagle-eyes-program-urges-people-to-say-something-if-they-see-something/.

4 *Dispositif* is "firstly, a thoroughly heterogeneous ensemble consisting of discourses, institutions, architectural forms, regulatory decisions, laws, administrative measures, scientific statements, philosophical and moral propositions – in short, the said as much as the unsaid. Such are the elements of that apparatus. The apparatus itself is the system of relations that can be established between these elements" (Agamben 2009, 2).

CHAPTER SIX

1 CPRLV, "Radicalization," CPRLV website, accessed on 30 May 2020 https://info-radical.org/en/definition-2/.

2 Many Canadians harbour negative feelings toward immigrant communities and what they see as their proclivity toward violence imported from their homeland. Such attitudes do not reflect how, in fact, most migrants come to Canada to escape conflict and live in peace. In a study on imported conflict (Monahan, Berns-McGown, and Morden 2014, 9), survey findings showed that "a majority of Canadians believe that people who have experienced conflict hold onto intercommunity tensions after coming to Canada, and many fear that those tensions may result in violence." However, the same study determined that "Canadians who come from conflict – regardless of community, conflict or generation – repudiate violence in Canada as a means of resolving or responding to conflict" (9).

3 The report notes that the views of Canadians on this question did not shift significantly since 2004 and that it was difficult to determine what effect, if any, the Quebec mosque massacre in 2017 may have had on the results.

4 What constitutes radicalization versus extremism is not clearly delineated in the literature (see also Abbas and Awan 2015). Some research problematically offers highly vague and generalized meanings, such as Joffé's (2014, 1) definition of radicalization being "dissent over normative and hegemonic assumptions about the nature of the state" while "extremism" is said to be "advocating drastic or immoderate measures." Trip et al. (2019) attempt to discern these terms from a psychological standpoint. They argue that "radicalization is [a] process by which people develop extremist ideologies and beliefs." They define extremism as referring both to "political ideologies and methods through which political actors try to achieve their aims. Extremist political ideologies oppose the fundamental values of society and the principles of democracy and universal human rights by advocating racial, political, social, economic, and religious supremacy" (Trip et al. 2019, 2). This definition of extremism promotes the dominance of secular liberal values and vilifies dissent from outside these epistemic boundaries. Radicalization is cited as a process of developing "extremist beliefs, emotions and behaviours" that fall along a spectrum of violent and non-violent manifestations. Yet, theorizing a linear chain of causality falls into the trap of overdetermination. While radicalization and extremism are theorized as related processes, there needs to be a clearer articulation of how these align and yet remain distinct concepts and processes. The stigmatizing effect of this terminology warrants more diligent analytical grounding or else these terms will continue to be loosely employed to target entire populations deemed "deviant" or "anti-Western," as has been the case with Muslims.

5 To illustrate the dialectics of civilizational discourse, Wiktorowicz (2004, 8) observes that some Islamists respond in a similar vein to Huntington's

clash of civilizations thesis by using the cultural infiltration argument to mobilize against "insidious western desires to undermine the culture of Muslim societies."

6 Roy (2017) found that in Europe, radicalization occurred among "born again Muslims" after leading a highly secular lifestyle that involved drug and alcohol use, petty crime, frequenting nightclubs – all actions that go against a traditionally religious Islamic lifestyle.

7 Roy (2017) notes that the European converts who figured in his research gravitated toward jihadist ideologues like Anwar al-Awlaki because they speak and write in English.

8 According to Hasan (2014), a classified briefing note on radicalization, prepared by MI5's behavioural science unit, was leaked to the *Guardian*. It revealed that "far from being religious zealots, a large number of those involved in terrorism do not practise their faith regularly. Many lack religious literacy and could ... be regarded as religious novices." The analysts concluded that "a well-established religious identity actually protects against violent radicalisation."

9 For example, Roy (1994, 4) remarks that "from Cairo to Tehran, the crowds that in the 1950's demonstrated in front of the red or national flag now march beneath the green banner."

10 Among the conceptual limitations Sayyid (2003, 16) points out is that "[f]undamentalism can only operate as a general category if it situates itself within the discourse of the liberal secularist enlightenment project and considers that project to be the natural state of affairs."

11 Scores of books have been published that promote the Islamophobic idea of an Islamist takeover by Muslims in the West. Canadian examples include Quiggin et al. (2017) *Submission: The Danger of Political Islam to Canada*; Christine Douglass-Williams (2017) *he Challenge of Modernizing Islam*; and Ezra Levant (2012) *The Enemy Within*.

12 Abbas (2019, 65), for example, notes that "[h]ypermasculinity encourages the need for young people to prove themselves – to seek recognition – to become somebody." Muslim men are the primary focus when it comes to radicalization; however, for a discussion of how Muslim women have been subject to scrutiny and surveillance as terror suspects in the UK see Saeed (2016).

13 The acronym SAW stands for the Arabic blessing bestowed on the Prophet Muhammad by Muslims after uttering his name, *Sallallahu Alaihi Wasallam*, which translates to "May God honour him and grant him peace."

CHAPTER SEVEN

1 This participant is my son Yusuf Zine. He was included in this study as his work is relevant to the issues at stake in this research, and he has made significant contributions to the Muslim youth cultural production in Canada. As noted previously, his input is included openly and transparently.
2 Conflict Relief. YouTube. Accessed 8 September, 2021. https://www.youtube.com/channel/UCqSa_GzRFZ_91V1nXoAOukw/about.
3 Conflict Relief. Accessed 15 July 2017. https://conflictrelief.com (site discontinued).

References

Abadi, Houda. 2018. "Introduction: The Carter Center Works to Understand and Counter the Rise of Islamophobia." In *Countering the Islamophobia Industry: Toward more Effective Strategies*, 5–7. Atlanta, GA: The Carter Center.

Abbas, Tahir, ed. 2007. *Islamic Political Radicalism: A European Perspective*. Edinburgh: Edinburgh University Press.

– 2011. *Islamic Radicalism and Multicultural Politics: The British Experience*. London: Routledge.

– 2019. *Islamophobia and Radicalization: A Vicious Cycle*. London: Hurst & Co.

Abbas, Tahir, and Imran Awan. 2015. "Limits of UK Counterterrorism Policy and its Implications for Islamophobia and Far Right Extremism." *International Journal for Crime, Justice and Social Democracy* 4 (3): 16–29. Accessed 3 June 2021. www.crimejusticejournal.com.

Abdel-Fattah, Randa. 2021. *Coming of Age in the War on Terror*. New South Wales, AU: NewSouth Publishing.

Abu-Lughod, Lila. 2013. *Do Muslim Women Need Saving?* Cambridge, MA: Harvard University Press.

Abu-Ras, Wahiba M., and Zulema E. Suarez. 2009. "Muslim Men and Women's Perception of Discrimination, Hate Crimes, and PTSD Symptoms post 9/11." *Traumatology* 15 (3): 48–63.

Agamben, Giorgio. 2005. *State of Exception*. Chicago: University of Chicago Press.

– 2009. *What Is an Apparatus?* Stanford, CA: Stanford University Press.

Aggarwal, Ricky. 2019. "Halalywood: The Rise of the Islamic Entertainment Industry." Aquila Style. 7 June. Accessed 3 June 2021. https://www.aquila-style.com/halalywood-the-rise-of-the-islamic-entertainment-industry/.

Aguilar, Luis Manuel Hernández. 2018. *Governing Muslims and Islam in Contemporary Germany*. Leiden, ND: Brill.

Ahmad, Fauzia, and Mohammad Siddique Seddon, eds. 2012. *Muslim Youth: Challenges, Opportunities and Expectations*. London, UK: Continuum.

Ahmad, Sidrah. 2019. "Islamophobic Violence as a Form of Gender-Based Violence: A Qualitative Study with Muslim Women in Canada." *Journal of Gender-Based Violence* 3(1): 45–66.

Ahmed, Sameera, and Hadiyah Muhammad. 2019. "Black American Muslim Youth." In *Political Muslims*, edited by Tahir Abbas and Sadek Hamid, 23–51. New York: Syracuse University Press.

Ahmed, Sara. 2000. *Strange Encounters: Embodied Others in Post-Coloniality*. London: Routledge.

Aidi, Hisham. 2014. *Rebel Music: Race, Empire, and the New Muslim Youth Culture*. New York: Pantheon Books.

Akseer, Tabasum. 2018. "Understanding the Impact of Surveillance and Security Measures on Muslim Men." Centre for International and Defence Policy, Queen's University. *Martello Papers*, 42. Accessed 10 September 2021. https://www.queensu.ca/cidp/sites/webpublish. queensu.ca.cidpwww/files/files/publications/Martellos/Martello42EN.pdf.

Al Jazeera. 2012. "NYPD under Fire for Spying on Muslim Students." 27 February 2012. Accessed 3 June 2021. https://www.aljazeera.com/ program/the-stream/2012/2/27/nypd-under-fire-for-spying-on-muslim-students.

Al-Natour, Ryan J. 2010. "Folk Devils and the Proposed Islamic School in Camden." *Continuum: Journal of Media & Cultural Studies* 24 (4): 573–85.

Ali, Arshad Imtiaz. 2014. "A Threat Enfleshed: Muslim College Students Situate Their Identities amidst Portrayals of Muslim Violence and Terror." *International Journal of Qualitative Studies in Education* 27(10): 1243–61.

– 2016. "Citizens under Suspicion: Responsive Research with Community under Surveillance: Citizens under Suspicion." *Anthropology & Education Quarterly* 47 (1): 78–95.

– 2018. "Off the Record: Police Surveillance, Muslim Youth, and an Ethnographer's Tools of Research." *Equity & Excellence in Education* 51 (3–4): 431–49.

Ali, Wajahat, Eli Clifton, Matthew Duss, Lee Fang, Scott Keyes, and Faiz Shakir. 2011. *Fear Inc.: The Roots of the Islamophobia Network in America*. Center for American Progress. Accessed 3 June 2021. https://www. americanprogress.org/issues/religion/reports/2011/08/26/10165/fear-inc/.

Alim, Samy H. 2005. "A New Research Agenda: Exploring the Transglobal Hip Hop Umma." In *Muslim Networks: From Hajj to Hip Hop*, edited by Miriam Cooke and Bruce Lawrence, 264–74. Chapel Hill, NC: University of North Carolina Press.

Allen, Christopher. 2010. *Islamophobia*. Farnham, Surrey: Ashgate.

Alsultany, Evelyn. 2012. *Arabs and Muslims in the Media: Race and Representation after 9/11*. New York: New York University Press.

Althusser, Louis. 1971. "Ideology and Ideological State Apparatuses." In *Lenin and Philosophy and Other Essays*, edited by Louis Althusser, 85–127. London: New Left Books.

Ambrozas, Diana. 1998. "The University as Public Sphere." *Canadian Journal of Communication* 23 (1): n.p. Accessed 3 June 2021. http://www.cjc-online.ca/index.php/journal/article/view/1024/930.

Anderson, Benedict. 1983. *Imagined Communities*. New York: Verso.

Angus Reid Institute. 2013. "Canadians View Non-Christian Religions with Uncertainty, Dislike." 2 October. Accessed 3 June 2021. http://angusreid.org/canadians-view-non-christian-religions-with-uncertainty-dislike/.

– 2017a. "Four-in-Ten Outside Quebec Would Prohibit Women Wearing Niqabs from Receiving Government Services." 27 October. Accessed 20 June 2021. https://angusreid.org/bill-62-face-covering/.

– 2017b. "Religious Trends: Led by Quebec, Number of Canadians Holding Favourable Views of Various Religions Increases." 4 April. Accessed 3 June 2021. http://angusreid.org/religious-trends-2017/.

– 2018. "Radicalization and Homegrown Terrorism: Four-in-Ten Say Radicalized Individuals Live in Their Communities." Angus Reid Institute and the Canadian Race Relations Foundation. 12 July. Accessed 3 June 2021. https://crrf-fcrr.app.box.com/s/xv7uxzwet3lo9v1mtdppc5xczu809sid.

Arat-Koç, Sedef. 2017. "Whose Transnationalism? Canada, 'Clash of Civilizations' Discourse and Arab and Muslim Canadians." In *Asian Canadian Studies Reader*, edited by Roland Sintos Coloma and Gordon Pon, 316–38. Toronto: University of Toronto Press.

Asen, Robert. 2000. "Seeking the 'Counter' in Counterpublics." *Communication Theory* 10 (4): 424–46.

Asmar, Christine, Elizabeth Proude, and Lici Inge. 2004. "'Unwelcomed Sisters?' An Analysis of Findings from a Study of How Muslim Women (and Muslim Men) Experience University." *Australian Journal of Education* 48 (1): 47–63.

Associated Press. 2012. "NYPD Kept Tabs on Muslims Not Just in New York, but Throughout the Northeast," *New York Daily News*, 20 February. Accessed 3 June 2021. https://www.nydailynews.com/news/national/nypd-tabs-muslims-not-new-york-northeast-article-1.1025644.

Associated Press. 2015. "The Muslim Boy behind #IStandWith Ahmed." *Maclean's*. 16 September. Accessed 3 June 2021. https://www.macleans.ca/news/world/the-muslim-boy-behind-istandwithahmed/.

Atasoy, Yildiz. 2006. "Governing Women's Morality: A Study of Islamic Veiling in Canada." *European Journal of Cultural Studies* 9 (2): 203–21.

Atran, Scott. 2010. *Talking to the Enemy: Faith, Brotherhood, and the (Un)Making of Terrorists*. New York: Harper Collins Publishers.

Awaad, Rania. 2015. "A Journey of Mutual Growth: Mental Health Awareness in the Muslim Community." In *Partnerships for Mental Health*, edited by Laura Roberts, Daryn Reicherter, Steven Adelsheim, and Shashank Joshi, 137–45. Switzerland: Springer.

Bahdi, Reem. 2003. "No Exit: Racial Profiling and Canada's War against Terrorism." *Osgoode Hall Law Journal* 41 (2/3): 293–317. http://digitalcommons.osgoode.yorku.ca/ohlj/vol41/iss2/7.

Bahr, Nan, and Donna Pendergast. 2006. "Adolescence: A Useful Concept for This Millennium." *Curriculum Perspectives* 26 (1): 67–73.

Bakali, Naved. 2016. *Islamophobia: Understanding Anti-Muslim Racism through the Lived Experiences of Muslim Youth*. Rotterdam: Sense Publishers.

Bakht, Natasha. 2014. "In Your Face: Piercing the Veil of Ignorance about Niqab-Wearing Women." *Social and Legal Studies* 24 (3): 419–41.

Bannerji, Himani. 2000. *Dark Side of the Nation*. Toronto: Canadian Scholar's Press.

Barber, Benjamin. 1996. *Jihad vs. McWorld: Terrorism's Challenge to Democracy*. New York: Ballantine.

Barlas, Asma. 2002. *Believing Women in Islam*. Austin: University of Texas Press.

Bayoumi, Moustafa. 2009. *How Does It Feel to Be a Problem?: Being Young and Arab in America*. New York: Penguin Books.

Bayrakli, Enes and Farid Hafez, eds. 2019. *Islamophobia in Muslim Majority Societies*. New York: Routledge.

Bazian, Hatem. 2015. "Islamophobia and the 'Three Evils of Society.'" *Islamophobia Studies Journal* 3 (1): 158–66.

– 2018. "Islamophobia, 'Clash of Civilizations,' and Forging a Post-Cold War Order!" *Religions* 9 (9): 282.

Bazzano, Elliot. 2010. "Muslim Students Associations." In *Encyclopedia of Muslim American History*, edited by Edward Curtis, 410–13. New York: Facts on File.

Bechrouri, Ibrahim. 2018. "The Informant, Islam, and Muslims in New York City." *Surveillance and Religion* 16 (4): 459–72.

Bell, Lee Anne. 2009. "The Story of the Storytelling Project: An Arts-Based Race and Social Justice Curriculum." *Storytelling, Self, Society* 5 (2): 107–18.

Bell, Stewart. 2006. "Nevermind Foreign Terrorists, Why Is Canada Growing its Own Extremists?" *National Post*, 3 June. Accessed 3 June 2021. http://circ.jmellon.com/docs/view.asp?id=965.

– 2020. "Canada's Terrorism Offenders Are Coming out of Prison Still Radicalized." *Global News*, 27 February. Accessed 3 June 2021. https://globalnews.ca/news/6574722/terrorism-in-canada-deradicalization-programs-parole/.

Berzengi, Azi, Latef Berzenji, Aladdin Kadim, Falah Mustafa, and Laura Jobson. 2017. "Role of Islamic Appraisals, Trauma-Related Appraisals, and Religious Coping in the Post Traumatic Adjustment of Muslim Trauma Survivors." *Psychological Trauma: Theory, Research, Practice, and Policy* 9 (2): 189–97.

Beydoun, A. Khaled. 2018. *American Islamophobia*. Oakland, CA: University of California Press.

Beyer, Peter. 2014. "Securitization and Young Muslim Males: Is None Too Many?" *Religious Radicalization and Securitization in Canada and Beyond*, edited by Lorne Dawson and Paul Bramadat, 121–44. Toronto: University of Toronto Press.

Bhabha, Homi K. 1994. *The Location of Culture*. New York: Routledge.

Bigo, Didier. 2002. "Security and Immigration: Toward a Critique of the Governmentality of Unease." *Alternatives (Special Issue)* 27:63–92.

– 2008. "Globalized (in)Security: The Field and the Ban-Opticon." In *Terror, Insecurity and Liberty: Illiberal Practices of Liberal Regimes after 9/11*, edited by Didier Bigo and Anastassia Tsoukala, 10–40. London: Routledge.

Boal, Augusto. 1994. *Theatre of the Oppressed*. London: Pluto Press.

Bouchard, Gérard, and Charles Taylor. 2008a. *Building the Future: A Time for Reconciliation*. Abridged Report. Quebec City: Bibliothèque et Archives nationales du Québec.

– 2008b. *Building the Future: A Time for Reconciliation*. Full Report. Quebec City: Bibliothèque et Archives nationales du Québec.

Bourdieu, Pierre. 1984. *Distinction: A Social Critique of the Judgement of Taste*. London, UK: Routledge.

– 1997. *Outline of a Theory of Practice*. Cambridge, UK: Cambridge University Press.

Bowen, John. R. 2012. *Blaming Islam*. Cambridge, MA: MIT Press.

Bracke, Sarah, and Luis Manuel Hernandez Aguilar. 2020. "'They Love Death as We Love Life': The 'Muslim Question' and the Biopolitics of Replacement." *British Journal of Sociology* 77 (4): 1–22.

Bramadat, Paul. 2014. "The Public, the Political and the Possible: Religion and Radicalization in Canada and Beyond." In *Religious Radicalization and Securitization in Canada and Beyond*, edited by Lorne Dawson and Paul Bramadat, 3–33. Toronto: University of Toronto Press.

Brown, Katherine E., and Tania Saeed. 2015. "Radicalization and Counter-Radicalization at British Universities: Muslim Encounters and Alternatives." *Ethnic and Racial Studies* 38 (11): 1952–68.

Bullock, Katherine. 2002. *Rethinking Muslim Women and the Veil: Challenging Historical & Modern Stereotypes*. Hearndon, VA: International Institute of Islamic Thought.

Bullock, Katherine, and Paul Nesbitt-Larking. 2011. *Canadian Muslim Youth and Political Participation: A Willingness to Engage*. Policy Report. Accessed 3 June 2021. http://www.tessellateinstitute.com/publications/.

Burstein, David. 2013. *Fast Future: How the Millennial Generation is Shaping our World*. Boston, MA: Beacon Press.

Burwell, Catherine. 2014. "'A Too Quick Enthusiasm for the Other': North American Women's Book Clubs and the Politics of Reading." In *Muslim Women Transnational Feminist Reading Practices, Pedagogy and Ethical Concerns: Contested Imaginaries in Post 9/11 Cultural Practice*, edited by Lisa K. Taylor and Jasmin Zine, 133–51. New York: Routledge Press.

Butler, Judith. 2009. *Frames of War: When Is Life Grievable?* London, UK: Verso.

Caidi, Nadia, and Susan MacDonald. 2008. "Information Practices of Canadian Muslims post 9/11." *Government Information Quarterly* 25 (3): 348–78.

Cainkar, Louise. 2002. "No Longer Invisible: Arab and Muslim Exclusion after September 11." *Middle East Report* 224:22–9.

CAIR (Council of American-Islamic Relations). 2017. "Unshakable: the Bullying of Muslim Students and the Unwavering Movement to Eradicate It." *CAIR-CA School Bullying Report*. 1–28. Retrieved from: https://ca.cair.com/sfba/publications/2017-bullying-report/.

Calhoun, Craig, ed. 1992. *Habermas and the Public Sphere*. Boston: MIT Press.

CAIR-CAN (Canadian Council on American-Islamic Relations). 2004. *Presumption of Guilt: A National Survey on Security Visitations of Canadian Muslims.* Accessed 28 September 2021. https://www.aph. gov.au/parliamentary_business/committees/house_of_representatives_ committees?url=pjcaad/asio_ques_detention/subs/sub107a.pdf.

– 2019. *Hijacked by Hate: American Philanthropy and the Islamophobia Network.* 19 June. Accessed 3 June 2021. http://www.islamophobia.org/ reports/243-hijacked-by-hate-american-philanthropy-and-the- islamophobia-network.html.

Canadian Press. 2013. "Fourth Former Student from London, Ont., High School being Investigated for Possible Terrorism Ties: Sources." *National Post,* 12 April. Accessed 3 June 2021. https://nationalpost. com/news/canada/fourth-london-ont-man-being-investigated-for- possible-terrorism-ties-sources.

– 2016. "48 Percent of Quebecers view Muslims Unfavourably: Poll." *CTV News,* 19, December. Accessed 3 June, 2021. https://montreal. ctvnews.ca/48-per-cent-of-quebecers-view-muslims-unfavourably- poll-1.3209179.

CBC News. 2011. "Harper Says 'Islamicism' Biggest Threat to Canada," 6 September. Accessed 3 June 2021. https://www.cbc.ca/news/politics/ harper-says-islamicism-biggest-threat-to-canada-1.1048280.

CBC Radio. 2015. "Boonaa Mohammed's Tug of War Takes a Frank Look at Radicalization." CBC Radio, 3 December. Accessed 3 June 2021. https:// www.cbc.ca/radio/q/schedule-for-thursday-december-3-2015-1.3348530/ boonaa-mohammed-s-tug-of-war-takes-frank-look-at-radicalization- 1.3348543.

Cecco, Leyland. 2018. "Canada Mosque Shooter Says He Was Motivated by Trudeau Welcoming Refugees." *Guardian,* 13 April. Accessed 3 June 2021. https://www.theguardian.com/world/2018/apr/13/canada-mosque- shooter-alexandre-bissonnette-trudeau-trump-refugees-travel-ban.

CFS (Canadian Federation of Students). 2007. *Final Report of the Task Force on Needs of Muslim Students.* Toronto: CFS.

Chalabi, Mona. 2018. "Terror Attacks by Muslims Receive 357% More Press Attention." *Guardian,* 20 July. Accessed on 30 July 2018. https:// amp.theguardian.com/us-news/2018/jul/20/ muslim-terror-attacks-press-coverage-study.

Chase, Steven. 2006. "Raids Prove That Canada Not Soft on Terror, Day Says." *Globe and Mail,* 5 June. Accessed 3 June 2021. https://www. theglobeandmail.com/news/national/raids-prove-that-canada-not-soft- on-terror-day-says/article1816481l/.

Christopher, Colin. 2019. "2019 Survey of MSA West Student Members: Perseverance in the Face of Adversity." *Institute for Social Policy and Understanding* (ISPU). Accessed 3 June 2021. https://www.ispu.org/wp-content/uploads/2019/07/ISPU-MSA-West-Survery-Report_Web-1.pdf?x22387.

CJPME (Canadians for Justice and Peace in the Middle East). 2018. *Islamophobia in Canada. Still a Grave Problem.* Accessed 3 June 2021. https://www.cjpme.org/islamophobia.

CNN Wire Staff. 2012. "Al-Shabaab Joining Al-Qaeda, Monitor Group Says." *CNN*, 10 February. Accessed 3 June 2021. https://www.cnn.com/2012/02/09/world/africa/somalia-shabaab-qaeda/index.html.

Cohen, Stanley. [1972] 2014. *Folk Devils and Moral Panics: The Creation of the Mods and Rockers.* London, UK: Routledge.

Collet, Bruce A. 2007. "Islam, National Identity and Public Secondary Education: Perspectives from the Somali Diaspora in Toronto, Canada." *Race Ethnicity and Education* 10 (2): 131–53.

CPRLV (Centre for the Prevention of Radicalization Leading to Violence). 2016. *Radicalization leading to Violence in Quebec Schools: Issues and Perspectives.* Montreal: CPRLV, 1–84. Accessed 3 June 2021. https://info-radical.org/wp-content/uploads/2016/10/rapport-cprlv.pdf.

Dabashi, Hamid. 2011. *Brown Skin, White Masks.* London, UK: Pluto Press.

Dawson, Lorne. 2014. "Trying to Make Sense of Homegrown Terrorist Radicalization: The Case of the Toronto 18." In *Religious Radicalization and Securitization in Canada and Beyond*, edited by Lorne Dawson and Paul Bramadat, 64–91. Toronto: University of Toronto Press.

Dei, George J. Sefa, and Ali Asgharzadeh. 2001. "The Power of Social Theory: The Anti-Colonial Discursive Framework." *Journal of Educational Thought* 35 (3): 297–323.

Dei, George J. Sefa, and Arlo Kempf, eds. 2006. *Anti-Colonialism and Education.* Rotterdam, NL: Sense Publishers.

Delshad, Carmel. 2019. "Mourning Nabra Hassanen: The Uncommon Aftermath of a Muslim Teen's Death." WAMU 88.5 American University Radio. Accessed 3 June 2021. https://wamu.org/story/19/05/17/mourning-nabra-hassanen-the-uncommon-aftermath-of-a-muslim-teens-death/.

Diab, Robert. 2008. *Guantánamo North Terrorism and the Administration of Justice in Canada.* Black Point, NS: Fernwood.

Dickson, Janice. 2019. "Terrorism Experts Applaud Minister's Clarifications on Returned Foreign Fighters." *Globe and Mail*, 16 January. Accessed 3 June 2021. https://www.theglobeandmail.com/politics/article-terrorism-experts-applaud-public-safety-ministers-clarifications-on/.

Dimoff, Anna, and Christine Coulter. 2017. "The 'Bystander Effect': Responding to Racist, Violent Incidents in Public." CBC News. Accessed 3 June 2021. https://www.cbc.ca/news/canada/british-columbia/bystander-effect-transit-attack-1.4437433.

Dion, Susan D., and Michael Dion. 2004. "The Braiding Histories Stories." *Journal of the Canadian Association for Curriculum Studies* 2 (1): 77–100.

Douglass-Williams, Christine. 2017. *The Challenge of Modernizing Islam*. New York: Encounter Books.

Du Bois, W.E.B. (1903) 1995. *The Souls of Black Folk*. New York: Signet Classic.

Eickelman, Dale, and Jon Anderson. 2003. "Redefining Muslim Publics," In *New Media in the Muslim World: The Emerging Public Sphere*, edited by Dale Eickelman and Jon Anderson, 1–19. Bloomington: Indiana University Press.

Elahi, Farah, and Omar Khan, eds. 2017. *Islamophobia: Still a Challenge for Us All: 20th Anniversary Report*. London, UK: Runnymede Trust.

Elkassem, Siham, Rick Csiernik, Andrew Mantulak, Gina Kayassi, Yasmin Hussain, Kathyrn Lambert, Pamela Bailey, and Asad Choudhary. 2018. "Growing Up Muslim: The Impact of Islamophobia on Children in a Canadian Community." *Journal of Muslim Mental Health* 12 (1): 3–18.

Fadil, Nadia, Martijn de Koning, and Francesco Ragazzi. 2019. *Radicalization in Belgium and the Netherlands*. London, UK: I.B. Taurus.

Fanon, Frantz. 1965. *A Dying Colonialism*. New York: Grove Press.

– 1967. *Black Skin, White Masks*. New York: Grove Press.

Finn, Melissa, Jenna Hennebry, and Bessma Momani. 2018. "Canadian Arab Youth at the Border: Cultural Dissociation, Fear Management, and Disciplining Practices in Securitized Spaces." *Journal of International Migration and Integration* 19 (3): 667–82.

Flatt, Jacqueline. 2012. "The Security Certificate Exception: A Media Analysis of Human Rights and Security Discourses in Canada's *Globe and Mail* and *National Post*." In *Islam in the Hinterlands: Muslim Cultural Politics in Canada*, edited by Jasmin Zine, 239–71. Vancouver: UBC Press.

Flower, Scott, and Birkett Deborah. 2014. "(Mis) Understanding Muslim Converts in Canada: A Critical Discussion of Muslim Converts in the Contexts of Security and Society". *Canadian Network for Research on Terrorism, Security and Society*. Working Paper Series 14 (6): 1–19.

Forum Poll. 2016. "Muslims the Target of Most Racial Bias." 19 December. Accessed 3 June 2021. https://poll.forumresearch.com/post/2646/muslims-the-target-of-most-racial-bias/.

Fraser, Nancy. 1992. "Rethinking the Public Sphere: A Contribution to the Critique of Actually Existing Democracy." In *Habermas and the Public Sphere*, edited by Craig Calhoun, 109–42. Boston, MA: MIT.

– 1995. "Politics, Culture and the Public Sphere toward a Post-Modern Conception." In *Social Postmodernism beyond Identity Politics*, edited by Linda J. Nicholson and Steven Seidman, 287–314. London, UK: Cambridge University Press.

– 2009. "Transnationalizing the Public Sphere: On the Legitimacy and Efficacy of Public Opinion in a Postwestphalian World." In *Scales of Justice: Reimagining Political Space in a Globalized World*, 76–100. New York: Columbia University Press.

Freire, Paulo. 1970. *Pedagogy of the Oppressed*. New York: Continuum Publishing.

Forrest, Maura. 2019. "Ottawa Unveils Anti-Racism Strategy, Which Includes Definition of Islamophobia." *National Post*. 26 June. Accessed 3 June 2021. https://nationalpost.com/news/politics/ottawa-unveils-anti-racism-strategy-which-includes-definition-of-islamophobia.

Foucault, Michel. 1991. *Discipline and Punish: the Birth of a Prison*. London, UK: Penguin.

– 1994. "The Subject and Power," In *Power: Essential Works of Foucault, 1954-1984*, edited by James D. Faubion, 328–49. New York: The New Press.

– 2000. "Interview with D. Deleule and F.P. Adorno: 'L'héritage Intellectuel de Foucault.'" *Cités* 2 (95): 107.

Fry, Hedy. 2018. "Taking Action against Systemic Racism and Religious Discrimination Including Islamophobia." Standing Committee on Canadian Heritage. 42nd Parliamentary Session. Accessed 3 June 2021. House of Commons. https://www.ourcommons.ca/Content/Committee/421/CHPC/Reports/RP9315686/chpcrp10/chpcrp10-e.pdf.

Geddes, John. 2013. "Canadian Anti-Muslim Sentiment Is Rising, Disturbing New Poll Reveals." *Maclean's*, 3 October. Accessed 3 June 2021. https://www.macleans.ca/politics/land-of-intolerance/.

Global News. 2017. "Nearly Half of Canadians View Islam Unfavourably, Survey Finds." Global News (website), 4 April. Accessed 3 June 2021. https://globalnews.ca/news/3356103/canadians-islam-religion-trends-study/.

Goldberg, David T. 1993. *Racist Culture*. Oxford, England: Blackwell Publishing.

Goldstein, Tara. 2000. "Hong Kong Canada: Performed Ethnography for Anti-Racist Teacher Education." *Teacher Education* 1 (3): 79–326.

Gottschalk, Peter, and Gabriel Greenberg. 2008. *Islamophobia Making Muslims the Enemy*. Lanham: Rowman & Littlefield Publishers.

Green, Todd. 2019. *Fear of Islam: An Introduction to Islamophobia in the West*. Minneapolis: Fortress Press.

Grosfoguel, Ramón, and Eric Mielants. 2006. "The Long-Durée Entanglement between Islamophobia and Racism in the Modern/ Colonial Capitalist/Patriarchal World-System: An Introduction." *Human Architecture: Journal of the Sociology of Self-Knowledge* 5 (2): 1–12.

– 2010. "Epistemic Islamophobia and Colonial Social Sciences." *Human Architecture: Journal of the Sociology of Self-Knowledge* 8 (5): 20–38.

Guest, Mathew, Alison Scott-Baumann, Sariya Cheruvallil-Contractor, Shuruq Naguib, Aisha Phoenix, Yenn Lee, and Tarek Al-Baghel. 2020. *Islam and Muslims on UK University Campuses: Perceptions and Challenges*. Durham: Durham University, London: SOAS, Coventry: Coventry University and Lancaster: Lancaster University.

Habermas, Jürgen. 1991. *The Structural Transformation of the Public Sphere: An Inquiry into a Category of Bourgeois Society*, translated by Thomas Burger and Frederick Lawrence. Cambridge, MA: MIT Press.

Habib, Jacky. 2019. "Far Right Groups and Hate Crime Rates Are Growing in Canada." *CBC Passionate Eye*. Accessed 3 June 2021. https://www.cbc.ca/passionateeye/m_features/ right-wing-extremist-groups-and-hate-crimes-are-growing-in-canada.

Hage, Ghassan. 2000. *White Nation: Fantasies of White Supremacy in a Multicultural Society*. New York: Routledge.

– 2003. *Against Paranoid Nationalism: Searching for Hope in a Shrinking Society*. Annandale, NSW: Pluto Press.

Hall, Stuart. 1997. "Old and New Identities; Old and New Ethnicities." In *Culture, Globalization, and the World-System: Contemporary Conditions for the Representation of Identity*, edited by Anthony D. King, 41–68. Minneapolis: University of Minnesota Press.

Haque, Eve. 2010. "Homegrown, Muslim and Other: Tolerance, Secularism and the Limits of Multiculturalism." *Social Identities* 16 (1): 79–101.

– 2012. *Multiculturalism within a Bilingual Framework*. Toronto: University of Toronto Press.

Hasan, Mehdi. 2014. "What the Jihadists who Bought 'Islam for Dummies' on Amazon Tell Us about Radicalisation." *NewStatesman*, 21 August. Accessed 3 June 2021. https://www.newstatesman.com/ religion/2014/08/what-jihadists-who-bought-islam-dummies-amazon-tell-us-about-radicalisation.

Hassan, Ghayda, Abdelwahed Mekki-Berrada, Cécile Rousseau, Gabrielle Lyonnais-Lafond, Uzma Jamil, Janet Cleveland. 2016. "Impact of the Charter of Quebec Values on psychological well-being of francophone university students." *Transcultural Psychiatry* 56 (6): 1139–54.

Hayes, Ben. 2006. "Arming Big Brother: the EU's Security Research Programme." *Transnational Institute*. 26 April. Accessed 3 June 2021. https://www.tni.org/es/node/14637.

– 2009. *NeoConOpticon: The EU Security-Industrial Complex*. Transnational Institute & Statewatch. Accessed 3 June 2021. https://www.statewatch.org/media/documents/analyses/neoconopticon-report.pdf.

Hefner, Robert W. 2001. "Public Islam and the Problem of Democratization." *Sociology of Religion* 62 (4): 491–514.

Helly, Denise. 2004. "Are Muslims Discriminated Against in Canada Since 2001?" *Canadian Ethnic Studies Journal* 36 (1): 24–47.

Hennebry, Jenna, and Bessma Momani, eds. 2013. *Targeted Transnationals: The State, the Media, and Arab Canadians*. Vancouver: UBC Press.

Hirschkind, Charles. 2001. "Civic Virtue and Religious Reason: An Islamic Counterpublic." *Cultural Anthropology* 16 (1): 3–34.

– 2006. *The Ethical Soundscapes: Cassette Sermons and Islamic Counterpublics*. New York: Columbia University Press.

Hirschkind, Charles, and Brian Larkin. 2008. "Introduction: Media and Political Forms of Religion." *Social Text* 26 (3): 1–9.

Holmlund, Christine Anne. 1993. "Displacing Limits of Difference: Gender, Race and Colonialism in Edward Said and Homi Bhahba's Theoretical Models and Marguerite Duras's Experimental Films." In *Otherness and the Media: The Ethnography of the Imagined and Imaged*, edited by Hamid Naficy and Teshome H. Gabriel, 1–22. Chur, Switzerland: Harwood Academic Publishers.

Hoodfar, Homa. 2001. "The Veil in Their Minds and on Our Heads: Veiling Practices and Muslim Women." In *Women, Gender, Religion: A Reader*, edited by Elizabeth Castelli and R. Rodman, 420–46. Palgrave Macmillan, New York.

hooks, bell. 1992. *Black Looks: Race and Representation*. Boston, MA: South End Press.

Hope Not Hate. 2018. "Bots, Fake News and the Anti-Muslim Message on Social Media." Accessed 3 June 2021. https://www.hopenothate.org.uk/bots-fake-news-anti-muslim-message-social-media/.

Hopkins, Peter. 2011. "Towards Critical Geographies of the University Campus: Understanding the Contested Experiences of Muslim Students." *Transactions of the Institute of British Geographers* 36:157–69.

Hoque, Aminul. 2019. "The Construction of a Multifaceted British Muslim Identity." In *Political Muslims:* Understanding Youth Resistance in a Global Context, edited by Tahir Abbas and Sadek Hamid, 99–124. Ithaca, NY: Syracuse University Press.

Howe, Neil, and William Strauss. 2000. *Millennial's Rising: The Next Great Generation.* New York: Vintage Books.

Huntington, Samuel. 1996. *The Clash of Civilizations and the Remaking of the World Order.* New York, NY: Simon and Schuster.

Innerspeak Media. 2017. *I Am Rohingya: A Genocide in Four Acts* (Documentary). 90 min. https://www.iamrohingyafilm.com/.

Irshaid, Faisal. 2015. "Isis, Isil, IS or Daesh? One Group Many Names." BBC News, 2 December. Accessed 3 June 2021. https://www.bbc.com/news/world-middle-east-27994277.

Jackson, Sherman. 2005. *Islam and the Blackamerican.* New York: Oxford University Press.

Jamil, Uzma. 2014. "The Impact of Securitization on South Asian Muslims in Montreal." In *Religious Radicalization and Securitization in Canada and Beyond*, edited by Lorne Dawson and Paul Bramadat, 145–63. Toronto: University of Toronto Press.

– 2017. "Can Muslims Fly? The No Fly List as a Tool of the 'War on Terror.'" *Islamophobia Studies Journal* 4 (1): 72–86.

Jamil, Uzma, and Cécile Rousseau. 2012. "Subject Positioning, Fear, and Insecurity in South Asian Muslim Communities in the War on Terror Context." *Canadian Review of Sociology/Revue canadienne de sociologie* 49 (4): 370–88.

Jiwa, Munir. 2010. "Imaging, Imagining and Representation: Muslim Visual Artists in NYC." *Contemporary Islam* 4:77–90.

Jiwani, Yasmin. 2004. "Gendering Terror: Representations of the Orientalized Body in Quebec's Post-September 11 English-Language Press." *Critique: Critical Middle Eastern Studies* 13 (3): 265–91.

– 2017. "Media Portrays Indigenous and Muslim Youth as 'Savages' and 'Barbarians.'" *The Conversation*, 26 June. Accessed 3 June 2021. https://theconversation.com/media-portrays-indigenous-and-muslim-youth-as-savages-and-barbarians-79153.

Jiwani, Yasmin, and Ahmed Al-Rawi. 2019. "Intersecting Violence: The Representation of Somali Youth in the Canadian Press." *Journalism*, 1–35.

Jiwani, Yasmin, and Matthew Dessner. 2016. "Barbarians in/of the Land: Representations of Muslim Youth in the Canadian Press." *Journal of Contemporary Issues in Education* 11 (1): 36–53.

Joffe, George. 2014. *Islamist Radicalization in North Africa.* New York: Routledge.

Johnston, Patrick, and Stephanie Ip. 2017. "On a Vancouver SkyTrain Full of People, just One Came to Help Teen in Religious Attack." *Vancouver Sun,* 7 December. Accessed 3 June 2021. https://vancouversun.com/news/local-news/police-investigating-alleged-racist-attack-monday-evening-on-board-canada-line.

Joosse, Paul, Sandra M. Bucerius, and Sara K. Thompson. 2015. "Narratives and Counternarratives: Somali-Canadians on Recruitment as Foreign Fighters to Al-Shabaab." *British Journal of Criminology* 55:811–32.

Joshi, Khyati Y. 2006. *New Roots in America's Sacred Ground.* New Brunswick, NJ: Rutgers University Press.

Kao, Josie. 2018. "Muslim Students' Association Says Executives Receiving Surprise Visits from Law Enforcement." *Varsity,* 12 November. Accessed 3 June 2021. https://thevarsity.ca/2018/11/12/muslim-students-association-says-executives-receiving-surprise-visits-from-law-enforcement/.

Karim, Karim Haiderali. 2003. *Islamic Peril: Media and Global Violence.* Montreal: Black Rose Books.

Kazem, Halima. 2016. "Funding Islamophobia: $206m Went to Promoting 'Hatred' of Muslim Americans." *Guardian,* 20 June. Accessed 3 June 2021. https://www.theguardian.com/us-news/2016/jun/20/islamophobia-funding-cair-berkeley-report.

Kazemipur, Abdolmohammad. 2014. *The Muslim Question in Canada: A Story of Segmented Integration.* Vancouver: UBC Press.

Kearns, Erin M., Allison E. Betus, and Anthony F. Lemieux. 2019. "Why Do Some Terrorist Attacks Receive More Media Attention Than Others?" *Justice Quarterly* 36 (6): 985–1022.

Keen, Sam. 1988. *Faces of the Enemy: Reflections of the Hostile Imagination.* San Francisco: Harper & Row Publishers.

Kenyon, Georgina. 2016. "The Man who Studies the Spread of Ignorance." BBC Future, 6 January. Accessed 3 June 2021. http://www.bbc.com/future/story/20160105-the-man-who-studies-the-spread-of-ignorance.

Khalema, E. Nene, and Jenny Wannas-Jones. 2003. "Under the Prism of Suspicion: Minority Voices in Canada after September 11." *Journal of Muslim Minority Affairs* 23 (1): 25–39.

Khan, Adnan R. 2014. "Muslim Brotherhood: The New Islamist Bogeyman in Canada." *Maclean's*, 2 June. Accessed 3 June 2021. https://www.macleans.ca/news/world/the-muslim-brotherhood-the-new-islamist-bogeyman-in-canada/.

Khan, Shahnaz. 2005. "Reconfiguring the Native Informant: Positionality in the Global Age." *Signs: Journal of Women in Culture and Society* 30 (4): 2017–37.

Khattab, Nabil, Sami Miaari, and Marwan Mohamed-Ali. 2019. "Visible Minorities in the Canadian Labour Market: Disentangling the Effect of Religion and Ethnicity." *Ethnicities* 20 (6): 1289-54.

Khosrokhavar, Farhad. 2009. *Inside Jihadism*. New York: Taylor Francis.

Kumar, Deepa. 2012. *Islamophobia and the Politics of Empire*. Chicago: Haymarket Books.

Kundnani, Arun. 2012. "Radicalization: The Journey of a Concept." *Race and Class* 54 (2): 3–25.

– 2015. *The Muslims Are Coming!* London, UK: Verso.

Lean, Nathan. 2017. *The Islamophobia Industry: How the Right Manufactures Hatred of Muslims*. London, UK: Pluto Press.

Levant, Ezra. 2012. *The Enemy Within: Terror, Lies, and the Whitewashing of Omar Khadr*. Toronto: McClelland & Stewart.

Lewis, Bernard. 1990. "The Roots of Muslim Rage." *The Atlantic*, September, n.p.

Limon, Elvia. 2018. "'Clock Boy' Ahmed Mohamed's Lawsuit against Irving ISD, City Dismissed." *Dallas News*, 14 March. Accessed 3 June 2021. https://www.dallasnews.com/news/irving/2018/03/14/clockboy-ahmed-mohamed-lawsuit-irving-isd-city-dismissed.

Lorente, Javier Rosón. 2010. "Discrepancies around the Use of the Term 'Islamophobia.'" *Human Architecture: Journal of the Sociology of Self-Knowledge* 8 (2): Article 11. Accessed 3 June 2021. http://scholarworks.umb.edu/humanarchitecture/vol8/iss2/11.

Mackay, Hugh. 1997. *Generations: Baby Boomers, Their Parents and Their Children*. Sydney, AU: Pan Macmillan.

MacLeod, Ian. 2008. "CSIS Focuses on Homegrown Terrorism Threat." *Ottawa Citizen*, 14 March. Accessed 3 June 2021. https://www.pressreader.com/canada/ottawa-citizen/20080314/281599531205178.

Magder, Jason. 2016. "Pig Head Left on Door of Quebec City Mosque during Ramadan." *Montreal Gazette*, 20 June. Accessed 3 June 2021. https://montrealgazette.com/news/local-news/pig-head-left-on-door-of-quebec-city-mosque-during-ramadan.

Mahr, Fauzia, and Tania Nadeem. 2019. "Muslim Women and Islamophobia." In *Islamophobia and Psychiatry*, edited by Steven Moffic, John Peteet, Ahmed Hankir, and Rania Awaad, 295–305. Cham: Springer.

Maira, Sunaina Marr. 2009. *Missing: Youth, Citizenship, and Empire after 9/11*. Durham: Duke University Press.

– 2012. "Islamophobia and Dissent: South Asian Muslim Youth in the United States." In *From the Far Right to the Mainstream: Islamophobia, Party Politics and the Media*, edited by Humayun Ansari and Farid Hafez, 112–30. Frankfurt, Germany: Campus.

– 2016. *The 9/11 Generation: Youth, Rights, and Solidarity in the War on Terror*. New York: New York University Press.

Mahmood, Saba. 2003. "Islam and the Challenge of Democracy: Questioning Liberalism Too." *Boston Review*, May 2003. Accessed 3 June 2021. https://bostonreview.net/forum/islam-and-challenge-democracy/saba-mahmood-questioning-liberalism-too.

– 2005. *The Politics of Piety*. New Jersey: Princeton University Press.

Mamdani, Mahmood. 2004. *Good Muslim, Bad Muslim: America, the Cold War, and the Roots of Terror*. New York: Three Leaves Press.

Marlow, Iain, and Kristin Rushowy. 2007. "School Assault Ignored: Sources." *Toronto Star*, 30 June. Accessed 3 June 2021. https://www.thestar.com/news/2007/06/30/school_assault_ignored_sources.html.

Massoumi, Narzanin, Tom Mills, and David Miller, eds. 2017. *What Is Islamophobia? Racism, Social Movements and the State*. London, UK: Pluto Press.

Mathelat, Siegfried L. 2015. "A Hidden Ideological Scheme under New Secularism: Explaining a Peak of Islamophobia in Quebec (2013–2014)." *Islamophobia Studies Journal* 3 (1): 29–43.

Mazarr, Michael, J. 2007. *Unmodern Men in the Modern World: Radical Islam, Terrorism and the War on Modernity*. Oxford: Cambridge University Press.

McCloud, Aminah. 1994. *African American Islam*. New York: Routledge.

McDonough, Sheila, and Hooma Hoodfar. 2009. "Muslims in Canada: From Ethnic Groups to Religious Community." In *Religion and Ethnicity in Canada*, edited by Paul Bramadat and David Seljak, 133–53. Toronto: University of Toronto Press.

McKenzie, Robert L. 2018. Keynote Address 3rd Annual Conference Report on *Youth Resiliency: Hate, Racism and Youth Radicalization*. Midaynta Community Services. Toronto, ON.

McSorley, Tim. 2021. *The CRA's Prejudiced Audits: Counter-Terrorism and the Targeting of Muslim Charities in Canada*. Toronto: Canadian Civil Liberties Monitoring Group.

Meer, Nasar, ed. 2014. *Racialization and Religion: Race, Culture and Difference in the Study of Antisemitism and Islamophobia*. London, UK: Routledge.

Memon, Nadeem. 2009. "From Protest to Praxis: A History of Islamic Schools in North America." PhD thesis, Ontario Institute for Studies in Education, University of Toronto.

Mignolo, Walter. 2000. *Local Histories/Global Designs: Coloniality, Subaltern Knowledges, and Border Thinking*. Princeton, NJ: Princeton University Press.

Milman, Oliver. 2016. "Southwest Airlines Draws Outrage Over Man Removed for Speaking Arabic." *Guardian*, 16 April. Accessed 3 June 2021. https://www.theguardian.com/us-news/2016/apr/16/southwest-airlines-man-removed-flight-arabic.

Minsky, Amy. 2017. "Hate Crimes against Muslims in Canada Increase 253% over Four Years," Global News, 13 June. Accessed 3 June 2021. https://globalnews.ca/news/3523535/hate-crimes-canada-muslim/.

Mir, Shabana. 2007. "American Muslim Women and Cross Gender Interaction on Campus." *The American Journal of Islamic Social Science* 24 (3):70–90.

– 2009. "Not Too 'College-Like,' Not Too Normal: American Muslim Undergraduate Women's Gendered Discourses." *Anthropology & Education Quarterly* 40 (3): 237–58.

– 2014. *Muslim American Women on Campus*. Chapel Hill, NC: University of North Carolina Press.

Mirza, Munira. 2007. "Being Muslim Is Not a Barrier to Being British." *Guardian*, 7 February. Accessed 3 June 2021. https://www.theguardian.com/commentisfree/2007/feb/02/comment.religion.

Mohammed, Boonaa. 2015. "Terror Is." YouTube (video). 9.37 min. Accessed September 28 2021. https://www.youtube.com/watch?v=DjET-FjFa2Q.

Moller Okin, Susan. 1999. *Is Multiculturalism Bad for Women?* Princeton, NJ: Princeton University Press.

Monahan, John, Rima Berns-McGown, and Michael Morden. 2014. *The Perception and Reality of "Imported Conflict" in Canada*. Mosaic Institute. Toronto.

Muslims Actually. 2017. "Timaj Garad: Using Poetry and Theatre to Bring Stories to Life." *Muslim Link*, 22 December. Accessed 3 June 2021. https://muslimlink.ca/stories/muslim-canadian-timaj-garad-poetry-theatre-toronto-spoken-word.

Mythen, Gabe, Sandra Walklate, and Fatima Khan. 2009. "'I'm a Muslim, but I'm Not a Terrorist': Victimization, Risky Identities and the Performance of Safety." *The British Journal of Criminology* 49 (6): 736–54.

Nadeau, Frederic, and Denise Helly. 2016. "Extreme Right in Quebec? The Facebook Pages in Favor of the 'Quebec Charter of Values.'" *Canadian Ethnic Studies* 48 (1): 1–18.

Nagra, Baljit. 2011. "'Our Faith Was Also Hijacked by Those People': Reclaiming Muslim Identity in Canada in a Post-9/11 Era." *Journal of Ethnic and Migration Studies* 37 (3): 425–41.

– 2017. *Securitized Citizens*. Toronto: University of Toronto Press.

Nagra, Baljit, and Paula Maurutto. 2020. "No-Fly Lists, National Security and Race: The Experiences of Canadian Muslims." *The British Journal of Criminology* 60 (3): 600–19.

Nasser, Shanifa. 2019a. "When CSIS Comes Knocking: Amid Reports of Muslim Students Contacted by Spy Agency, Hotline Aims to Help." CBC News, 7 August. Accessed 3 June 2021. https://www.cbc.ca/news/canada/toronto/csis-students-university-muslim-campus-1.5229670?__vfz=medium%3Dsharebar&fbclid=IwAR0YnpXxf4xXxSiQxQDtnsOB MW6HUJaumdQZGrFMv7TRl5h7wKu-W2IHppY.

– 2019b. "Ontario Man Dubbed 'High Risk to Public Safety' after Trying to Join Terror Group Set for Release." CBC News, 22 February. Accessed 3 June 2021. https://www.cbc.ca/news/canada/toronto/canadian-terror-release-kevin-omar-mohamed-parole-1.5030090.

Nasir, Na'ilah Suad, and Jasiyah Al-Amin. 2006. "Creating Identity-Safe Spaces on College Campuses for Muslim Students." *Change: The Magazine of Higher Learning* 38 (2): 22–7.

Nazim, Zabedia. 2007. "Interrogating Restructuring: A Critical Ethnography of Ethno-Racial Women Bank Workers in Canadian Retail Banking." PhD dissertation. Ontario Institute for Studies in Education/ University of Toronto.

Nguyễn, Thúy Ann, and Maya Pendleton. 2020. "Recognizing Race in Language: Why We Capitalize 'Black' and 'White.'" Center for the Study of Social Policy. 23 March. Accessed 13 September 2021. https://cssp. org/2020/03/recognizing-race-in-language-why-we-capitalize-black-and-white/.

Nilan, Pam. 2017. *Muslim Youth in the Diaspora*. New York: Routledge.

Noël, Brigitte. 2015. "New Survey Exposing Quebec's Islamophobia Is Just Tip of Iceberg, Muslim Group Says." *Vice*, 4 November. Accessed 3 June

2021. https://www.vice.com/en_ca/article/8gkkna/new-survey-exposing-quebecs-islamophobia-is-just-tip-of-iceberg-muslim-group-says.

Odartey-Wellington, Felix. 2009. "Racial Profiling and Moral Panic: Operation Thread and the Al-Qaeda Sleeper Cell That Never Was." *Global Media Journal – Canadian Edition* 2 (2): 25–40.

Ontario Human Rights Commission. 2005. *Policy and Guidelines on Racism and Racial Discrimination.* Accessed on 27 September 2021. http://www.ohrc.on.ca/sites/default/files/attachments/Policy_and_guidelines_on_racism_and_racial_discrimination.pdf.

– 2008. "Commission Statement Concerning Issues Raised by Complaints Against *Maclean's* Magazine." Accessed 30 June 2020. http://www.ohrc.on.ca/en/news_centre/commission-statement-concerning-issues-raised-complaints-against-macleans-magazine.

Opratko, Benjamin. 2019. "Devils from Our Past. Liberal Islamophobia in Austria as Historicist Racism." *Ethnic and Racial Studies* 42 (16): 159–76.

Pape, Robert A. 2006. *Dying to Win.* New York: Random House Trade Paperbacks.

Pape, Robert A., and James K. Feldman. 2010. *Cutting the Fuse: The Explosion of Global Suicide Terrorism and How to Stop It.* Chicago: University of Chicago Press.

Patel, Shaista. 2012. "The Anti-Terrorism Act and National Security: Safeguarding the Nation against Uncivilized Muslims." In *Islam in The Hinterlands: Muslim Cultural Politics in Canada,* edited by Jasmin Zine, 272–98. New York: Palgrave Macmillan.

Patriquin, Martin, and Charlie Gillis. 2010. "About Face." *Maclean's,* 7 April. Accessed 20 June 2021. https://www.macleans.ca/news/canada/about-face/.

Peek, Lori. 2003. "Reactions and Response: Muslim Students' Experiences on New York City Campuses Post 9/11." *Journal of Muslim Minority Affairs* 23 (2): 271–83.

– 2005. "Becoming Muslim: The Development of a Religious Identity." *Sociology of Religion* 66 (3): 215–42.

– 2011. "Behind the Backlash: Muslim Americans after 9/11." Philadelphia, PA: Temple University Press.

Perry, Barbara. 2014. "Gendered Islamophobia: Hate Crime against Muslim Women." *Social Identities* 20 (1): 74–89.

Perry, Barbara, and Ryan Scrivens. 2015. "Uneasy Alliances: A Look at the Right-Wing Extremist Movement in Canada." *Studies in Conflict and Terrorism* 39 (9): 819–41.

Pilkington, Ed. 2018. "NYPD Settles Lawsuit after Illegally Spying on Muslims." *Guardian*, 5 April. Accessed 3 June 2021. https://www. theguardian.com/world/2018/apr/05/nypd-muslim-surveillance-settlement.

Porter, John. 1965. *The Vertical Mosaic: An Analysis of Social Class and Power in Canada*. Toronto: University of Toronto Press.

Postmedia News. 2017. "Most Canadians Favour Values Test for Immigrants, while 23 Per Cent Think Muslims Should Be Banned: Poll." *National Post*, 13 March. Accessed 3 June 2021. https://nationalpost. com/news/politics/most-canadians-favour-values-test-for-immigrants-while-23-per-cent-think-muslims-should-be-banned-poll.

Proctor, Robert N., and Londa Schiebinger, eds. 2008. *Agnotology: The Making and Unmaking of Ignorance*. Stanford, CA: Stanford University Press.

Quayle, Amy, Christopher Sonn, and Pilar Kasat. 2016. "Community Arts as Public Pedagogy: Disruptions into Public Memory through Aboriginal Counter-Storytelling." *International Journal of Inclusive Education* 20 (3): 261–77.

Quiggin, Thomas, Tahir Gora, Saied Shoaaib, Jonathon Cotler, and Rick Gill. 2017. *Submission: The Danger of Political Islam to Canada*. Canadian Centre for the Study of Extremism.

Quijano, Anibal, and Michael Ennis. 2000. "Coloniality of Power, Eurocentrism, and Latin America." *Nepantla: Views from South* 1 (3): 533–80.

Rabasa, Angel, and Cheryl Bernard. 2015. *Eurojihad*. Oxford, UK: Cambridge University Press.

Ramji, Rubina. 2008. "Creating a Genuine Islam: Second Generation Muslims Growing Up in Canada." *Canadian Diversity* 6 (2): 104–9.

Rappaport, Julian. 2000. "Community Narratives: Tales of Terror and Joy." *American Journal of Community Psychology* 28 (1): 1–24.

Razack, Sherene. 2008. *Casting Out: The Eviction of Muslims from Western Law and Politics*. Toronto: University of Toronto Press.

Rousseau, Cécile, Uzma Jamil, Kamaldeep Bhui, and Meriem Boudjarane. 2015. "Consequences Of 9/11 and The War on Terror on Children's and Young Adult's Mental Health: A Systematic Review of the Past 10 Years." *Clinical Child Psychology and Psychiatry* 20 (2): 173–93.

Rousseau, Cécile, Youssef Oulhote, Vanessa Lecompte, Abdelwahed Mekki-Berrada, Ghayda Hassan, and Habib El Hage. 2019. "Collective Identity, Social Adversity and College Student Sympathy for Violent Radicalization." *Transcultural Psychiatry*, June 2019.

Roy, Olivier. 1994. *The Failure of Political Islam*. Cambridge, MA: Harvard University Press.

– 2017. *Jihad and Death*. London, UK: Oxford University Press.

Runnymede Trust. 1997. "Islamophobia: A Challenge for Us All." London, UK: Runnymede Trust.

Russell, Andrew. 2015. "RCMP In Quebec Arrest 10 Youths on Suspicion of Planning to Join Jihadist Groups." Global News, 19 May. Accessed 3 June 2021. https://globalnews.ca/news/2006777/rcmp-in-quebec-arrest-10-suspects-planning-to-join-jihadist-groups/.

Saeed, Tania. 2016. *Islamophobia and Securitization*. Cham, Switzerland: Palgrave Macmillan.

Sageman, Marc. 2008. *Leaderless Jihad: Terror Networks in the Twenty-First Century*. Philadelphia: University of Pennsylvania Press.

Said, Edward. 1979. *Orientalism*. New York: Vintage Books.

Samari, Goleen. 2016. "Islamophobia and Public Health in the United States." *American Journal of Public Health* 106 (11): 1920–5.

Saylor, Corey. 2014. The U.S. Islamophobia Network: It's Funding and Impact. *Islamophobia Studies Journal* 2 (1): 99–118.

Sayyid, Salman. 2003. *A Fundamental Fear: Eurocentrism and the Emergence of Islamism*. London, UK: Zed Books.

– 2014a. "A Measure of Islamophobia." *Islamophobia Studies Journal* 2 (1): 10–25.

– 2014b. *Recalling the Caliphate: Decolonization and World Order*. London, UK: Hurst.

Sayyid, Salman, and AbdoolKarim Vakil. 2010. *Thinking through Islamophobia: Global Perspectives*. London, UK: Hurst.

Sayyid, Salman, Ruth Mas, AbdoolKarim Vakil, and Uzma Jamil. 2015. "Reorient: A Forum for Critical Muslim Studies." *Reorient* 1 (1): 5–10.

Schmidt, Garbi. 2002. "Dialectics of Authenticity: Examples of Ethnification of Islam among Young Muslims in Sweden and the United States." *The Muslim World* 92 (1–2): 1–17.

Selby, Jennifer, Amelie Barras, and Lori G. Beaman. 2018. *Beyond Accommodation: Everyday Narratives of Muslim Canadians*. Vancouver: University of British Columbia Press.

Semati, Mehdi. 2010. "Islamophobia, Culture and Race in the Age of Empire." *Cultural Studies* 24 (2): 256–75.

Sensoy, Özlem, and Christopher Darius Stonebanks, eds. 2009. *Muslim Voices in Schools: Narratives of Identity and Pluralism*. Boston: Sense Publishers.

Shaheen, Jack. 2016. *Reel Bad Arabs: How Hollywood Vilifies a People.* Documentary. 50 min.

Shahzad, Farhat. 2014. "The Discourse of Fear: Effects of the War on Terror on Canadian University Students." *American Review of Canadian Studies* 44 (4): 467–82.

Sharify-Funk, Meena. 2014. "Marketing Islamic Reform: Dissidence and Dissonance in a Canadian Context." In *Islam in the Hinterlands: Muslim Cultural Politics in Canada,* edited by Jasmin Zine, 137–60. Vancouver: UBC Press.

Sheehi, Stephen. 2011. *Islamophobia: The Ideological Campaign against Muslims.* Atlanta, GA: Clarity Press.

Shephard, Michelle. 2010. "Star Story Inspires Project Ismael." *Toronto Star,* 19 October. Accessed 3 June 2021. https://www.thestar.com/news/world/2010/10/19/star_story_inspires_project_ismael.html.

Sian, Katy Pal. 2015. "Spies, Surveillance and Stakeouts: Monitoring Muslim Moves in British State Schools." *Race Ethnicity and Education* 18 (2): 183–201.

Sirin, R. Selcuk, and Michelle Fine. 2007. "Hyphenated Selves: Muslim American Youth Negotiating Identities on the Fault Lines of Global Conflict." *Applied Development Science* 1 (3): 151–63.

Smith, Linda Tuhiwai. 1999. *Decolonizing Methodologies.* London, UK: Zed Books.

Smith, Marie-Danielle. 2017. "Senate Passes Bill to Remove Mention of 'Barbaric Cultural Practices' from Harper Era Law." *National Post,* 12 December. https://nationalpost.com/news/politics/senate-passes-bill-to-remove-mention-of-barbaric-cultural-practices-from-law-passed-by-harper-conservatives.

Snowden, Wallis. 2021. "Muslim Women Call for Increased Protection Following Latest Alberta Attack." CBC News, 25 June. Accessed 26 June 2021. https://www.cbc.ca/news/canada/edmonton/muslim-women-attacks-edmonton-1.6081152.

Solórzano, Daniel G., and Tara J. Yosso. 2002. "Critical Race Methodology: Counter-Storytelling as an Analytical Framework for Education Research." *Qualitative Inquiry* 8 (1): 23–44.

Solyom, Catherine. 2016. "Radicalization of CEGEP Students: Long-Awaited Report Reveals Perfect Storm." *Montreal Gazette,* 19 August. Accessed 3 June 2021. https://montrealgazette.com/news/radicalization-of-quebec-cegep-students-long-awaited-report-reveals-perfect-storm/.

Speck, Bruce W. 1997. "Respect for Religious Differences: The Case of Muslim Students." *New Directions for Teaching and Learning* 70:39–46.

Spivak, Gayatri. 1988. "Can the Subaltern Speak?" *Die Philosphin* 14 (27): 42–58.

Stanley, Jay. 2004. *The Surveillance Industrial Complex*. American Civil Liberties Union. Accessed 3 June 2021. https://www.aclu.org/sites/default/files/FilesPDFs/surveillance_report.pdf.

Starrett, Gregory. 2008. "Authentication and Affect: Why the Turks Don't Like Enchanted Counterpublics." *Comparative Studies in Society and History* 50 (4): 1036–46.

Statistics Canada. 2011. *Religion: National Household Survey 2011*. Government of Canada. Accessed 3 June 2021. https://www150.statcan.gc.ca/n1/daily-quotidien/130508/dq130508b-eng.htm.

Steyn, Mark. 2006. "The Future Belongs to Islam." *Maclean's*. 20 October. Accessed 15 May 2021. https://www.macleans.ca/culture/the-future-belongs-to-islam/.

Tahseen, Madiha, Sawssan R. Ahmed, and Sameera Ahmed. 2019. "Muslim Youth in the Face of Islamophobia: Risk and Resilience." In *Islamophobia and Psychiatry*, edited by H. Steven Moffic, John Peteet, Ahmed Z. Hankir, and Rania Awaad, 307–19. Cham, Switzerland: Springer.

Taylor, Charles. 1992. *Multiculturalism and the "Politics of Recognition."* New Jersey: Princeton University Press.

Taylor, Lisa K., and Jasmin Zine. 2014. "Introduction: The Contested Imaginaries of Reading Muslim Women and Muslim Women Reading Back." In *Muslim Women Transnational Feminist Reading Practices, Pedagogy and Ethical Concerns: Contested Imaginaries in Post 9/11 Cultural Practice*, edited by Lisa K. Taylor and Jasmin Zine. New York: Routledge Press.

Thobani, Sunera. 2007. *Exalted Subjects: Studies in the Making of Race and Nation in Canada*. Toronto: University of Toronto Press.

Toronto Police Service. 2001. *2001 Hate Bias Crime Statistical Report*. Accessed 3 June 2021. http://www.torontopolice.on.ca/publications/files/reports/2001hatecrimereport.pdf.

Towns, Eleni. 2011. "The 9/11 Generation." Center for American Progress, 8 September. Accessed 3 June 2021. https://www.americanprogress.org/issues/religion/news/2011/09/08/10363/the-911-generation/.

Townsend, Mark. 2017. "Anti-Muslim Online Surges Driven by Fake Accounts." *Guardian*, 27 November. Accessed 3 June 2021. https://www.theguardian.com/media/2017/nov/26/anti-muslim-online-bots-fake-acounts.

Trip, Simona, Carmen H. Bora, Mihai Marian, Angelica Halmajan, and Marius I. Drugas. 2019. "Psychological Mechanisms Involved in Radicalization and Extremism. A Rational Emotive Behavioral Conceptualization." *Frontiers in Psychology* 10:437.

Trispiotis, Ilias. 2017. "Islamophobia in European Human Rights Law." In *Counter Islamophobia Kit*, July. Accessed 3 June 2021. https://cik. leeds.ac.uk/wp-content/uploads/sites/36/2017/07/2017.07.25-Law-Report-IT-final-1.pdf.

Tuhiwai-Smith, Linda. 1999. *Decolonizing Methodologies*. London: Zed Books

Van Driel, Barry. 2004. *Confronting Islamophobia in Educational Practice*. Stoke on Trent, Inglaterra: Trentham Books.

Van Nieuwkerk, Karin. 2011. *Muslim Rap, Halal Soaps, and Revolutionary Theatre: Artistic Developments in the Muslim World*. Austin: University of Texas Press.

Wadud, Amina. 1999. *Quran and Woman*. New York: Oxford University Press.

Walia, Harsha. 2006. "Responding to the Toronto Terror Arrests." Znet, 13 June. Accessed 3 June 2021. https://zcomm.org/znetarticle/ responding-to-the-toronto-terror-arrests-by-harsha-walia/.

Warner, Michael. 2002. "Publics and Counterpublics." *Public Culture* 14 (1): 49–90.

Wiktorowicz, Quintan, ed. 2004. *Islamic Activism: A Social Theory Approach*. Bloomington: Indiana University Press.

– 2005. *Radical Islam Rising*. Lanham, MD: Roman & Littlefield.

Wise, Robert. 2011. "Al-Shabaab." Center for Strategic and International Studies. AQAM Futures Project Case Study Series Number 2, (July).

Yegenoglu, Meyda. 1998. *Colonial Fantasies: Toward a Feminist Reading of Orientalism*. Cambridge: Cambridge University Press.

Zaal, Mayida. 2012. "Islamophobia in Classrooms, Media, and Politics." *Journal of Adolescent & Adult Literacy* 55 (6): 555–8.

Zaal, Mayida, Tahani Salah, and Michelle Fine. 2007. "The Weight of the Hyphen: Freedom, Fusion and Responsibility Embodied by Young Muslim-American Women during a Time of Surveillance." *Applied Development Science* 11 (3): 164–77.

Zedner, Lucia. 2007. "Pre-Crime and Post-Criminology." *Theoretical Criminology* 11 (2): 261–81.

Zilio, Michelle. 2017. "Canadians Prioritize Prosecution over Rehabilitation for Jihadi Suspects: Poll." *Globe and Mail*, 27 December. Accessed 3 June 2021. https://www.theglobeandmail.com/news/politics/ canadians-prioritize-prosecution-over-rehabilitation-for-jihadi-suspects-poll/article37432097/.

Zine, Jasmin. 2000. "Redefining Resistance: Toward an Islamic Sub-culture in Schools." *Race Ethnicity and Education* 3 (3): 293–316.

– 2001. "Muslim Youth in Canadian Schools: Education and the Politics of Religious Identity." *Anthropology and Education Quarterly* 32 (4): 399–423.

– 2004. "Anti-Islamophobia Education as Transformative Pedagogy: Reflections from the Educational Frontlines." *American Journal of Islamic Social Sciences*, Special Issue: Orientalism, Neo-Orientalism and Islamophobia 21 (3): 110–19.

– 2006a. "Unveiled Sentiments: Gendered Islamophobia and Experiences of Veiling among Muslim Girls in a Canadian Islamic School." *Equity and Excellence in Education. Special Issue: Ethno-Religious Oppression in Schools* 39 (3): 239–52.

– 2006b. "Between Orientalism and Fundamentalism: Muslim Women and Feminist Resistance." *(En)Gendering the War on Terror War Stories and Camouflage Politics*, edited by Krista Hunt and Kim Rygiel, 27–50. Farnham, Surrey, UK: Ashgate Publishing.

– 2008. *Canadian Islamic Schools: Unravelling the Politics of Faith, Gender, Knowledge and Identity*. Toronto: University of Toronto Press.

– 2009a. "Unsettling the Nation: Gender, Race and Muslim Cultural Politics in Canada." Special Feature Article, *Studies in Ethnicity and Nationalism* 9 (1): 146–63.

– 2009b. "Living on the Ragged Edges: Latin Americans and Muslims and the Experience of Homelessness in Toronto." In *Finding Home: Policy Options for Addressing Homelessness in Canada*, edited by J. David Hulchanski, Philippa Campsie, Shirley Chau, Stephen Hwang, and Emily Paradis, 1–23. Toronto: Cities Centre, University of Toronto. Accessed 3 June 2021. https://www.homelesshub.ca/sites/default/files/attachments/5.1%20Zine%20-%20Latin%20Americans%20and%20Muslims.pdf.

– ed. 2012a. *Islam in the Hinterlands: Muslim Cultural Politics in Canada*. Vancouver: UBC Press.

– 2012b. "Shar'ia in Canada? Mapping Discourses of Race, Gender and Religious Differences." In *Sharia Tribunals in Canada*, edited by Anna Korteweg and Jennifer Selby, 279–306. Toronto: University of Toronto Press.

– 2017. "Rescuing Islamophobia from the Melting Pot of Oppression." Accessed 3 June 2021. https://irdproject.com/rescuing-islamophobia-melting-pot-oppression/.

– 2018a. "A National Day of Remembrance: Lessons from the Quebec Massacre" The Conversation, Edition Canada, 25 January. Accessed 3 June 2021. https://theconversation.com/a-national-day-of-remembrance-lessons-from-the-quebec-massacre-90520.

– 2018b. "The Alt-Right and the Weaponization of Free Speech on Campus." *Academic Matters*, Fall Issue. Accessed 3 June 2021. https://academicmatters.ca/the-alt-right-and-the-weaponization-of-free-speech-on-campus/.

– 2019. "I Had a Front-Row Seat to Hate and Was Physically Assaulted: The Liberal Washing of White Nationalism." *The Conversation*, Edition Canada, 1 April. Accessed 3 June 2021. https://theconversation.com/i-had-a-front-row-seat-to-hate-and-was-physically-assaulted-the-liberal-washing-of-white-nationalism-114002.

– 2021. "Muslim Family Killed in Terror Attack in London, Ontario: Islamophobic Violence Surfaces Once Again in Canada." The Conversation, Edition Canada. 8 June. Accessed 8 June 2021. https://theconversation.com/muslim-family-killed-in-terror-attack-in-london-ontario-islamophobic-violence-surfaces-once-again-in-canada-162400.

Zine, Jasmin, and Asma Bala. 2019. "Faith and Activism: Muslim Students' Associations and Campus-based Social Movements." In *Political Muslims*, edited by Tahir Abbas and Sadek Hamid, 52–74. New York: Syracuse University Press.

Zine, Yusuf. 2016. "'I Am Rohingya': A Pedagogical Study on the Roles of Ethnographic Theatre for a Refugee Youth Population." MA thesis, Social Justice and Community Engagement, Wilfrid Laurier University.

Index

Abbas, Tahir, 4, 95, 116–17, 120, 130, 156–62, 164, 167, 173, 177, 180, 222n12

Abdel-Fattah, Randa, 4, 5, 50, 56, 76, 125, 213

Adil (participant): on extremism, 111–12

Agamben, Giorgio, 35, 84, 120–1

Aisha (participant): on double surveillance, 48; on hyper-securitization, 126; on legacy of Muslim storytelling, 190; on patriarchal hegemony of MSAS, 102–4; on the risk of challenging Islamophobia, 200

Ali, Arshad Imtiaz, 4, 27–8, 151

Althusser, Louis, 37–8, 137

Amin (participant): on diversity of Islam, 109–10; on perception of MSAS, 134

Anela (participant): on Islamophobia and Muslim identity, 53–4

Anisa (participant): on being Muslim and Canadian, 59; on entrapment, 178–9; on social and mental health drivers of violence, 164–5

anti-Semitism, 11, 97, 99

Arif (participant): on dealing with taunts and bullying, 70

Ateeka (participant): alienation as driver of extremism, 164; on the burden of representation, 40–1; on interiorizing surveillance, 148; on internalizing bullying post-9/11, 65–6; panoptic fears, 152; on women's prayer space at university, 105–6

Awad (participant): on ethno-racial diversity of Muslims, 47–8; on lack of MSA support for Black Muslims, 116; on MSAS as apolitical, 118–19; on MSAS and community, 96–7

Bazian, Hatem, 16, 24, 34–5

belonging, 6, 7, 16, 20–1, 37, 51, 59; anti-citizen, 21, 27, 52, 120; citizenship, 20, 52, 57–61, 120; diasporic, 4, 8, 164, 170–1; integration, 61–63; and MSAS, 95–7, 106–10; and multiculturalism, 7; policing of, 3–6, 108–10; and radical movements, 161, 164,